Bearing Witness against Sin

Bearing Witness against Sin

The Evangelical Birth of the
American Social Movement

MICHAEL P. YOUNG

THE UNIVERSITY OF CHICAGO PRESS   CHICAGO AND LONDON

Michael P. Young is assistant professor of sociology at the University of Texas.

The University of Chicago Press, Chicago 60637
The University of Chicago Press, Ltd., London
© 2006 by The University of Chicago
All rights reserved. Published 2006
Printed in the United States of America

15 14 13 12 11 10 09 08 07 06   1 2 3 4 5

ISBN-10: 0-226-96085-4 (cloth)
ISBN-13: 978-0-226-96085-2 (cloth)

ISBN-10: 0-226-96086-2 (paper)
ISBN-13: 978-0-226-96086-9 (paper)

Library of Congress Cataloging-in-Publication Data

Young, Michael P.
  Bearing witness against sin : the evangelical birth of the American social movement /
Michael P. Young
    p.   cm.
  Includes bibliographical references and index.
  ISBN 0-226-96085-4 (cloth : alk. paper) — ISBN 0-226-96086-2 (pbk. : alk. paper)   1. So-
cial movements—United States—History—19th century.   2. Church and social problems—
United States—History—19th century.   3. Social movements—United States—Religious
aspects.   4. United States—Moral conditions—History—19th century.   1. Title.
  HN90.M6Y68   2006
  261.80973'09034—dc22

                                                                    2006015466

⊗ The paper used in this publication meets the minimum requirements of the American
National Standard for Information Sciences—Permanence of Paper for Printed Library
Materials, ANSI Z39.45-1992.

For Naomi

ועל־פתחינו כל־מגדים

Contents

Illustrations

Figures

Tables

Maps

Acknowledgments

Research for this book started in the 1990s when I was a graduate student at New York University (NYU). As luck would have it, I could not have been in a better place to be schooled in the historical sociology of social movements. I wish I could take some credit in researching and selecting the ideal department, but I enrolled in the sociology program at New York University because of a pitch Jim Jasper made over lunch during a recruitment period. And I stuck with it largely because of Jim's friendship.

At NYU I was blessed with four amazing advisors that guided me through the research and writing of this book. Jeff Goodwin's courses on contemporary and Marxist theory inspired my initial curiosity about the origins of modern social movements. Independent studies with Jeff on Weber and the sociology of emotions shaped my theoretical approach to social movement research. Jeff also provided close and critical readings of my dissertation. Edwin Amenta taught me the rigors of research in historical sociology and sparked my interest in America's past. This book is the result of my efforts to immerse myself in a pivotal period of American history and make sociological sense of it; it is an attempt to emulate the kind of historical sociology exemplified by Edwin's research. He also challenged me to answer the scariest and most important question a graduate student faces: so what? I think I've answered the question. He is the best mentor a student and young scholar could ask for. I am one of many graduate students in political and historical sociology that passed through NYU that owes his career to Edwin's mentorship. Craig Calhoun became chair at NYU just as I was thinking about a dissertation topic, and it was my great fortune that in spite of his many responsibilities he agreed to chair my committee. He pushed me to think big, suggested exemplars for the kind of research I was doing, read multiple drafts of my dissertation and a draft of the book, and boosted my confidence at critical moments. Craig recognized at the beginning what should be the controlling ideas of this study. He helped me frame the puzzle, engage with social theory, and present my empirical research. If Craig had stayed at the University of North Carolina at Chapel Hill, I do not know where I or this research would be.

From beginning to end, Jim Jasper was there for me. During periods when I despaired about a career in academe, conversations in Jim's living room recharged my intellectual interests. From the time I enrolled in graduate school to his line-by-line critical comments of my last draft of chapters for this book, Jim has pushed me to think straight, write well, and be bold. I hope I have come close.

A number of other people read drafts of parts or the whole of this book and provided important comments and suggestions. Gideon Sjoberg read the theory chapter and provided key insights. Dinners with Gideon at Kerbey Lane on Guadalupe Street in Austin discussing Blumer, frame analysis, cultural schemas, and the power of confession helped me finish the book. Sidney Tarrow read the entire manuscript and gave me comments that greatly improved the final product. I also benefited greatly from anonymous reviews solicited by the University of Chicago Press and another press. Christine Williams provided sage and steadying advice throughout the publication process. Stephen Cherry provided critical engagement with my arguments, encouragement, and indispensable help with my many competing responsibilities as an assistant professor. Kim Baker made the maps in this book possible.

I also owe a great debt of gratitude to Drew Halfmann and Scott Appelrouth. Throughout graduate school and after, Drew and Scott were faithful sounding boards and encouraging friends. I formulated and rehearsed many of the arguments made in this book in discussions with them. They have probably heard more about the United States in the 1830s than they ever cared to know.

All of this expert help would have been wasted if not for Naomi Hanser. She knows why. To Maya, Eli, and Noah, in years to come, you will understand how grateful I am that you played joyfully with Dad's seemingly endless struggle to publish so he would not perish. And finally, to my parents, thank you for making it all possible.

Introduction

As I left my native state on account of slavery, and deserted the home of my fathers to escape the sound of the lash and the shrieks of tortured victims, I would gladly bury in oblivion the recollection of those scenes with which I have been familiar; but this may not, cannot be; they come over my memory like gory spectres, and implore me with resistless power, in the name of a God of mercy, in the name of a crucified Savior, in the name of humanity; for the sake of the slaveholder, as well as the slave, to bear witness to the horrors of the southern prison house.—Sarah M. Grimké's testimony in *American Slavery as It Is* (1839)

God is my witness that, great as is my detestation of slavery and the foreign slave trade, I had rather be a slaveholder—yea, a kidnapper on the African coast—than sell this poison to my fellow-creatures for common consumption. Since the creation of the world there has been no tyrant like INTEMPERANCE, and no slaves so cruelly treated as his.—William Lloyd Garrison, "An Address to the Second Annual Convention of the People of Color in Philadelphia" (1832)

In the 1830s, a wave of moral protests broke out across the United States. Not since the Revolution had Americans engaged in such widespread movements for change. This *national* wave of protests included the movements for temperance, the immediate abolition of slavery, and a host of lesser-known moral reforms. These efforts prefigured in important ways forms of social protest in the late twentieth- and early twenty-first centuries. It is difficult at the outset to specify the affinity between antebellum reformers and the social activists of more than a century later, but a story published in 1842 in a New York monthly periodical provides a glimpse of the family resemblance. Published anonymously in the *Knickerbocker* and entitled "The Ultra Moral-Reformer," this piece satirized the activists behind a decade of moral protests. It poked fun at the all-too-earnest moral reformer by spoofing the formulaic narrative structure of popular religious tracts. In the story, the undoing of the "ultraist" begins when he links public reform to personal lifestyle. Speaking to his wife, the moral reformer explains the link.

I have fully adopted the principles of Teetotalism, Abolitionism, and Non-Resistance. Upon reflection I have come to the conclusion that principles are of no use whatsoever, unless put in practice; and I have determined to carry them out to their full extent, and be governed by them in every act of my life, however apparently trivial.

The practical implications were radical:

We must discontinue the use of sugar and molasses. They are products of slavery; and I will not uphold that institution, how indirectly soever. . . . And there is another thing; you must not buy anything more of Mr. Winkle the grocer. I hear he sells wine by the gallon, and I cannot conscientiously patronize such a man.

In short order, he and his family are reduced to poverty on account of his fanatical drive to achieve absolute consistency between the uncompromising principles of moral reform and personal conduct. Finding no aspect of his mercantile business untainted by the filthy lucre of slavery and spirits, the reformer quits his business without compensation. In despair, his wife begs him to draw on dividends from stock he holds in a railroad in order to support his family and put an end to this *"madness."* But the saint will not be tempted:

[N]ow that my eyes are open, my conscience will not allow me to draw any support from that polluted source. . . . A large proportion of the revenue of the road is derived from the transportation of cotton, a slave product, from Boston to Lowell, and from the freight of manufactured cotton goods from Lowell to Boston. This is the great business to which the road is devoted; this, and the conveyance of persons engaged in the manufacturing of cotton. The Lowell rail-road is one great prop of the tottering edifice of slavery. I will touch none of the unhallowed spoil.

Toward the end of the morality tale, the reformer, reduced to vagrancy, wanders the land eating and conversing only with ultraists as pure in their reform commitments as him—a rapidly diminishing lot because "every day found" him "engaged in some new vagary."

The last [vagary] was the wildest of all. He laid it down as a fact not to be controverted, that our ancestors obtained possession of this country by fraud and murder. He thought the receiver as bad as the thief, and one who would prosper

by murder as bad as the murderer. . . . He *had* shared in the unholy spoil, but he
would partake of it no longer, either directly or indirectly.

Pushed by conscience to the American strand as the seventeenth-century
Puritans before him, but this time from the opposite direction, trapped by
his code of ultrareform, unable to find a mode of transport untainted by
unholy spoil to remove him from this guilty land, he finds himself on an
overhanging cliff.

> Behind him lay the depraved and vicious earth; above him from the countless
> eyes of heaven glared Almighty wrath; before him was peace and rest. His brain
> whirled; he leaped from the cliff, and plunged into the waves below.[1]

This account exaggerated true features of the moral reformer.

The antebellum reformer had a cosmopolitan appreciation of how a
market society deeply implicated individuals in injustices that seemed remote to many other Americans of the period. "Ultraism" refused to excuse mediated contact with evils. Even indirect contact with sin was an immediate moral failing, and ultraists tracked the serpentine extensions of
these evil mediations like few before them ever had. The *Knickerbocker*
morality tale appreciated, albeit through denigration, that teetotalers and
abolitionists, the leading moral reformers of the period, were *visionaries.*
By interlacing individual and social reform—in effect fusing the personal
and the public in moral protest—they led the way for future generations
of social activists.

Over the past few decades, activists and social theorists alike have
commented on how protest has become increasingly mixed with personal
matters. In this book, I not only argue that antebellum moral reformers
anticipated the "life politics" of contemporary protest in their reflexive
reference to social and personal axes of change but also that this interlacing of a sense of intimate responsibility and attention to far-flung social problems propelled the first national wave of social movements in the
United States.[2] The antebellum reformer's connection of the intimate and
the far-flung, her fusion of personal reform and social change, was religious in origin, stemming from an evangelical sense of the dynamic of
sin, repentance, and reformation. This reflexive force projected personal
sins onto national problems and introjected national evils into personal
affairs. The moral bond the reformer claimed between the personal and
the national made sense of feelings of guilt and longings to repent and

gave expansive social purpose to these emotions. It also made sense of national struggles by making them axial to personal reform. This evangelical
dynamic, linking the spiritual fates of the individual and nation, launched
and sustained these movements.

The sudden popular support and impressive geographic reach of these
movements can be tracked through the spread of auxiliary societies to
the two most prominent moral reform associations of the period: the
American Temperance Society and the American Anti-Slavery Society.
The American Temperance Society first reported on auxiliary societies
in April 1829, and they numbered barely two hundred. Over the next two
years, the national society kept detailed records of support for the cause.
It was strongest in New England but by no means limited to this region.
In the first few years of the movement, support emerged in places as far
away as Illinois and Mississippi (map 1). By 1835, the national society
claimed more than eight thousand auxiliaries and 1.5 million members.
The emergence of a national movement for the immediate abolition of
slavery lagged these developments by a few years. The first signs of interregional support for abolition appeared in 1833 with the formation of the
American Anti-Slavery Society. Over the next five years, auxiliary societies organized across the North. A few short-lived societies formed in
border states. By 1838, auxiliaries numbered over thirteen hundred with
an estimated membership of one hundred twenty thousand. Support, like
that for temperance, was widespread although, after repression, it was
confined to the free states (map 2).[3]

From the very start, these movements were far-flung social phenomena.
Support for temperance was genuinely national. The antislavery movement was broadly sectional in its support and national in its purpose and
ultimate impact. They were both national social movements. In their interregional and popular appeal, they were the first of their kind in American history. The personal dimensions of these moral reform movements
underpinned their widespread appeal and the forms of protest they initiated. Temperance and antislavery emerged as national movements when
drinking and slavery *suddenly* appeared as problems demanding immediate personal reform and when personal guilt over intemperance and racial
prejudice *suddenly* appeared as central to the fate of the country. This was
not a necessary or obvious formulation. Indeed, for more than a century
of extensive slaveholding and hard drinking, it had occurred to few Americans to link these different registers of social experience.

The United States was a rapidly expanding country with weak national

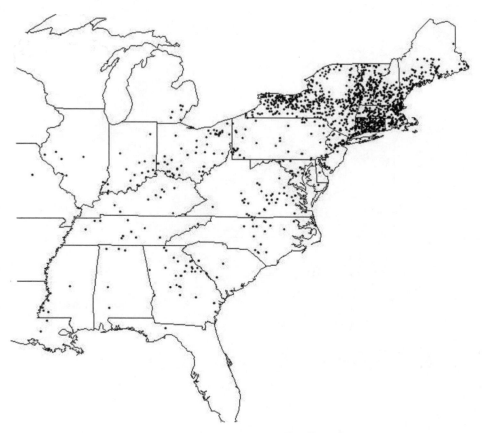

MAP I. Auxiliaries to the American Temperance Society, 1831.
SOURCE: *Journal of Humanity,* vol. 2, nos. 36–44 (January–April, 1831).
NOTE: Each dot represents a society formed by the spring of 1831. There are some missing data because not all societies could be located. Most of the missing data come from the western states.

institutions when this wave of protests emerged. There were few institutions with sufficient reach and influence to support and motivate, let alone coordinate, extensive social movements. In this unsettled social context, these moral reform movements generated extensive popular support by banding together diverse evangelicals through causes that were at once abstract in their national scope, vagaries according to the *Knickerbocker,* and deeply felt in their personal significance.[4] In this wave of movements, widely scattered Americans came together, in spite of few intermediary institutional connections, to address issues of public and personal import.

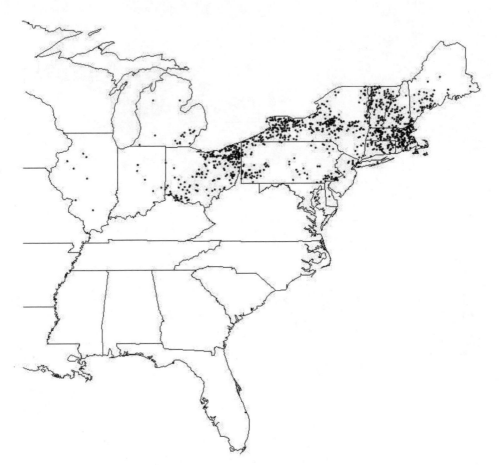

MAP 2. Auxiliaries to the American Anti-Slavery Society, 1838.
SOURCE: American Antislavery Society, *Annual Report*, 1838.
NOTE: Each dot represents a society operating in the spring of 1838. There are some missing data because not all societies could be located. Most of the missing data comes from the western states.

A novel combination of the evangelical schemas of sin and confession created these moral commitments by hinging personal reform and extensive social problems. This combination linked schemas from the genteel orthodoxy of Presbyterians and Congregationalists and from the boisterous populism of sects like the Methodists and Baptists. From the orthodox side came a rationalized variation of the schema of sin. From the populist side came a public variation of the schema of confession. The combined schemas shaped the protests that launched and sustained these interregional movements.

When this wave of reform movements was near its peak, the Reverend Leonard Bacon, Congregationalist minister of the prestigious First Church of New Haven, described the form of dissent in a letter to the wealthy philanthropist Gerrit Smith this way:

> A clergy independent of the churches, an itinerating clergy—a clergy distributed into various orders, each charged with its single topic of instruction or agitation, is making its appearance amongst us. . . . One class of itinerants preaches temperance, according to the *latest discoveries*. Another is determined to know nothing but anti-slavery. . . . What surer method can be devised to make him (the lecturer) a flaming enthusiast? The man may draw people after him; he may easily acquire an influence and reputation far beyond his talents. And if the churches instead of being instructed by men, each of whom is to declare the whole counsel of God, are to fall under the tuition of such men, each of whom is a man of one idea, what can be expected but that the church will be overrun with extravagances of opinion and practice. There is such a thing as ecclesiastical order.[5]

Bacon's description remains apt. He recognized the movements for temperance and antislavery as originating in religious protests lodged against ecclesiastical institutions. With the phrase "itinerating clergy" and "flaming enthusiast" he correctly associated these movements with religious revivals and the public confessions made popular by populist sects like the Methodists and the Baptists. With the phrases "single topic of agitation" and "latest discoveries" he also linked them to the newly publicized special sins that had been articulated within the orthodox benevolence societies of Presbyterians and Congregationalists.

Bacon's letter was prompted by Smith's very public conversion to the principles of immediate abolitionism. Smith had recently fallen "under the tuition" of these preachers of "one idea." In the 1820s, Smith and Bacon had been leaders in the nation's most prestigious benevolence societies, central figures in a united Presbyterian and Congregationalist effort to evangelize the nation. This effort rationalized the holistic, evangelical mission of orthodox Calvinists, dividing it into discrete campaigns or specialized causes like temperance. Bacon and other religious conservatives contributed to this development, but they never envisioned that the specialized agencies might rebel against the greater evangelical mission, against "the whole counsel." In the late 1820s and early 1830s, the religious revivals of populist sects that had swept the western periphery of the nation came into contact with the agencies of orthodox benevolent societies centered in the northeastern cities. The combination proved radical. As public confessions, the dramatic centerpiece of the populist revival, became central to the specialized campaigns of orthodoxy, a wave of social movements independent of ecclesiastical order broke out across the United States. This unprecedented national wave of social movements emerged as hundreds of thousands of Americans joined together to bear witness against special sins.

First and foremost, reformers pressured evangelical churches to join them in bearing witness against particular sins like intemperance and slavery. They demanded that churches expel liquor merchants, unrepentant drinkers, and slaveholders from their communion. They agitated to convert ministers and communicants of America's churches to the belief that *immediate* repentance of the sins of drinking and slavery was demanded by God. When churches proved less than zealous in their condemnation of these particular sins or limited in their social impact, antebellum reformers turned to other means. These measures included organizing a massive publishing and mailing campaign, coordinating boycotts, building counter-institutions like temperance taverns and free-produce associations, petitioning Congress, forming independent political parties, lobbying for new legislation, and even engaging in unlawful actions to counter the particular sins.

Temperance advocates and abolitionists triggered fierce counter-mobilizations. Churches split over the moral duty to renounce all intoxicants. Antitemperance conventions formed in many American cities. By the end of the decade, the temperance movement initiated a century-long political and legal struggle for prohibition. Churches and denominations split over the issue of immediate abolitionism. In the South, abolitionism was almost immediately repressed by local governments. At the national level, the state attempted to censor debate on the issue. In the North, mobs moved to shut down abolitionist meetings and destroy antislavery presses. Across these two issues, temperance and antislavery, and a host of others including campaigns against adultery, prostitution, and Sabbath violations, a culture war split Americans and foreshadowed the Civil War.

This book presents an account of the development of these movements and their novel form of moral protest. Chapter 1 reviews the sociological literature on historical ruptures in the forms of protest and the origins of national social movements. Synthesizing these arguments with insights from the historiography of antebellum reform movements and collective behaviorist theories of social movements, I present a cultural and social-psychological theory to guide the empirical account that follows. Chapters 2, 3 and 4 discuss the development of national institutions and events preceding this wave of movements. In chapter 2, I discuss the broad demographic, economic, political, and religious context of the period leading up to the rise of the movements. In chapter 3, I track the prolific institution building of Presbyterians and Congregationalists and their organization of a united front to promote and rationalize evangelical efforts. In chapter 4, I trace the emergence of a form of mass confession of faith and sin among the populist sects—Methodists, Baptists, and a host of smaller sects—and its influence on the middling classes of westward Presbyterians and Congregationalists. Chapter 5 establishes how these separate cultural currents, the rationalization of Presbyterian and Congregationalist evangelism and populist revivals, came together in the late 1820s and 1830s in a series of moral protests that propelled a national wave of reform movements. I follow this development throughout the decade to a point of devolution. In this chapter, I also analyze the common dimensions of these movements in a comparative analysis of the reform causes. Chapter 6 recounts the main arguments in biographical accounts of six leading reformers, highlighting the personal dimensions of moral reform. In the concluding chapter, I return to the cultural and social-psychological theory introduced in chapter 1 and discuss how it not only explains the first national social movements in the United States but can be extended to make sense of a wider history of modern social movements.

CHAPTER ONE

Modern Social Movements and Confessional Projections of the Self

How did the first national wave of social movements emerge in the United States? Historians of antebellum reform and sociologists of social movements have not directly addressed this puzzle. Historians have focused instead on explaining the coming of the Civil War, the origins of civil rights movements, or the class bases of moral reform movements. In spite of growing interest in the historical sociology of American movements, few sociologists have researched antebellum protests. Concerned with the intersection of movements, state expansion, and industrial capitalist growth, most studies have focused on movements after the Civil War. As a result, few scholars have explored how, or even if, the American protests that took hold in the early nineteenth century created a new and enduring form of social movement.[1]

The works of Charles Tilly and Sidney Tarrow are something of an exception. Tilly's research of centuries of Western protest, or what he prefers to refer to as "contention," pinpoints processes central to the emergence of sustained and interregional social movements. Tilly's account of a nineteenth-century rupture in the Western repertoire of contention relies primarily on the systematic data he has gathered on centuries of French and British protest. His research demonstrates that sustained sequences of interregional contention first appeared as a repeating social phenomenon in the late eighteenth and early nineteenth centuries, and it identifies features of the new forms of collective action that enabled the spatial and temporal extension of protest. Tarrow, drawing in part on research on late eighteenth- and early nineteenth-century American protests, has further specified the new forms of action that structured the earliest examples of sustained and interregional protests.[2] Together, Tilly and Tarrow provide the best starting point for an account of the novel dimensions of antebellum reform movements. In this chapter, I build on this start and develop a cultural and social-psychological approach to explain the first U.S. national social movements.[3]

A Historic Rupture in the Forms, Purposes, and Identities of Protest

Tilly's extensive and systematic catalogs of French and British protests establish a historic rupture in the very forms of popular collective action: a relative decline in particular, parochial, and patronized forms of contention—for example, rough music, grain seizures, the destruction of toll gates—and the emergence and recurrence of public meetings and demonstrations planned by autonomous, special-purpose associations. Tilly introduced the notion of "repertoires of contention" to account for this change. The term highlights the endurance of traditions of popular struggle and captures as a puzzle the dramatic transformation of Western patterns of protest occurring in the century after 1750. At any given point in history, protests follow a delimited repertoire: a set of means or routines of banding together that people learn and share. Changes in this cultural know-how generally occur "at the perimeter of the existing repertoire." Only rarely is a repertoire junked and replaced. But such a radical transformation did occur during the early nineteenth century with a new repertoire showing unmistakable signs of displacing the old throughout Western Europe and America. Before the late eighteenth century, the Western repertoire was made up of a rich variety of local traditions and semiauthorized public ceremonies. Starting in the late eighteenth century, the repertoire changed. Among other things, the new forms extended the spatial and temporal reach of protests.[4]

Tarrow has joined Tilly in specifying the characteristics of the new repertoire of contention and the contours of this historic rupture. Reading across a range of Tilly's and Tarrow's work, three novel and interrelated characteristics appear central in extending the time horizon and geographical scope of protest. First, Tarrow argues that the collective action of protesters shifted from particular to "modular forms" of collective action, a concept borrowed from Benedict Anderson, and that this more than anything else distinguished the new repertoire from the old. Modular collective action transposes across different circumstances and locales and can be utilized by different actors and against an array of targets. The flexibility and inclusiveness of imitable and transposable models of action enabled protesters to break out of a militant parochialism that characterized the old repertoire and to contend for power across regional communities and changing events. Before the rupture in eighteenth-century patterns of popular struggle, inflexibility, direct action, and corporate-based organization combined in the most common types of protest. The old repertoire limited protests to local and particular forms of action that did not travel well. The problems of spatial scale and limited time horizons that have always dogged popular struggles were partially addressed by new modular forms of collective action.[5]

Second, as the form of collective action shifted from the particular to the general, the claims making of protesters became more specialized. The new repertoire featured special purposes. It was not just an increased generality that was new to protest but also a sharp focus in stated goals or ends. This sharpness enabled protesters to establish common goals that cut through regional differences and changing events. These particularized goals not only bridged spatial divides but provided coherent lines for action across time. In the new repertoire, these first two characteristics, modular forms of action and specialized goals, regularly combine in the standard formation of special-purpose associations. Tilly's empirical research of France and Britain suggests that if one thing is characteristic of the new repertoire of contention it is the planned meetings of special-purpose associations.[6]

Third, Tilly argues that this new form and purpose to Western protests constituted and was constituted by new actors with detached contentious identities. The old forms of contention—for example, the collective shaming rituals of rough music, donkeying, and tar and feathering—enacted embedded identities or identities established in local cultures and networks of social relations. The collective identities of the nineteenth-century men and women who followed the new repertoire of protest were not as deeply tied to local traditions of resistance or local networks of social exchange. The new forms and purposes of nineteenth-century protest involved increasingly cosmopolitan social activists. Detached protest identities emerged with associations and purposes that transcended local commitments and problems. With this new form, purpose, and collective identity, the protests of Westerners moved "from the alien world of the eighteenth century into our own era."[7]

Explaining the Nineteenth-Century Rupture

According to Tilly and Tarrow, a gradual but extensive shift in social power explains the emergence of this new repertoire. Sweeping economic, demographic, and political processes worked to undermine the old forms of protest and shape the new. As interregional markets linked far-flung communities, the targets of protest were more often remote, demanding new ways of influencing nonlocal parties. As Tilly demonstrates, until the nineteenth century, protests were typically bifurcated in the way they sought to influence social conditions. They either reached directly out in local affairs to coerce or shame an offending party, or they pressed local patrons to bring their concerns to bear on more remote forces. Market forces rendered these parochial forms increasingly impractical. Offenders were no longer as likely to be in immediate reach, and the influence of local patrons who mediated more extensive affairs declined. New interregional markets not only placed the targets of protest at a distance, but they made long-distance mobilizations possible. The development of print capitalism, in particular, facilitated the spread of protest events across time and space by shaping modular forms of collective action, articulating specialized purposes, and publicizing distant protests and leading activists.[8]

The demographic changes that accompanied these expanding markets also disrupted local traditions that comprised the old repertoire of protest. Take, for example, rough music or the charivari. Into the nineteenth century, variants of rough music were commonly practiced across Western Europe and North America. Rough music was in a weak sense modular in that across time and space Europeans engaged in a recognizably similar form of collective action for related purposes. Directed against a particular community offender, rough music involved subjecting the target to a public ritual of humiliation. This much was standard, but the practice and full meaning of a particular instance of rough music and of its publicity of disgrace varied from place to place and across time. The actual practice of rough music admitted to a great diversity or particularity of forms. An experienced "player" of *katzenmusik* in western Germany could not be expected to know how to "get up the lads" for a *skimmington* in Britain. A New Englander might know how to ride a teetotaler out of town on a rail but not be able to follow the rites of "Judge Lynch" in the South. The proper nominy, props, instruments of noise, and public stage were all subject to regional variation and posed cultural barriers to the interregional extension of these forms of collective action. Moreover, the rites of rough music belonged to cultures that started to decompose in the nineteenth century. As demographic forces disrupted local communities, the know-how to perform the acts and the significance of such acts were lost on many who were caught up in this social change.[9]

According to Tilly and Tarrow, strategic interactions with centralizing political institutions provided a key mechanism to lift protesters out of their particular local routines of claims making, to establish new and extensive lines of action, and to articulate novel claims pitched at a new social register. As state building expanded and centralized authority, it penetrated local communities providing a centralized target for protest and causes that superseded local concerns. As challengers targeted centralized state agencies or sought to draw them into conflicts with other social actors as mediators, they adapted their forms of contention. Protests became modular and the objects of their claims national and specialized. In short, as a result of these economic, demographic, and political processes, the old repertoire, with its traditional routines and direct attacks, lost much of its place and purpose. The challenge to deliver claims to the new locations of power required adaptation, innovation, and the assembly of a new repertoire of contention.

According to Tilly's research, Great Britain took the lead in this innovation. In the mid-eighteenth century, mass mobilizations around national issues were quite literally inconceivable due to weak or nonexistent national institutions. By the 1830s, British public "campaigns had crystallized into social movements, with their meetings, marches, demonstrations, slogans, banners, colors, pamphlets, and special-interest associations orbiting around one major issue at a time." In the intervening years increasingly cosmopolitan political entrepreneurs learned to coordinate public campaigns with parliamentary deliberations over bills.

> In 1833, the great themes of public meetings were elections, the behavior of the national government, treatment of the Irish, administration of local affairs, maintenance of trade, the abolition of slavery, and taxes—essentially the same issues Parliament was debating that very year.[10]

Drawing on the work of Pauline Maier, Tarrow argues that American colonists in their resistance of British taxation utilized key elements of the new repertoire, giving rise to the first truly national social movement, the American Revolution. In the years leading up to the Revolution, local mobilizations and protests in different colonies led steadily to increased coordination across colonies and ultimately to a sustained and intercolonial movement. This novel movement was structured by modular forms of collective action like the boycott, special purposes like resisting the Stamp Act, and widespread identification with interregional associations like the Sons of Liberty.[11]

The Problem with Explaining Antebellum Reform Movements

After the Revolution, American protest reverted to the older form. Through the first quarter of the nineteenth century, there were no prolonged, interregional social movements. Given Tilly's and Tarrow's explanations, this reversion makes good sense. The political processes structuring the interregional and sustained protests leading up to the American Revolution did not obtain after independence was secured. The Revolution, after all, was a rebellion against "the European-style notion of concentrated political sovereignty."[12] If, as Tarrow and many historians argue, the taxation of a centralizing British state drew the regional protests of colonialists together into a national revolution, this center of political gravity disappeared with American victory.

It is an overstatement to claim that the early American republic was without a central state. Nonetheless, in comparative terms, the federal system of the United States succeeded in arresting the centralizing processes of sovereignty promoted extensively in Western Europe by the bureaucracies of absolute monarchs and national parliaments. In the 1830s, sustained and interregional protests dramatically reappeared in America but without the institutional target of a strong central state. At the same time the national social movement "crystallized" in Great Britain, a range of special-purpose associations with pledges, slogans, newspapers, agents, constitutions, and auxiliary societies flourished across the United States. Unlike Great Britain, the United States had not developed a state with "locality-penetrating" administrative capacities headed by a representative body capable of channeling protest into discrete national issues. The issues around which the most contentious and popular of these movements revolved—antislavery and temperance—were not addressed by the federal government and the national political parties and would not be for some time. To the extent that the American federal government held power over public affairs, that power was in decline when these movements burst on the scene.[13] How then did these moral reforms manage to mobilize and sustain interregional protests?

Tilly and Tarrow's work still guides. The use of modular forms of collective action, the articulation of specialized purposes, and the construction of detached identities distinguish these movements as the first of their kind in U.S. history and help explain their national appeal. Demographic upheaval and market revolution opened the possibility and, for many, the need for sustained and interregional movements, but they also brought havoc to many of the institutions around which protest could be mobilized. The rapid expansion of markets uprooted individuals and groups embedded in local cultures, undermining traditional forms and purposes of collective action. In the face of these sweeping and decentralizing changes, state and political institutions provided little leverage for lifting collective action out of parochial forms. They were not central to the mechanisms that shaped modular forms of action, special purposes, and detached protest identities. Religion was the primary social force that shaped the form, purpose, and identity of the first national movements in the United States.

Religious forces of course mixed with political processes. Political processes remade American Christianity by making sure there would be no established religion, but religious dissent shaped these political forces of disestablishment. Market and religious forces were similarly intertwined. In the context of the social upheaval caused by rapid market expansion, evangelical Christianity proved exceptionally adaptable.[14] Even as certain traditional religious beliefs and institutions faltered under rapid economic changes, popular concern for sin, repentance, and reformation grew. Affinities between this concern and the material interests of a rising middle class cannot be denied nor their impact ignored. But economic forces cannot take credit for why these religious schemas ran deep and wide through the social institutions of early nineteenth-century America. Evangelicals relied on the saliency of sin and the power of repentance to adjust their religious commitments to worldly affairs.

Evangelical forces mediated the rapid spread of the temperance and antislavery movements. Evangelical support for these causes did not come automatically. There was heated competition between populist and orthodox evangelical camps and even within these camps. Many devout individuals, churches, benevolent societies, and denominations resisted or stood aloof from the movement for temperance, and most attacked the movement for the immediate abolition of slavery. Activists had to fight for what support they gained from evangelicals and their religious institutions. To the extent this fight succeeded, it did so by drawing "confessional" support that challenged the authority structures of evangelical institutions and that crossed deep sectarian divides.

Despite their differences, evangelicals shared what C. Wright Mills described as a "vocabulary of motive." The syntactical structure of this vocabulary centered on the corrupting power of sin and the redeeming power of confession. Disagreement abounded over the true nature of sin and confession, but all evangelicals proclaimed the centrality of these religious schemas to the human trial. In the late 1820s, an innovative combination of confession and sin generated support for these movements. In short, a cultural mechanism combining schemas constitutive of the evangelical cosmos launched and sustained these movements by mobilizing human and material resources within parachurch institutions to new and startling purposes.[15]

A Social-Psychological Approach to the Problem

This confessional mechanism shaped a modular form of protest aimed at special and national purposes and carried out by protestors with emergent collective identities detached from traditional religious associations and local communities. When institutional political processes could not shape the basic characteristics of national social movements as identified by Tilly and Tarrow, religious forces did and they propelled nationwide movements. Any adequate account of the source of these new movements must explore the cultural and social-psychological dynamics that shaped the *religious* actions, purposes, and identities of the evangelicals that joined these protests.

Historians of antebellum reform have long recognized this imperative. Although they have not directly addressed the puzzle of the emergence of the first national social movements, they offer some oblique answers to how cultural and psychological forces might have shaped and sustained these novel movements in the absence of strong or centralized political and economic institutions. Over the past century, there have been a number of radical interpretive shifts in the historiography of antebellum reform. For much of the period, the retrospective shadow of the Civil War haunted historians and their research. Early in the twentieth century, so-called progressive historians did not pay much attention to antebellum reformers because they considered them all but irrelevant to the coming of the Civil War. They viewed the war as an "irrepressible conflict" between an agrarian South and an industrializing North—a clash between incompatible civilizations.[16] In the 1930s and 1940s, "revisionist" historians recast the reformers as part of a "blundering generation" largely to blame for a "repressible war." J. G. Randall summed up this view: "If one word or phrase were selected to account for the war, that word would not be slavery, or state-rights, or diverse civilizations. It would have to be such a word as fanaticism."[17]

In their revision of the sources of the Civil War, these historians articulated a novel social psychology to explain the actions of reformers. They identified a common temperament in the leading antebellum activists. For these historians radical abolitionists epitomized a wider range of reformers that included advocates for temperance, women's rights, Sabbatarianism, dietary reforms, and many more obscure causes.[18] Avery Craven, speaking of the nation's leading abolitionist, William Lloyd Garrison, argued that "temperament" set him against the institutions of society. Garrison's life, he contended, "would probably have been spent in protesting even if slavery had never existed." Craven also found Theodore Weld, the nation's other great abolitionist, to be "unusual." Weld not only crusaded against slavery but was also "much given to 'anti-meat, -butter, -tea, and -coffee, etc. -ism[s].' He indulged in excessive self-effacement and in extravagant confessions of selfishness, pride, impatience of contradiction, personal recklessness and 'a bad, unlovely temper.'"[19]

Although abolitionists like Weld and Garrison were emotionally predisposed to protest, revisionists also found an objective source to their disquiet. They argued this source was to be found in the North, not the South. Slavery was not at the root of antislavery protests. The real source was the rapid advance of capitalism in both industry and agriculture. By the third decade of the nineteenth century, economic changes had undermined the cultural identity and self-sufficiency of rural northerners. This market revolution displaced people from long-standing social patterns and undermined traditional sources of social status, stirring discontent and a misguided search for the cause of the nation's ills. This search found a remote target—the slaveholder. As Craven put it, the slaveholder was in the eyes of declining northern elites "un-matched" in his *sinfulness.* "His licentious conduct with Negro women, his intemperance in the use of intoxicating liquors, his mad dueling, and his passion for war against the weak were enough to mark him as the nation's moral enemy number one!" Emotion fueled a collective episode of what Freud termed "mésalliance." "Thus it was that the slaveholder began to do scapegoat service.... To him were transferred resentments and fears born out of local conditions."[20]

Critical accounts of antebellum reformers continued through the 1950s. In the years after World War II, historians concerned with the causes of totalitarianism saw in movements like abolitionism early signs of the pathologies of protest in mass societies. This research deepened the psychological and structural analysis of reform movements. Stanley Elkins presented the most sophisticated articulation of this social psychology of reform. He saw in movements as different as the transcendentalism of Emerson and immediate abolitionism of Garrison a common impulse to sweep away social institutions as well as a naive trust in the moral compass of the individual. He identified reformers as ego-centered anti-institutionalists. According to Elkins, the fragmentation of the Church and the absence of other strong public institutions in early nineteenth-century America fueled an "antinomian" spirit in the North. This spirit privileged the individual's conscience over social institutions, intuition over intellect, moral ideals over practicality, and absolute truths grasped personally over common sense anchored in traditions.[21]

This antinomianism shaped the defining characteristic of reformers: a mind-set of exaggerated personal guilt and tendency for abstract thought. Detached from the stable workings of social institutions, reformers lacked a sense of proportion when it came to the workings of society. They were simultaneously prone to believe abstract simplifications of complicated social problems like slavery or drinking and to magnify their personal responsibility for these (abstract) problems. Although Elkin's judgment of the reformers was too harsh, he hit on something central. A bipolar mix of introspective guilt and high-flying abstractions shaped the reform movements of the period.[22]

At roughly the same time, theories of collective behavior in sociology arrived at a similar mix of psychological and structural factors to explain social movements. In the 1930s, Herbert Blumer developed the first theory of collective behavior, covering a range of social phenomena that included crowds, mobs, stampedes, fads, and social movements. As the historiography of antebellum reform linked abolitionism with other collective phenomena like dietary and intellectual movements, Blumer thought social movements shared basic features with a wide range of collective behavior. He not only linked these phenomena in their elemental components but also in their causes. Emotional reactions to social unrest were the motive forces behind all such behavior.

According to Blumer, the frustration of desires leads to a state of unrest, and in this state people become excited, apprehensive, irritable, and in severe cases neurotic. This emotional state spreads through interaction, leading to what he termed social unrest. The emotions of social unrest are "the crucible" out of which all collective behavior emerges, but important mediating cultural factors determine the form of behavior to emerge. In the continuum of collective behavior, social movements are shaped by the highest degree of symbolic mediation. Movements give direction to frustrated desires "through ideas, suggestions, criticisms, and promises." In movements, mediating symbols interject a process of interpretation between collective emotional stimulus and collective action. Blumer viewed movements less as expressions of social-psychological pathologies than as creative yet emotional sources of new moral orders. Through symbolic mediation, the restless individual "has his sentiments focused on, and intertwined with, the objective of the movement." The experience of participating in a movement is purposeful and transforming. The feeling is one of personal "expansion" as frustrated desires "surge forth" in the direction of the articulated social cause of the movement and toward a "new order of life."[23]

In the early 1960s, Neil Smelser presented the most comprehensive theory of the collective behavior tradition. For Smelser, as for Blumer, the formation of social movements begins with experiences of insecurity. Smelser argued that structural strain, broadly understood, leads to ambiguity and ambiguity to anxiety, as individuals are unable to explain the source of their insecurity. Movements, as well as other forms of collective behavior, emerge when "generalized beliefs" speak to the experience of anxiety and restructure the ambiguity brought on by structural strain. The difference between social movements and less organized forms of collective behavior, like panics or hostile crowds, rests with the articulation between the generalized belief and practical circumstances. All such beliefs reconstitute an ambiguous situation by linking concrete experiences with higher levels of general significance. Smelser referred to this link as a "short-circuit." Short-circuiting resolves ambiguity and drives social action as it operates as an anxiolytic.

Hysteria is a simple and extreme form of short-circuiting. With episodes of collective hysteria, the link between the abstract and the concrete leaves the believer's self-conception comparatively untouched by positing that the ambiguity and anxiety results from a threat that is absolutely other. Collective behavior structured by beliefs that make a big leap of faith between lived experience and extensive social problems may be—as Elkins described antebellum reformers—weak in its grasp of reality and distorted in its sense of responsibility. All collective behavior, however, depends on generalized beliefs that short-circuit: that jump from concrete situations of action to abstractions. Social movements, at the other end of the spectrum of collective behavior, involve beliefs that, as they jump levels of generality, disturb and reconfigure those levels of meaning. At this limit, the generalized belief and ensuing collective behavior envision and enact a regeneration of self *and* society. This twinning of personal and public transformations is a defining characteristic of social movements.[24]

The key insight provided by the revisionist historiography of antebellum reform and the sociology of collective behavior is the role of emotional projections of the self into extensive social issues, the telescoping of the feelings of individuals with great social projects. This social-psychological mechanism can help explain how individuals could imagine themselves joined in far-flung movements for social change even in a context of relatively weak institutional connections.

The Promises of Social Psychology Almost Lost

Starting in the 1960s, new research both in the history of antebellum reform and the sociology of social movements challenged traditional explanations that emphasized structural strain and emotional reactions. In both disciplines, this research countered the conservative bias inherent in much of the social psychology of earlier accounts, but it also chased from the field of inquiry insights that are key to understanding what was new about antebellum reform movements and how these movements managed to sustain widespread support.

In sociology, the collective behaviorist paradigm of structural strain and psychological insecurity came under sharp attack. In the wake of the 1960s, sociologists increasingly emphasized organizational, material, and rational aspects of activism. Structural strain was viewed by a new generation of sociologists as a nearly constant feature of modern societies, and, as such, a poor explanation for variable phenomena like social movements. The new paradigm depicted activism as more similar to than distinct from the institutional behavior of formal organizations. Whereas the collective behavior models of social movements assumed them to be inherently similar to crowds, this model treated movements as similar to organizations operating in competitive markets. Whereas collective behaviorists distinguished social movements from the normal workings of politics, this new organizational and materialist perspective viewed movements as engaged in the same political processes as other institutional actors, but at a serious structural disadvantage. Movements were an extension of normal political action, not an extension of spontaneous crowds.

Tilly's and Tarrow's explanations of the nineteenth-century rupture in Western forms of protest fit squarely within—and helped define—this organizational, materialist, and rational approach. This political process and resource mobilization theory of social movement dynamics displaced the collective behavior tradition and supplanted the rich psychology of collective behavior with the parsimonious assumptions of a rational actor model. The historiography of antebellum reform experienced a similar and contemporaneous interpretive shift, but the rebellion against traditional approaches was not as total as in sociology.

For historians in the 1960s, it was no longer the nation's greatest catastrophe, the mass fratricide of the Civil War, but one of its shining moments, the emancipation of slaves, that illuminated antebellum reforms, or at least abolitionism. Whereas earlier critical accounts of antebellum reformers tended to lump many causes and movements together, these more favorable readings of abolitionists tended to distinguish the particular cause of antislavery from the other reforms. For historians involved in the civil rights and student movements, it was easier to identify with the abolitionists than with reformers of abstemious campaigns like temperance.[25]

At the outset of the 1960s, a series of essays challenged the revisionist view, asking anew about the abolitionists and their states of mind.[26] These questions were answered, in part, through biographical studies. Deep descriptions of leading activists did not suggest that reformers were particularly isolated and detached from institutions or that their life chances were in steady decline. In fact, many leading reformers were organizers in powerful evangelical institutions and members of a "middling" class with rising material expectations. Bertram Wyatt-Brown's classic study of Lewis Tappan, for example, placed the abolitionist at the center of a thriving network of evangelical benevolent societies and showed him to be much more benefactor than victim of the market revolution.[27]

These studies also emphasized how "normal" reformers were. To use the example of Tappan again, he was deeply religious, even zealous, but his agitation for moral reforms was in no way irrational. Tappan was of even temper, and he maintained stable ties with friends, family, and fellow reformers throughout his years of activism. More comprehensive studies of the antislavery movement came to similar conclusions. Aileen Kraditor's study of abolitionists, for example, challenged Elkin's characterization of reformers as anti-institutional. She pointed out that they were only opposed to certain institutions. Many if not most of the leading reformers of the age were embedded in networks of churches, benevolent societies, schools, and other civil associations. Kraditor offered a "less psychological explanation for the abolitionists' guilt feelings." Because slavery was integral to the economic, political, and religious institutions of the nation, northerners had real cause for feeling guilty. "The unrealism was not the abolitionists' for feeling guilty but their neighbors' for *not* feeling guilty." In short, these studies revealed that abolitionists were firmly embedded in a network of social organizations, emotionally well-adjusted, and rather circumspect about how to tackle the obstacles to their cause.[28]

Further research on the members of reform societies revealed a profile of youthful, upwardly mobile men and women following an energetic evangelical spirit, not declining elites holding on to a bygone era. Marxist historians argued that the "humanitarian" sensibility of the reform movements was tied to the material interests of capitalists. Antislavery, temperance, and other moral reform campaigns served to legitimate and discipline wage labor. More interestingly and on topic, they argued that the extensive temporal and geographic horizons of market sensibilities shaped the new humanitarianism and its moral concern for distant suffering. Feminist historians uncovered the independent and sometimes rebellious role of women in benevolent and reform societies. These images clashed strongly with the revisionist visions of "an elite without function, a displaced class."[29]

Rich social histories of local communities interlaced these themes of the rising influence of a younger generation, a new middle class, and activist women. These community studies documented the emergence of popular support for a range of reform causes, occurring at roughly the same time, and tied this support to the social ascendancy of a new middle class and especially the women of this emerging class. Paul Johnson, in a study of revivals and reforms in Rochester, New York, argued that the efforts of wealthy evangelicals associated with benevolent societies to influence their poorer neighbors on issues such as temperance and Sabbath observance reached an impasse in the 1820s. With the arrival of the revivalist Charles Grandison Finney in the winter of 1830–31, the residents of Rochester pushed through this impasse, unleashing reform campaigns that reached into the lower classes of the industrializing city. Johnson highlighted the prominent role of shopkeepers and entrepreneurial mechanics in Finney's revival and the reform movements that followed in its wake. He argued that as market pressures separated workplace from home, evangelical members of an emerging middle class suffered guilt for their part in expelling workers from their homes. The developing middle class of Rochester sought through the revivals and reform movements to reestablish the moral control they had exercised over their apprentices when they lived and worked under the same roof. Through these movements, an emerging middle class pushed for moral influence in the places where laborers carried on their lives after work: the boardinghouses, taverns, and theaters of a new market society.

Mary Ryan's study of Utica supported central aspects of Johnson's account while it illuminated the central role of women in these events. Interrogating the same social process from the anxious perspective of mothers and would-be mothers, Ryan established the disproportionate role of women in the middle-class revivals and reforms of the period. In the first quarter of the nineteenth century, the frontier household based on subsistence farming collapsed under the expansion of agrarian capitalism and the attending demographic pressures. Rural New York households could no longer ensure sustainable growth on family land or through the acquisition of new property. Forced to turn out their children into a new market economy, women mobilized to influence the civic morality of this new social order. In the revivals and evangelical reforms of the 1830s, women sought to reconstitute a moral order lost with the passing of family-based production. Under these pressures, the moral vigilance of the family had to take new form, and women took the unprecedented step of making claims against the *public* affairs of men.[30]

These community studies were more sensitive to class and gender than to religion. To their credit, they acknowledged the influence of religious experiences, but they betrayed uneasiness with letting these stand as motives in the last instance. In this sense, they continued to share in a long tradition of scholarly work on reform that sought to answer questions about the "real" motivations behind movements, but a shift in the interpretation of antebellum reform was unmistakable. Reformers were no longer viewed simply as declining in status, alienated, impractical, and disturbed. Acknowledgment of the role of organizations and material resources in the reform movements—particularly the influence of evangelical organizations and the material support from a rising middle class and women—replaced revisionist claims of the anti-institutionalism of reformers. The antebellum movements no longer appeared so much as the fruits of emotionalism, as that of professional organizing and the material interests of a new middle class. Finally, the fanaticism of reformers—or at least of abolitionists—was no longer an issue of central significance, and their pragmatism and strategy for organizing public pressure not as likely to be disparaged.

Evangelical Sin and Confession: Toward a New
Theory of the Sources of Antebellum Reform

This change in the historiography of antebellum reform paralleled the contemporaneous interpretive shift in the sociology of social movements, but it was something less than a paradigm shift. As evident in the works of Ryan and Johnson, reforms and revivals were in part innovative reactions to anxiety and guilt. The new form of activism transformed the way a new middle class understood itself and the way it made public claims for moral order. This innovative form of collective action did not simply reflect class interests. It established the cultural and material expectations of an emerging class, and it was shaped by religious reactions to the guilt and anxiety of shopkeepers, women, and mothers.

Ryan and Johnson echoed an insight from Elkins's work: The reform movements intertwined personal and emotional struggles over social identity and recognition with complicated and large-scale social issues. In the final analysis, they concluded that the direction this anxiety and guilt typically took—the imperative of spiritual rebirth through the reformation of sins like drinking, profaning the Sabbath, adultery—was at best a displacement or at worst a cover for material or domestic interests. Nonetheless, the collective and religious articulation of anxiety provided a form and purpose to extensive social movements that material interests and resources alone could not.

Unlike the contemporary trends in sociology, in history the religious expression of emotions retained significant explanatory power and for good reasons. Honest observers could not fail to notice that these movements were shot through with guilt. Even if material and domestic imperatives did lurk behind these anxieties, the emotional dimensions of reform most often found religious expression. Even before revisionists like Craven articulated their social-psychological accounts, historians Gilbert Barnes and Dwight Dumond presented what we might today term a cultural explanation for the emergence of the reform movements—an explanation that found in the religious schemas of evangelical Christianity the keys to the development of antebellum reform.

Barnes's classic book *The Antislavery Impulse* described the abolitionist movement as a religious revival against the sin of slavery. In Barnes's account and in later accounts by Dumond, the moral universe of evangelicals emerged as the key to understanding the spread of the antislavery movement—and by implication other reforms like temperance. A new recognition of sin and guilt and a new sense of optimism in the ability of people to perfect themselves shaped antebellum reforms. Unlike the revisionists, Barnes and Dumond did not see a distorted reality in these responses to the sin of slavery. They did not impugn the religious sentiments of the evangelicals driving abolitionism and reform. As Dumond would make clear decades later, they viewed the antislavery impulse as heroic.[31]

Seventy years of historical and sociological research on the relationship between evangelicalism and antebellum reform has amended but not overturned Barnes's and Dumond's interpretation.[32] For example, David Brion Davis argued that the emergence of widespread support for antislavery after 1830 was clearly much more than a shift in organization or interests; it was a transformation in "total outlook from [a] detached, rationalistic perspective on human history and progress to a personal commitment to make no compromise with sin." Anne Loveland made more explicit the link between evangelicalism and the reformist disposition: the evangelical experience of conversion "crystallized" a sense of sin and "provided the vocabulary and method of [antislavery] immediatism."[33] Most historical accounts of temperance and other antebellum reforms now acknowledge the influence of evangelicalism and, in particular, religious revivals on popular reform mobilizations.[34]

Ronald Walters, in his excellent survey of a broad range of antebellum reform movements, captures the enduring value of the culturalist approach initiated by Barnes and Dumond. Looking beyond the psyches, material resources, and class interests of activists, a reform movement, Walters argues, "starts when a few men and women declare that something is evil and they know the cure for it." As broad popular support for attacking slavery emerged, there were "hundreds of objections that could have been made," but reformers "made only a handful of them. Why those and not others?" The answer to this type of question, Walters correctly notes, leads to an exploration of the "cultural conditions that *permitted* . . . reformers to see reality as they did."[35]

In the 1980s, as sociologists made a "cultural turn," many took up an exploration very much like the one Walters described. Although there were many efforts to develop cultural explanations of social movements, including work on the formation and maintenance of collective identities and the role of narrative in protests, "frame analysis" became the dominant approach in the American sociology of social movements.[36] Drawing on the work of Erving Goffman, David Snow and his colleagues defined a frame as a "schemata of interpretation" that enables individuals to "organize experience and guide action" by simplifying and condensing the "world out there."[37] Cultural frames help potential movement participants make sense of the conditions they confront and clarify what is to be done about these conditions. In Walters's terms, frame analysis specifies the "cultural conditions" that permit activists to see circumstances as unjust and as changeable.[38]

Frame analysis emerged to address the neglect of cultural and, in particular, ideational elements in social movement research. And by the response to the work of Snow and his close collaborator Robert Benford, it has clearly succeeded. Over the next two decades, a wave of new research on framing processes was published in leading sociology journals. It is not much of an exaggeration to describe the cultural turn in American social movement research as a turn toward framing.

Frame analysis has not been without critics—even critics sympathetic to the cultural turn in sociology. Pamela Oliver and her colleagues argue that the theory does not account for why frames do or do not resonate. Frames that resonate strike a responsive chord, they speak compellingly to people, they win adherents. Snow and Benford contend that the fit between a movement's frames and the "life world of adherents and constituents as well as bystanders" determines resonance, but Oliver is right to point out that the analysis basically stops there. This problem of resonance is linked to a second. There is a clear ideational or cognitive bias in frame theory. As Benford himself acknowledges, frame theory has yet to find a place for emotions. If it does, it might also find a key to the missing matter of resonance. Sociologists, in their rebellion against the critical accounts of social protest before the 1960s, banished almost all talk of emotion. The cultural turn of the 1980s, and frame analysis in particular, did little to incorporate emotions into explanations of movements. Because historians did not entirely abandon the social-psychological interpretations of the 1950s, the finest of the cultural studies of antebellum reform movements are riveted to the forces of guilt, anxiety, doubt, and sensitivity, and they reveal much of what is needed in the sociology of social movements.[39]

From the beginning, the culturalist approach in history was laced with emotions. As Barnes argued, the abolitionists' recognition of slavery as a sin meant "more than a change of opinion; . . . it meant a change in their lives." Similarly, Davis described the commitment to immediate abolitionism as an expression of "an immediate transformation within the reformer himself" and a "freedom from guilt." Loveland came to a similar conclusion about the nature of antislavery commitments: "immediatism signaled a change in disposition, not of discourse." [40] Robert Abzug, in his masterful overview of antebellum reform movements, argues that a religious imagination and passion that hoped to reorder society at large and the intimate details of everyday life animated these movements. This religious passion offered a "self-scrutinizing national piety." Those who took to this offer with abandon—the leaders of the reform movements—were the "religious virtuosos" of an evangelical middle class. Abzug uses Max Weber's term to identify the vanguard of the movements as individuals "who craved religious experiences." Although committed to a dramatic transformation of society, reformers were attuned to "the inward interests of a truly religiously 'musical'" temperament. Similarly, Bertram Wyatt-Brown's work describes reformers as deeply sensitive men and women caught up in large-scale social processes. Abolitionists, Wyatt-Brown contends, "were romantics, racked with feelings they did not fully understand." Even so, "fed by their own romantic meditations, abolitionists guessed with some precision the [social] effects of total masterhood and bondage." [41]

The romantic saints or religious virtuosos of antebellum reform were relatively few in number. The mass movements of temperance and antislavery mobilized support from people less religiously musical, but among the rank and file the offer or challenge of a self-scrutinizing national piety proved popular and motivating. As with religious movements in general, believers are attracted to the sacralizing power of virtuoso leaders even as they may fall short of the same heights of religious experience. The promise of reforms spoke to a wider audience than those who could answer it in full.

The present study is not a call to return to the social psychology of collective behaviorism or the revisionist historiography of antebellum reform. The mobilization of resources mattered. Reformers were architects of organizations essential to the success of their movements. They also exploited opportunities provided by political processes, and they were not especially irrational or fanatical. But the driving force behind these movements was the coming together of religious schemas that alloyed self-scrutiny to national piety. Elkins was not all wrong when he characterized antebellum reform as a mix of introspective guilt and high-flying abstractions, and appreciating this emotional and cultural power reminds us that something valuable in collective behaviorism should be recovered. There was a good degree of what Smelser terms short-circuiting in this. The result was to relate anxious personal situations to broad social problems in a fashion that motivated collective action. As Blumer theorized, antebellum reforms presented individuals with the chance for personal expansion in extensive social causes. The last section of this chapter draws on theories of cultural schemas *and* emotions to better specify how this cultural mechanism—this fusing of the intimate and the extensive, the personal and the political—could propel a national wave of social movements.

The Role of Intensive and Extensive Schemas in the First U.S. National Social Movements

The concepts of cultural frames and cultural schemas are closely related. Erving Goffman defined frames as "interpretive schemata." The rules of frames, according to Goffman, are analogous to the syntactical structures of language. These linguistic structures, as William H. Sewell, Jr., points out, have been, for better or worse, treated as paradigmatic of the operation of cultural schemas. Moreover, recent sociological research on social movements has made good use of conjoining the two theoretical concepts. Schemas, however, seem to connote a more generative and embodied cultural phenomena than frames.[42]

In the social movement literature, frames are largely treated as cognitive devices subject to an instrumental logic. Frames belong to a wider cultural toolkit that activists employ for mostly strategic purposes to motivate others. The conceptual roots of cultural schemas in structural anthropology, semiotics, and hermeneutic theory provide for a deeper and more generative image. Schemas pattern, compel, and even constitute actors. Actors belong to schemas as much as schemas belong to them. This is not to suggest that they cannot be strategically deployed or factor into strategic action. Schemas also suggest embodied practices and dispositions or temperaments as well as more ideational constructs. This embodied aspect to schemas provides the link between the cultural and emotional dimensions of movements that has been missing in the framing literature.

On the other hand, an important advantage frame analysis holds over a theory of cultural schemas is its easy handling of issues of agency. The mechanism of framing is the hallmark of this cultural approach, and there is no simple conceptual counterpart to this form of agency in a theory of schemas. By emphasizing the structuring power of schemas, cultural theory runs the risk of denying agency. In response to this risk, the following discussion draws from the pragmatist tradition to open a space for agency within a cultural theory of schemas.[43]

Cultural schemas give form to experiences. They structure social life as they mediate experiences, making them meaningful and practical. As Sewell describes schemas, they provide people with "meanings, motivations, and recipes for social action." Symbols, metaphors, frames, scripts, conventions, rituals, and even habits provide schematic shape to social life. As actors transpose these intersubjective schemas across changing circumstances, as they apply them to manifold sense perception, they construct coherence, significance, and purpose out of their otherwise chaotic experiences. Through these schemas, actors render social life continuous, meaningful, practical, and more or less routine. They often operate at a prereflexive, taken-for-granted level of awareness; they shape how the world unfolds or flows from practical sensibilities. In this sense, schemas can be "embodied," shaping the way people stand, walk, feel, speak, as well as think. Schemas enable social actors to trust their experiences; they provide what Anthony Giddens calls "ontological security."[44]

Cultural schemas are transposable or modular, but not all schemas are equally so. Some are very extensive and others less so. The range of subjective and intersubjective experiences that schemas subsume can be more or less wide. For a particular individual, a schema like sin or joke may inform a wide or narrow range of her acts, thoughts, or feelings. Some find the human experience shot through with sin. Others find a much more limited range of experience as worthy of moral condemnation. For a particular type of act, thought, or feeling, a wide or narrow range of individuals may make sense of it under a schema of sin or joke. Some acts or statements may transpose widely as a joke. Others may not travel well turning incomprehensible or even offensive.

Extensive schemas, ones that travel well, may only touch lightly on the understandings, motives, and actions of people. The handshake, for example, is currently widely practiced and recognized. In most instances, the significance of this act is superficial or diffuse. Boxers shake hands before they pummel each other, and Christian congregants shake hands as they wish each other peace. Although widely recognized as a gesture of courtesy, the handshake often conveys little else about the motives of the people shaking. There was a time and there remain particular situations when the handshake expresses something much less diffuse—a gesture of not carrying a weapon, a contractual agreement backed by the reputations of the shakers, or a heartfelt expression of care; but in its present and widest practice the handshake often controls little more than a perfunctory action surrounding comings and goings.

Intensive schemas, on the other hand, tightly control meaning, motives, and action.[45] A code of vengeance, for example, may control matters of life and death. The extent of influence of a particular schema of revenge, say the Corsican vendetta, may be narrow compared to conventions governing greetings, but it may deeply affect the intentions of those it does reach. The schematic structure of a vendetta depends on nuances in the extent and salience of the blood ties of honor, the related reach of the stain of shame, and the measures that are called for to remove the stain of shame and defend family honor. Codes of vengeance can trigger cycles of bloodshed that direct the affairs of kinsman over and above all other material and spiritual concerns. Intensive schemas claim a supreme and total right of primacy over social experience. Intensive schemas strike a deep emotional resonance; individuals are deeply and psychologically invested in these schemas. Intensive schemas do not change without disrupting an individual's sense of self, without disrupting their identity.

How extensive a schema is often mitigates against how intensive it is and vice versa. This is not a necessary relationship. As will become clear, an extensive *and* intensive evangelical schema (or fusion of schemas) shaped antebellum moral reforms. Nonetheless, the extension of a schema tends to attenuate its tight control over meanings, motives, and actions. With the worldwide extension of the handshake as a universal form of greeting, it lost much of its earlier significance. Very intensive schemas, on the other hand, tend toward an inwardness that can inhibit their spread. The deadly dynamics of the vendetta do not extend easily beyond or even within blood ties.[46]

As cultural schemas shape meanings, motives, and forms of action, they generate and command material and human resources. Schemas are also enabled and constrained by these resources. In Clifford Geertz's terms, cultural schemas can be both "models of" and "models for" the coordination of material and human resources. The relationship between schemas and resources is recursive; they are both input and output for the other. Resources embody or instantiate schemas, but at the same time they convey and reproduce schemas.[47]

To draw on an example central to this book, the material and human resources of Christian churches convey the schema of confession: Churches enshrine confession, ministers preach confession, a liturgy scripts confession, and congregants model confession. At the same time, confession generates and regenerates these human and material resources: Confession brings converts, structures the liturgy, provides a message for ministers, and renews congregants' spiritual and material commitments to the church. The recursive relationship between schemas and resources is often tightly coupled and resists change. It provides for institutional stability. Social movements emerge when schemas are transposed in creative ways that turn material and human resources to new purposes.

Creative transpositions of schemas come about regularly and for many reasons. In institutionally differentiated societies, opportunities for the novel extension of schemas regularly emerge. Most often transpositions do not redirect collective action and material resources to radically new ends. But in culturally diverse settings, with multiple connecting and overlapping social spheres structured by distinct constellations of schemas, the control of resources can be unpredictable as schemas from one context are extended to another, transforming the meaning and purpose of accumulated resources. In these situations of imbricated social domains, actors move from one sphere of activity to another and transpose schemas. In the process, schemas may be transformed and resources redirected.[48]

Social change can also disrupt the recursive organization of schemas and resources. As with movement across social spheres, in changing social conditions, people are forced to extend cultural schemas to make sense of new experiences. Societies are, of course, always changing, but the pace, reach, and, more importantly, the cultural fallout of this change are not constant. Even in the face of sweeping social change, traditional cultural schemas may only need adaptation to make sense of what is going on, to guide action, and to stabilize resource control. Individuals and collective actors may reassuringly manage changing circumstances. The recursive relationship between schemas and resources, though dynamic, remains smooth. It is also possible that cultural schemas will not prove adaptable. Under rapid social change, as schemas extend to make sense of new circumstances, they may become so attenuated that they no longer cohere, stop making sense, and lose their command over resources. Finally, it is also possible that as schemas extend to make sense of new circumstances they may generate surprising new meanings, motives, and even identities and may convert material and human resources to new purposes.

The unsettling processes unleashed by social change and by mobility among social spheres regularly interact in modern societies. Change drives mobility and mobility drives change, creating further dynamism within and across social spheres. Change surrounds actors regardless of whether they are moving or staying put. This change can lead to what Blumer described as "social unrest." In these instances, change disorients and disrupts actors. The comfortable mediation of experience by cultural schemas falters. Restless actors balk at the reality they face. Reality shatters their routines, habits, and assumptions. Restlessness calls for more than an adaptation of the cultural schemas to reconstruct familiar experiences and lines of conduct; it calls for what John Dewey termed an "adjustment in life."[49]

In these crises, as the familiar lines of action rebound and shatter, actors must free themselves from stymied routines and discover new possibilities to move beyond the arresting situation. Intentional and creative responses emerge as actors search for new lines of action, new meanings, and new identities. This is an assertive and creative act. Some may adapt more or less comfortably through the stable mediation of existing cultural schemas, some may become disoriented and disassemble, and still others may make radical adjustments extending cultural schemas to new purposes. This last and third way is the way of movements. In adjusting to the changing circumstances, these actors *project* themselves into the change. When this projection is a collective act it constitutes *a social movement.*[50]

As described so far, a social movement might appear simply as a creative response to an epistemological challenge brought on by changing circumstances, but the grounds for creative movement are as emotional as they are cognitive. What is disrupted and challenged when experience and practice balk at a changing or unfamiliar circumstance is first and foremost the affective disposition of individuals toward the social world. Cultural schemas provide ontological security by mediating experience and rendering social life familiar and routine. Restlessness undermines that trust in social experience. Disruption of routine life is first *felt* and only then does a definition or conceptual grasp of the situation, of the problem, and of the way to proceed begin to emerge. In order for actors to reorient themselves in the unfamiliar setting, they must feel their way. It is the uneasiness of losing the familiar and the excitement of new horizons opened up by this disruption that prompt the creative force driving social movements.[51]

For Blumer and Smelser, anxiety is the primary emotional reaction to these situations of disruption, frustration, and ambiguity. According to their social-psychological approach, the restlessness or strain that stems from rapid social change or mobility awakens a fear without a clear object. Social movements take form when this diffuse emotion is focused by a novel symbolic mediation. From this perspective, it follows that an emotional response relatively unmediated by cultural schemas cannot provide direction to individual actors, let alone to collective actors. As people who suffer from phobias know too well, anxiety can be paralyzing and is not a straightforward motive for action. Hysteria may lead to action, but it is typically unimaginative and without clear purpose or direction. In the event of radical collective disorientation and anxiety, social movements are unlikely to form and collective actors are more likely to disassemble than they are to react.

Adaptation and adjustment to the disruption of experience depend on fighting off or mediating disorientation and anxiety. Adaptation does so quite easily whereas adjustment is a more emotionally charged response. Movements are collective adjustments and emerge somewhere between the collapse and the easy adaptation of cultural schemas, and somewhere between pervasive anxiety without a clear object and the comfortable emotional management of change. In this in-between zone, movements provide schemas that channel emotions into action. They provide a vocabulary of motives that makes sense of what people are feeling and suggest how they should act on these feelings.

Given the recursive relationship between schemas and resources, individuals most disconnected from institutions and stable social networks are least likely to respond purposefully to emotional disorientations. They are least likely to discover a symbolic mediation to make purposeful sense of their insecurity. Individuals deeply embedded in stable institutions are likely to find ways to easily accommodate change and will experience little disorientation. It is actors in between these limits that will respond to insecurity not by disassembling or adapting but by adjusting. They are potential activists. They can project themselves in creative ways into the uncertain circumstances.

Intensive schemas, ones that provide firm control over meaning, motives, and actions, would seem key to movements that adjust action and actors in times of unrest. Intensive schemas shape and are shaped by emotions that fix a personal sense of security in the world. Intensive schemas inform an actor's sense of self and the practices she is most committed to and least willing to abandon. Intensive schemas are most likely to guide purposeful action in the face of disorientation. However, as noted above, the salience of intensive schemas is easily attenuated with wide extension. In informing new experiences and constructing collective action across diverse settings, intensive schemas are tested. Extensive schemas would seem to hold the key to movements that spread across changing events and settings, but as noted above, the influence of extended schemas over material and human resources are often weak, and their control over these resources most easily disrupted. The wide extension of schemas often runs counter to the tight control of meanings, motives, and forms of action; and movements cannot succeed without such control if they are to mobilize people and resources in the face of unrest. Extensive schemas seem at once central to widespread social movements in differentiated and changing societies and unlikely catalysts of forms of collective action that demand resolve.

An important aspect of cultural schemas helps resolve this seeming paradox. As classical sociology introduced and semiotic theory developed, cultural schemas interrelate—sacred with profane, good with evil, purity with pollution, wet with dry, milk with blood. Cultural theory tends to emphasize the interrelations among cultural schemas as binary oppositions or equivalences, but different schemas can combine, producing surprising outcomes.[52] In Christianity, for example, sin is axial to confession, and confession overcomes sin. If the meaning of sin changes, then confession is redirected; if the form of confession is altered, then the battle against sin changes. With interrelated schemas like sin and confession, the extension of a particular schema may activate a related schema in the new context to surprising directions, and because the extending schema combines with an embedded schema, the human and material resource effects may be quite intensive. The opportunity for these interactions, the likelihood of such a cultural mechanism taking hold, depends upon lineaments spanning changing circumstances and different social domains. As Elisabeth Clemens argues, cultural transpositions across institutional boundaries follow a logic of appropriateness. The extending schema must fit or mesh with established cultural and emotional patterns, but the resulting interaction can produce creative moments not fully anticipated by the actors transposing the schemas. In its combination of intensive and extensive schemas, this mechanism can provide at once deeply personal adjustments and wide cultural resonance.[53]

Cultural mechanisms that combine intensive and extensive schemas command significant material and human resources, including emotions. Even across changing and institutionally differentiated settings, these mechanisms exercise deep and diffuse control. In early nineteenth-century America, activists working to mobilize widespread support had to speak to split registers of social life. Although the citizens of the new republic were no strangers to social change, historians generally agree that the scope and speed of the upheaval during this period were unprecedented. For many, the experience was profoundly disorienting. In a social context of demographic upheaval, expanding markets, and traditional social

institutions outpaced by these social forces, interregional movements had
to tap meanings and forms of actions that gripped and adjusted individuals disembedded from traditional arrangements. They had to speak to
and shape emotional responses to these conditions, and they had to make
sense of bewildering circumstances created by anonymous and far-flung
market and demographic processes. Across these polarized registers of
social experience, antebellum reform movements had to provide coherent
meaning and motivations. Bearing witness against special sins—the dominant form of protest—accomplished this. It provided a simultaneously intensive and extensive collective project: a confessional project that was at
once "self-scrutinizing" and "national." [54]

Theories of contemporary life politics specify a similar dynamic of successful movement mobilization.[55] Characteristic of life politics is a telescoping of intensive and extensive projects: commitments of personal significance and purposes of great social abstraction. Recent work on cultural frames in social movement research comes to a similar conclusion:
the popular mobilization of resources by movements is effected by "collective action frames" that "align" broad social conditions to personal sys-
tems of motivation. But these theoretical approaches do not explain how
this process works. The process is similar to the symbolic mediation introduced by Blumer. As he argued, in a social movement the activist's being is
intertwined with the objective of the movement. This experience is one of
personal "expansion" as intensive concerns "surge forth" in the direction
of the extensive cause of the movement. It involves what Smelser termed
a process of short-circuiting as the polarized registers of social life are
linked. Historians like Elkins and Craven disparaged this intensive and
extensive dynamic in antebellum moral reformers as an unstable mix of
"introspective guilt" and "high-flying abstractions." Although their judgment against the reformers was too harsh, they rightly recognized that the
combination of different registers, the emotional introspection and the
high-flying moral cause, were formative and distinctive of these new moral
reform movements. But, there is nothing necessarily fanatical in this projection of the self into abstract causes; to the contrary, it is indispensable
for anyone trying to make sense of a life caught up in extensive and complex social processes. It is, however, an inherently emotional process.

* * *

In the first three decades of the nineteenth century, sweeping social change
pressed Americans to adapt, withdraw, or adjust. Some adapted to the ex-

tensive and rapid change without a radical reorientation of life, but many others became, in a word, restless. There was no simple or uniform emotional response to this restlessness. It stirred pervasive feelings of anxiety, excitement, and a mix of both. Political, economic, and demographic pressures made many feel scared, trampled on, and powerless; still others felt exhilarated, unleashed, and newly powerful. Data on the consumption of alcohol suggest that many Americans sought courage and shelter in drink. Some seized opportunities to amass great wealth and to move aggressively to control the fate of others. Some turned more inward to build self-reliance and control their own fate (for example, transcendalists), and still others turned to communal withdrawal (for example, Mormons).

For the subjects of this book—the antebellum reformers—the challenge led to amplification and moral extension of the self into a dynamic nation that had to be redeemed. Under political, economic, demographic, and religious pressures, the cosmos of many evangelicals started to crumble. For many evangelicals, the loss of ecclesiastical authority over communities and fundamental changes in religious doctrine and practices compounded their sense of disorientation. At the same time, certain evangelical schemas through transposition gained new and unexpected salience. It was in this cultural adjustment that widespread reform movements got their start. This creative response expressed and sharpened deep and pervasive feelings of guilt. These men and women were driven by a sense of expanded (critics said distorted) personal moral responsibility for distant and vast arrangements. Historically speaking, it was a new moral outlook.[56]

Given their religious temperament, evangelicals were disposed to interpret the mix of anxiety and excitement experienced by many fellow Americans as guilt feelings. Even as theological truths, established authority structures, and liturgical practices crumbled, an evangelical temperament extended across the religious uncertainty. As evangelicals moved to adjust their beliefs and their engagement with the world during a period of unsettling change, emotions became a sounding board for the adjustment of cultural schemas. Evangelicals felt their way through the unrest, and the emotion of guilt served as a gyroscope keeping reformers questing. As their cosmos crumbled, they were thrown back onto certain core sentiments about their engagement with the world. Reform movements offered a way out of crisis by addressing and channeling these sentiments. Abolitionists and teetotalers felt their way, as much as thought their way, into movement, and the dominant feeling they followed was guilt. The dynamics of evangelical guilt, and the cultural mediation of this emotion by variations in the schemas of sins and confession were at the heart of the

interregional success of temperance, abolitionism, and a host of other reform movements.

Over the next five chapters, empirical analyses will ground these abstract claims. After covering some solid history of the events and people
shaping the first U.S. national social movements, the conclusion to this
book revisits this theory. It explores in greater detail the evangelical emotion of guilt and how a schematic mediation of this emotion shaped the
modular form, the special purposes, and the new identities of a national
wave of protests. It also explains in more concrete terms how guilt mediated by a call to bear witness against special sins led to type of life politics
in early nineteenth-century America: a form of protest that was decisive
in the formation of the first U.S. national social movements and that continues to shape modern social movements.

CHAPTER TWO

Mammon, Church, and State in a Restless America

S ustained and interregional protests were central to the revolutionary activities of American colonists. The American Revolution may have been the first national social movement, but after the Revolution, protest reverted to an older form of collective action. The uprisings of poor farmers in Shays's Rebellion in Massachusetts and in the Whiskey Rebellion in Pennsylvania were relatively short-lived, regionally contained, and involved more traditional forms of direct action and local patronage. The collective action of mechanics and apprentices relied on an old repertoire of contention. Citywide associations of laborers did not emerge until the 1830s, and only for a brief period in that decade was there coordination among worker associations across northeastern cities. Before the 1820s, religious campaigns for moral reforms were also regionally contained and relatively short-lived. Antivice campaigns in Calvinist-dominated communities were common during this period. In these campaigns, congregants and the minister of the local church, often with the help of the magistrate, would for a period of time step up public sanctions against Sabbath violations, public drinking, and other moral failings. These campaigns were not coordinated across communities, let alone the nation. In short, for almost the first half-century of the new republic, there were no prolonged, interregional social protests. The U.S. national social movement had yet to appear.[1]

In the late 1820s and 1830s this all changed. Widespread campaigns to change or protect institutions central to American life suddenly reappeared. Labor movements or state-centered movements did not lead. The first national social movement was for temperance. Soon after, a series of similar moral reform movements followed, including most notably the movement for immediate abolitionism. Alexis de Tocqueville visited America just as this wave of movements started to gather force. Unlike the events of 1848 in his native France, which he famously predicted, Tocqueville did not anticipate the conflict that was about to erupt. He did recognize that the nation was restless, possibly dangerously so. "Scarcely have you descended on the soil of America when you find yourself in the midst of a sort of tumult; a confused clamor is raised on all sides." This restlessness, he concluded, owed much to the nation's unique political institutions, its voluntary associations, and above all else, its ceaseless economic activity.

> Americans arrived only yesterday on the soil they inhabit, and they have already overturned the whole order of nature to their profit. They have united the Hudson to the Mississippi and linked the Atlantic Ocean with the Gulf of Mexico across more than five hundred leagues of continent that separate these two seas. The longest railroads that have been made up to our day are in America.

He saw an "innumerable multitude of small enterprises"—not any particular great project or ambition—as driving this unprecedented social assertion over space.[2]

According to Tocqueville, what saved this gigantic, enterprising nation with its democratic institutions and weak central government from descending into disorder or tyranny was that the people were engaged primarily in local political and material ambitions. Americans had directed their boundless energy into the "meandering rivulets of private interest and local associations." This unfettered populace was too busy in its own immediate affairs to combine in movements of a factious majority that might threaten the political stability of the nation.[3]

Christianity seemed to Tocqueville to be one of the few social institutions capable of exercising some discipline over this tumult. Indeed, the first thing in America that struck his eye was not the commotion of commerce or the "very excess of democracy" but the "religious aspect of the country." He marveled, in particular, at the American Sabbath:

> In the United States, when the seventh day of each week arrives, the commercial and industrial life of the nation seems suspended; all noise ceases. A deep

repose, or rather a sort of solemn meditation, follows; the soul finally comes back into possession of itself and contemplates itself. . . . Thus at times the American in a way steals away from himself, and as he is torn away for a moment from the small passions that agitate his life and the passing interests that fill it, he at once enters into an ideal world in which all is great, pure, eternal.

This account may have best described New England townships and Calvinist-dominated communities outside that region, but Tocqueville had good cause to consider Christianity as Americans' "first" social institution. He correctly sized up the importance of American religion, but he guessed badly on the direction of its civic and political impact. He did not foresee the unfolding conflict of the 1830s because he failed to appreciate that it was precisely religion that could assemble a factious, mass movement capable of asserting its will across the extent of a restive nation. In this, religion was a unique social force in early nineteenth-century America.[4]

A Booming Nation

The type of "agitation" displayed by individual Americans was not entirely unfamiliar to Tocqueville, but it seemed to compass "the whole people" and this, he thought, represented something historically new. He may have been right. The nation he visited was in the midst of a period of unequaled demographic growth. In 1790, 3.9 million people lived in the United States. By 1830, there were 12.8 million Americans. This rate of population growth outpaced all other countries over the same period. This population boom was almost entirely the result of high fertility rates among "native" Americans. The main influx of European immigration was still to come. This booming population was also very mobile.[5]

It is likely that "not since the seventeenth century had such a high proportion of the white [American] population lived in newly settled communities."[6] Migration was predominantly from east to west. In 1790, 5 percent of the population lived west of the Appalachian Mountains. By 1830, more than 25 percent of a population that had tripled lived in states west of the Appalachian Mountains. The net in-migration was greatest to the Old Northwest. The population of Ohio jumped from 45,356 in 1800 to 932,903 in 1830. In three decades, Ohio went from frontier land with a population smaller than Delaware to the fourth largest state in the nation. Because this migration tended to cross latitudes, not longitudes, some of

the North-South cultural differences that existed on the seaboard repro-
duced themselves in the interior. That said, the western settlements were
typically more diverse than the established communities back east. In the
Northwest, for example, New Englanders, upland southerners, and migrants from Pennsylvanian lived in close proximity.[7]

This broad social change cannot explain the precise timing or the uneven geographic spread of support for the national wave of social movements that broke out across the country in the 1830s. At best, this demographic upheaval provided widespread but diffuse restlessness that could
be channeled into social movements, but as Tocqueville observed, there
seemed to be few extensive social forces capable of disciplining or coordinating this restive activity. These restless Americans had left behind many
of the traditional forms of collective action and patterns of institutional
authority that shaped movements in the past. One of the few purposes
that did unite a broad segment of Americans was commercial ambition.
Indeed, this ambition was driving much of the internal migration.

A Transportation and Market Revolution

The subsistence culture of American farm families initiated this population boom and western movement. After the War of 1812, plentiful new
territories and capitalist transformation hastened the mobility. Political
treaties, turnpikes, canals, steamboats, and railroads opened up the fertile lands and natural resources of the interior to emerging interregional
markets. Market interests centered in Boston, New York, Philadelphia,
and Baltimore pushed for the commercial development of the hinterland.
Eastern property values soared as the price of farm products dropped.
The combination made many eastern household farms unviable. Whereas
earlier generations of farmers had been able to subdivide their land hold-
ings or acquire nearby land in order to set each of their male offspring
with his very own household farm, this became increasingly difficult in
the East. Many families were forced to send their children to work in industrial or commercial trades in the cities or to sell off their eastern farms
and purchase larger tracts of land out west in a bid to keep the household farm. Markets pulled migrants toward opportunity but also repelled
them. Many migrants moved west to escape a life of wage labor back east.
In some cases, entire communities moved west trying to reproduce their
eighteenth-century producer societies on the frontier.[8]

The same transportation network that conveyed farm products from the periphery to core cities brought millions of emigrants and finished products westward to newly settled regions. New forms of transportation dramatically cut the time it took to travel long distances. For example, the relatively short trip of 150 miles from New York City to Albany took two days to two weeks by sailing packets. By the 1830s, steamboats made the trip in under ten hours. In the first quarter of the century, the grain products of western farmers could only find distant markets by roads in a distilled form of whiskey or through long river trips down to New Orleans and then via ship to the eastern cities. By the 1830s, cities like Philadelphia, New York, and Baltimore tapped grain markets in the Ohio and Mississippi valleys directly through canals and railroads.[9]

Farmers producing for the markets also became consumers of commodities produced in the eastern cities or in Europe. By the 1820s, middleclass farmers were replacing the home's hearth with stoves and homespun with calico. They were substituting specialty agricultural products grown on the more expensive farmland close to the commercial centers for a diet of grains and salted pork. By the 1820s, four port-hinterland market axes flourished. The most powerful and extensive reached from New York City up the Hudson River, across western New York along the newly built Erie Canal, and into the Ohio and Mississippi valleys. In the early nineteenth century, as the dominant port of foreign trade with the best access to the nation's interior, New York City surpassed the economic influence of other major cities. This commercial route was also fed by Boston and the western and northern New England market region. New England émigrés moved in large numbers along this route to western New York, Ohio, and beyond. Other booming port-hinterland market regions extended from Philadelphia west to Pittsburgh and the Ohio River, and from Baltimore west and south.

To describe these economic changes as a market revolution may be a little misleading. Eighteenth-century American farmers had allotted some of their production for the market and were never entirely self-sufficient. The economic change most American farmers experienced in the early nineteenth century was not from pure household production to an entirely market business. Nonetheless, the degree of market dependency among Americans was staggering when compared to the first years of the new republic. This reality was painfully brought home in 1819 when the United States suffered its first *national* economic crisis. Increasingly the material interests and needs of Americans intertwined with the interests and needs of others hundreds and even thousands of miles away. Farmers produced for consumers they only read about, and consumers used commodities produced in settings and in ways that they never directly experienced. A statistical table of trade on the Schuylkill Canal in 1826 published in *Niles Register* provides a glimpse of the types of goods and their direction in this commerce. The canal ran west from Philadelphia to Port Carbon, Pennsylvania. Raw materials like iron ore, foodstuffs like flour, and whiskey flowed east in large amounts. Store goods, plaster of paris, specialty food items, and empty containers flowed west.[10]

Within a generation, extensive and complex market forces mediated most aspects of everyday life. Americans increasingly appreciated that distant events and forces impacted their immediate livelihood, even though they dimly understood how. The transportation networks and commercial newspapers of this new market society provided resources that moral reformers used to build and extend support for their causes. Expanding market institutions presented a material and informational infrastructure that made interregional movements possible, but they alone cannot explain the precise timing, the uneven geographical spread, and, most importantly, the form and purposes of these movements.

Markets cannot explain why the movements appeared in the period between the late 1820s and mid-1830s or why support came from where it did. This was a period of rapid economic expansion, but the same could be said for numerous other seven-year periods in the first half of the nineteenth century. The geographic distribution of support for antislavery and temperance societies suggests that the commercial routes extending from New York and New England west to Ohio were a conduit for these movements. These movements did not generate support on a similar scale across the other major port-hinterland axes, but they were not confined to this interregional transverse, and support varied within these port-hinterland axes in ways that market forces cannot easily explain.[11] If market forces, in particular the spread of wage labor, the need for greater labor discipline, and the legitimation of both, propelled these movements, they did so in a geographically selective fashion. Moreover, as Tocqueville observed of the American passion for material ambition, its focus was narrowly limited by time and space. In the early nineteenth century, a great multitude of small ambitions transformed America, but this national passion was almost incapable of great, coordinated social projects. A compelling explanation for the timing and spread of these extensive social movements, let alone their form, must go beyond market institutions.

Midget Government and Mass Parties

Beyond markets there were few institutions with sufficient reach and influence to support and motivate, let alone coordinate, the wave of moral reforms that broke out across the nation. Political institutions were among the few. It is common to think of the early republic as almost without a state—"a midget institution in a giant land." Tocqueville's experience in Albany, the state capital of New York, comes to mind—the Frenchman searching in vain to find physical signs of the government. But this picture is misleading. The institutions of a centralized governing structure were slight but critical to national development. More importantly, in the historical development of American political institutions, state-building processes and electoral processes followed distinct logics, and they often worked at cross-purposes.[12] Although the United States on the eve of this wave of extensive movements had little central government, popular elections were building mass political parties.

In the years leading up to this wave of movements, the United States was not without a central state. The republic negotiated treaties with other states, fought a second war against Britain, levied taxes, raised tariffs, organized a central bank, forcefully displaced Native Americans, more than doubled its territorial acquisitions, distributed land among its citizens, and regulated property relations, but in comparison with most Western European nations, its state capacities were weak and declining. Federalists, the strongest advocates for an active central government, were politically irrelevant by the end of the War of 1812. Their vision of a powerful federal government lost out to the Jeffersonian vision of decentralized governance. In a reversal, after the War of 1812, Jeffersonian Republicans warmed to a version of the Federalist philosophy of state building. Through the early 1820s, they put forth a set of interrelated policies to build what some called the "American system." These policies sought an improved transportation and communication infrastructure, a central banking system, and increased tariffs. In the decade following the War of 1812, the federal government pursued these policies with some consistency and force, but the American system faltered in the 1820s.[13]

From 1820 to 1830, expenditures by the central government actually fell in real terms (see table 1). Total spending by the federal government for the five-year period of 1826 to 1830 was the lowest for any previous half-decade since 1810. Given the growth of the state's population, geographic space, and economic markets, this marked a sharp decline in

TABLE 1 **U.S. Government Spending, 1810–1850**

	Total Expenditures*		Per Capita Expenditure**		Expend. as Percent of GNP	
Year	Central	All	Central	All	Central	All
1810	8.7		9		1.5	
1820	19.3	27.7	18	8	2.9	4.2
1830	17.0	33.1	14	8	1.8	3.5
1840	28.9	67.6	16	13	1.7	4.0
1850	44.8	89.2	22	14	1.7	3.4

SOURCE: Mann (1993).
*Total expenditures are in millions of dollars.
**Per capita expenditures are at constant prices controlling for both inflation and population growth (see Mann 1993, p. 364).

strength. The capacities of state-building institutions were weakening precisely when far-flung social movements first emerged. There was an exception to this decline of influence: a central and expanding institution of the federal government was the postal system. In Massachusetts, for example, there was one post office before the Revolution. By 1820, there were 443 offices throughout the state. Critical to the internal communication of the nation and the reform movements, the mail did become the focus of struggles between moral reformers and the government in the early years of the development of these movements. This was one of the only direct interactions between the movements and the central state in their first decade of development.[14]

Overall, direct or indirect interaction with the institutions of the central government had little to do with the development of these movements, but these state-building institutions were not the most significant political institutions of the time.[15] In the 1820s, the capacities of the central state were weakened just as the mass political party emerged and gathered power. These two processes were related. The sharp rise in electoral participation clearly marked by the turnout in the 1828 presidential election was linked to a popular attack on the state-building institutions of the American system.[16] In 1828, electoral participation more than doubled from four years earlier (see table 2). This rise in participation coincided with the landslide victory of Andrew Jackson over John Quincy Adams. In this presidential election, an emerging Jacksonian Democratic Party mobilized recently enfranchised voters (state constitutions had recently struck down property requirements for voters in most states across the nation) with a new form of political campaigning. By the 1830s, heated electoral competition and organized political parties made their presence felt in every sizeable American community.

TABLE 2 **Voter Turnout Rates for Presidential Election Years,**
1812–1852

Year	Outside the South	South	Total
1812	47.1	17.8	41.6
1816	26.8	8.3	20.5
1820	12.0	3.8	9.8
1824	26.5	27.4	26.7
1828	62.8	42.6	57.3
1832	64.2	30.1	56.7
1836	58.5	49.2	56.5
1840	81.6	75.4	80.3

SOURCE: Burnham (1987).

State politics, like those in New York, revolutionized electoral campaigns and gave rise to the mass political party. Political committees organized at the local level generated broad support through popular forms of collective action like parades, barbecues, militia musters, and tippling at taverns. The emergence of mass party politics, a process that unfolded state by state, invigorated local forms of organizing over and against the designs of the central state. For example, in the early 1820s, the Bucktails in New York forged popular electoral support around antistatist sentiments and a melding of regional grievances. The Jacksonian national electoral campaign of 1828 patched together regional loyalties to parties like the New York Bucktails and the Richmond Junto into a national coalition.[17]

Interregional coordination in the presidential election by Jackson supporters came not from a coherent national agenda or organization but through the informal agreement of a network of local nongentry politicians and newspaper editors who had turned popular sentiments against elites benefiting from the American system and the market revolution. Jacksonians mobilized a popular constituency by weaving together disparate regional grievances against the elite interests driving the American system of internal development and central banking. Apart from voicing an antistatist sentiment of a periphery against a central state, the emerging party politics avoided articulating national issues or programs. A negative political philosophy that "the world is too much governed" and a strong party identification cemented at the local level through innovative forms of collective action blurred the party's stand on important national issues like tariffs. Before the 1830s, Jacksonian Democrats were in fact loosely coordinated and did not constitute a *centralized* national institution.[18]

Jacksonians had nonetheless mobilized unprecedented popular support under one party "standard." Once in office, the Jacksonian Democrats cemented party loyalty and identification with collective rituals and an elaborate system of spoils. The timing suggests that the expansion of electoral participation influenced the rise of this wave of movements. But this influence was at best indirect. The leaders and rank and file of these new movements did not directly interact with the emerging parties to leverage themselves into national public life. The issues they supported were not shaped by party politics. Like most patronage parties throughout history, Jacksonians (and later Whigs) were averse to programmatic and national purposes. Jacksonians sought to contain the specifics of party policy within the rivulets of local politics. Nor did reformers adopt the form of collective action that shaped electoral politics. Quite the opposite: as party politics took form, moral reformers attacked electioneering with its tippling and opportunism as morally corrupt. As the 1830s unfolded, moral reformers increasingly defined themselves in contradistinction to party politicians and loyalists, and in particular against Jacksonian Democrats—the primary architects of mass party politics.[19]

This antithesis is nicely captured in cross-sectional comparisons of support for Jacksonian Democrats and for temperance and antislavery. The states where temperance and antislavery generated the greatest support did not, for the most part, go to Jackson in the 1828 election. In states like New York that went to Jackson by a narrow margin, reform movements found the greatest support in counties that voted against Jacksonians. Moral reformers were unlikely to be loyal party men and even less likely to be loyal Jacksonian Democrats. If they learned lessons about how to mobilize popular support from party politics, the lessons were largely negative ones. The issues and forms of collective action Jacksonians used to invent the mass political party were not models reformers imitated.[20]

Evangelizing a Restless People

If the average reformer was *not* a party man, he or, just as likely, she *was* an evangelical Christian and part of a rapidly expanding and increasingly influential subculture in America. Evangelical forces did more in the three to four decades after the Revolution to Christianize Americans than in any period before or after.[21] The Second Great Awakening is the "vague" designation given to this period of rapid religious growth. In this "awakening," evangelicals fought for, and to an extent achieved, institutional influence over American society. Because there were so many different aspects to this historical surge in religious influence, any summary statement risks serious misrepresentation. The awakening did *not* effect a *straightforward* change in the beliefs, practices, fellowships, or institutions of religious Americans. Diverse and even countervailing forces buffeted this religious surge. During this period, however, religious competition among evangelical Protestants created a national religious audience before there was a truly national economic market or a national electorate. No region of the new republic was left untouched by this evangelism. Among a restless people with otherwise weak national institutions, evangelicals proved to be proficient builders of extensive institutions.

As Tocqueville observed, religion presented possibly the only social institution that could discipline the many material and political ambitions that kept Americans in constant motion. This is not to suggest that the surging popularity of evangelical Christianity was not intertwined with political and economic forces. It was, and the mix created genuinely American religious streams that departed from their European sources. The overthrow of the colonial church establishment system with the Revolution foreclosed the possibility of an exclusive state church tradition taking hold in the United States, but it left open possibilities of different forms of government support for religion. For a number of years after independence and even after the First Amendment to the Constitution passed, Americans debated the merits of government sanctions for religion and a few states supported multiple establishments. Under these arrangements blasphemy was often punishable by law and tax support was given to a number of different Protestant churches. Evangelical dissenters, particularly Baptists and Methodists, took absolutist positions in the debate, rejecting all forms of government activity in religion. They were instrumental in shaping the "free market" of religion that ultimately took hold, but government support for religion did not disappear all at once. In particular, the descendents of the Puritans resisted disestablishment. In New England, government support for churches lasted the longest, with a variant of the establishment not formally ending in Massachusetts until 1833.[22]

Unfettered by government sanction, religion flourished. And the religion of evangelical dissenters who had fought for an absolute separation of church and state flourished most of all.[23] This is not to suggest that evangelicals stood aloof from the politics of the times. To the contrary, they regularly invoked the Revolution's spirit of egalitarianism and freedom as they tried to win converts. In advance of politicians, they honed the "democratic art of persuasion," and in step with expanding markets they articulated an ethos of individualism. As Mark Noll argues, the energetic evangelical Christianity that emerged in the early nineteenth century was an American original. It departed from its European sources by fusing a republican ideology *and* a commonsense faith in human powers into a worldly ethic with deep affinities for an emerging democratic market society. But evangelical Christianity grew strong because it resisted tight institutional identification with political and economic forces. American evangelicals achieved religious influence unique for its reach and depth in the Western world by concentrating their efforts on shaping civil society. Religion became the most compelling and popular form of voluntary association in the United States. It did so by avoiding identification with particular political and market interests.

As a result, in the years just before the first national wave of social movements broke out, evangelical Christianity provided some of the only intermediary institutions that connected large numbers of Americans to a nation with its weak central state, decentering popular party politics, and restless markets.[24] As Donald Matthews argues, the awakening was above all else a "recruiting impulse." From 1790 to 1820, growth in religious organizations and religious adherents far outpaced the impressive growth in population. The number of Christian congregations grew from 2,500 in 1780 to 11,000 in 1820. In terms of church attendance, this meant an increase from around one in six to one in four Americans and rising. By 1850, Finke and Stark estimate that 34 percent of Americans were "churched." Most of this growth came from evangelical congregations. As American evangelicals competed for souls they invented social techniques for mass recruitment. The most dramatic examples of innovation appeared on the periphery of the early republic.[25]

Through informal, public, and emotional appeals for confession, itinerant preachers far removed from the centers of market and government revolutionized religious gatherings. In the backwoods of America, meetings centered on emotional public confessions spread religious fellowship throughout the new settlements of a booming population. It was the itinerant preachers of the upstart sects that perfected what Perry Miller termed the "invincible persistence of the revival technique." All evangelicals supported religious revivals, but the revivals of populist sects like the Methodists and the Baptists with their emotional and public displays of repentance were qualitatively different from those of the more orthodox

Presbyterians and Congregationalists. They also proved more popular. Public confessions have a long history in Christianity. They were present in the "barbarian" conversions of the early medieval period. The Church hierarchy grew to mistrust these events because they were difficult to control. They reappeared within Reformation movements—most notably in the eighteenth century pietistic revivals. As the historian Paul Johnson observed, public confession has always been a kind of "rude democracy" and prominent during periods of rapid Christian growth.[26]

The growth of Baptist and Methodist congregations during the first few decades of the early republic was startling. There may have been 400 Baptist congregations in 1780. By 1820, there were around 2,700. Methodists had no formal congregations in 1780. By 1820, they had organized roughly the same number as the Baptists. Growth was slower among the orthodox evangelical denominations. Presbyterian and Congregationalist churches numbered around 1,250 in 1780. By 1820, after two decades of a united evangelical plan to expand, they numbered 2,800. On top of these local churches, religious leaders built supralocal ecclesiastical organizations. The regional presbyteries of American Presbyterianism, for example, increased from 9 in1776 to 59 in 1820; and the larger regional ecclesiastical unit, the synod, increased from 1 to 11. The growth of Baptists and Methodist interregional organizations was still greater. From 1780 to 1820, the number of Baptist associations jumped from 6 to over 100. In 1784, Methodists were formally organized in one conference. By the 1840s, they made up 32 conferences.[27]

The interregional coordination of this growth in churches should *not* be exaggerated. The circuits of itinerant preachers were often quite extensive and planned by the interregional administrative bodies of denominations. The revival techniques these preachers employed united Americans in shared practices that were also quite extensive. And for some Americans, strong identification with religious denominations brought them into fellowship with brothers and sisters in Christ across the nation and even the world. Nonetheless, this growth in religious adherence came from forces that were essentially centrifugal. For example, although Methodist preachers were organized in a centralized administrative episcopacy, local societies and regional circuits exercised great autonomy. Baptist associations might appoint itinerant preachers to travel to certain regions, but they controlled little else about the small, local groups through which the denomination grew in strength and numbers. As with the mass recruitment of voters by Jacksonian Democrats, but years in advance of it, the evangelical recruitment of congregants was nationwide but not centrally coordinated. Insofar as it was a recruiting impulse to get Americans to join churches, the religious art of persuasion unfolded and thrived first and foremost at the local level. From this aspect, the Second Great Awakening was a decentralized multitude of local religious phenomena.[28]

There was a more centralizing aspect to the awakening. The awakening involved more than emotional revival meetings and the growth of local churches and competing denominational ecclesiastical structures. At the turn of the nineteenth century, cooperation between leading ministers and wealthy laity of what amounted to orthodox Calvinism constructed a rationalized network of interdenominational missionary organizations. Commonly referred to as benevolent societies, these missionary organizations united Presbyterians, Congregationalists, and members of smaller Calvinist churches in a united evangelical enterprise to redeem Americans *and* America. Central to this mission was the spread of special-purpose voluntary associations and the mass publication and distribution of religious literature. To raise support for the work of missionaries in places as far away as Ceylon and Liberia or in places closer to home as among the Cherokees and migrants to the Western Reserve, national benevolent societies promoted a network of thousands of auxiliary societies that stretched across all the states of the Union. Benevolent societies also created a publishing empire to link these societies and to spread the missionary work among all Americans, even the unchurched. In 1790, there were 14 religious newspapers; by 1830, there were perhaps 300. Beyond newspapers, a primary product of this publishing enterprise was the religious tract. Published by the millions, these tracts broadcast tales of sin, damnation, and salvation. This evangelical publishing empire reached a national audience of readers even before the print enterprise of capitalists. If early nineteenth-century Americans were, in the words of the historian Jon Butler, "awash in a sea of faith," they were also awash in a sea of religious print.[29]

These different aspects to the awakening were far from united. Evangelicals were divided by sharp differences in social class and geography, as well as doctrine and liturgy. The competition between populist and orthodox evangelicals pitted paradoxical configurations of attitudes toward personal religious experiences and commitments to civic morality. Orthodoxy prized private religious conversions and public intervention in matters of civic order. Populists, in almost mirror image, prized public testimonies of personal experiences of piety but resisted ecclesiastical meddling in matters of public morality. Curtis Johnson aptly described this opposition between orthodox and populist as "formalists" versus "antiformalists." The formalists valued an "orderly faith," doctrinal consistency, decorum in liturgy, and cleaved to the notion of a collective covenant between the saints and God. In sharp contrast, the antiformalists valued an "emotional faith," were suspicious of religious elites, and promoted a democratic and voluntary process of individual religious conversions (albeit in mass). Antiformalists were prevalent among the poor yeomanry that took part in the western land grab of the early nineteenth century. Formalists dominated the religious communities of those that settled with and prospered from the mercantilist economy of the eastern seaboard. Although this opposition did not exactly conform to denominational distinctions, Presbyterians, Congregationalists, Dutch and German Reformed, low-church Anglicans, and some conservative Baptists comprised the formalist or orthodox camp. Methodists, most Baptists, the African American churches, and a host of nineteenth-century schismatics were typically antiformalist or populist. Most orthodox counted themselves Calvinists. Although many antiformalist Baptists also considered themselves Calvinists, a growing majority of populists promoted an Arminian doctrine of free will.[30]

Because of these deep divisions, evangelical institutions were unlikely sources for extensive social movements. The popular power of the populist sects was too centrifugal to unite Americans to a particular national agenda for social change. The benevolent societies of orthodoxy were elitist in their composition and alienated the majority and the fastest-growing segment of evangelical Americans. On the eve of this wave of movements, although religious adherence was extensive in America, it was for many a local affair they intimately shared with a small number of people and a commitment to values and practices that divided them from most of their fellow Americans. Nonetheless, in the late 1820s, these two sides in a growing evangelical subculture mixed, and the peculiar but powerful religious recombination that resulted was crucial to the rise of national social movements. How did these religious forces combine to launch these movements? To answer this it is necessary to track the development of the two different evangelical trajectories—the orthodox and the populist—and their coming together. The next chapter charts the efforts of orthodoxy and its construction of a rationalized structure of national benevolent societies. Chapter 4 charts developments in the religious revivals of populist evangelicals.

CHAPTER THREE

The Benevolent Empire and the Special Sins of the Nation

In 1829, the American Education Society published in its *Quarterly Register* the results of a survey of the mission, income, and leadership of American benevolent societies. This Congregationalist and Presbyterian association for the education of Calvinist clergy had published similar reports in the previous four years. These statistical and descriptive reports attempted to capture the scope and the scale of an expanding network of Christian philanthropy and evangelism—an empire of orthodox benevolence. The largest of the societies in the survey championed *broad* missions and were the product of a Presbyterian and Congregationalist "evangelical united front." These parachurch institutions included societies like the American Bible Society and the American Board of Commissioners for Foreign Missions and constituted the spiritual and material core of organized benevolence. By 1829, one third of the societies in the report had *narrower* missions defined by specific "worldly" problems. The *Register* reported one society each for intemperance, war, prisons, seamen, conversion of Jews, the deaf and the dumb, the colonization of free blacks, and Sabbath violations. These "special-purpose" societies were smaller and newer than the broadly evangelical organizations like the Bible and missionary societies, but at the end of the decade they represented the fastest-growing wing of organized benevolence.[1]

The same edition of the *Register* betrayed uneasiness with the growing role of societies organized to address special, worldly problems. In a long letter appearing at the beginning of the report, Professor Archibald Alexander, president of Princeton Theological Seminary and an architect of a conservative response to an emerging activist bent within orthodoxy, launched a thinly veiled attack against the young ministers associated with these societies. Alexander's letter listed "being too much in public," "an ardent spirit of disputation," and "too much social intercourse" as obstacles to their ministerial piety. He also warned that too many were "under the direction and influence of weak, hot-headed men, who push themselves forward when there is any excitement, from a belief that they can be of great service." "Now," Alexander warned, "although these young men may be zealous, noisy, and active professors; and may take the lead in revivals, and in all benevolent enterprises, they will be found on careful examination, to be shallow christians." To combat this "spiritual pride," he counseled that these young men study their own hearts by attending to "the duties of the closet."

Alexander foresaw the religious type Rev. Leonard Bacon described seven years later as "an itinerating clergy charged with a single topic of agitation." But Alexander was too severe in placing the better part of the responsibility on the young professors themselves; these men had developed their controversial public roles within orthodox institutions like the one he was writing to, the American Education Society, and even the conservative orthodox bastion he presided over, Princeton. Systematic efforts to rationalize and nationalize orthodox evangelism, efforts Alexander had contributed to, set the stage for the radicalization of reform-minded ministers and their supporters.[2]

Little else in the *Register*'s report led the reader to believe that orthodoxy's organized benevolence faced serious internal trouble. The editors of the report presented the pieces of benevolence, including the newer special-purpose societies, as fitting together in a coordinated plan to minister to an expanding and diverse America. This plan had developed over three decades as part of an orthodox bid for national influence. After the American Revolution, with the collapse of the Anglican Church, Congregationalism and Presbyterianism became the two "mainline" denominations in the United States. Congregationalism held sway in New England and Presbyterianism in the Middle Atlantic. These two Calvinist denominations shared the same basic doctrines and a similar liturgy. The major difference between the two was in ecclesiastical structure. Congregationalist churches were independent, linked only by associations, and congregants freely elected their ministers; Presbyterian congregations were under the authority of a hierarchy of synods and presbyteries, and these ecclesiastical orders appointed ministers to particular congregations. Although the two denominations shared a history of sometimes bitter conflict, with the end of established churches and the growing presence of Baptists, Methodists, Unitarians, Universalists, Catholics, and worse, seventeenth- and eighteenth-century differences over ecclesiastical structure appeared rather insignificant to America's orthodox Calvinists.[3]

At the turn of the nineteenth century, Presbyterians and Congregation-alists represented around 40 percent of all religious adherents and con-trolled vast material resources, but this position of influence was precari-ous. By the end of the War of 1812, representatives of orthodoxy were on the defensive, and organized benevolence developed as an interdenomi-national effort to counter a steep loss of influence.

The Presbyterian and Congregationalist Response to a Restless Nation

The building of orthodoxy's empire of benevolence started around the turn of the nineteenth century with the separate efforts of Presbyteri-ans and Congregationalists. After 1815, a pattern of cooperation was set between the two denominations. This cooperation extended to smaller, like-minded sects such as the Dutch Reformed. In a climate of national development and expansion, orthodox elites followed the mold of British benevolent societies. They constructed a network of interdenominational societies for the promotion of Christian wisdom and the suppression of vice. Orthodoxy was shaped by its role of ministering to the covenanted communities of the eighteenth and seventeenth centuries. Social change was obliterating the corporate structure of these communities. In response to this crisis, national benevolent societies were a radical organizational departure. These societies were the first organized attempt to coordinate a national effort to shape civil society based on the principles of volun-tary association. Organized benevolence was an attempt by orthodoxy to reinvent itself.[4]

Membership in these national societies was open to all contributors. Claims of interdenominational cooperation and nonsectarian goals were important to the leaders of benevolence because they legitimized their national ambitions. Although these claims were not entirely unfounded, organized benevolence retained a strong orthodox bias. A few Method-ists and Baptists, typically ministers of well-established congregations in the East, joined the boards of national benevolence societies, but Presbyterians and Congregationalists dominated these parachurch institutions. Suspicious of the intentions of orthodox institutions and their elite clergy, most leaders and followers of the populist sects shunned organized benevolence.[5] Their suspicions were warranted. The earliest national societies planned missions to counter "the errors of enthusiastic and false teachers" circuit riding the backwoods. In the organization of benevolent societies, orthodox clergy and laymen sought to curb the success of Baptists and Methodists or, at least, temper their doctrinal and liturgical excesses. The populist religion that penetrated the continent and held sway with the yeomanry stood either aloof or in opposition to organized benevolence.[6]

Unlike the decentered organizing of populist upstarts, the national benevolent societies of Presbyterians and Congregationalists developed broadcast strategies from the core commercial cities of New York, Philadelphia, and Boston. These societies directed massive publishing campaigns, raised funds for targeted Christian missions, and organized a national network of auxiliary societies. Before the War of 1812, the missionary efforts of orthodox Calvinists remained regional and were closely tied to particular congregations and denominations. After the war, national societies emerged to organize American civil-religious society on a mass scale. As this network of societies grew in size and strength, it developed considerable independent moral authority. Money and talent that once flowed to ecclesiastical institutions were redirected to these parachurch institutions.

The work of organized benevolence was the polite and consensual affair of an educated ministry supported by the resources of pious merchants. With the association of men like William Jay, Richard Varick, Stephen Van Rensselaer, Theodore Frelinghuysen, and Henry Clay, organized benevolence commanded considerable public deference. For these luminaries, wealthy merchants, and their pastors, religious education through Sunday schools, tracts, Bibles, and a trained ministry was a means to temper and redeem what they feared was an increasingly anarchic democracy. Launching the national parachurch institutions of the benevolence empire was an elite effort to recover and expand orthodoxy's moral authority threatened by the disestablishment of religion, the decline of deferential politics, fierce competition from populist Christian sects, and the mammon of a market revolution.[7]

The organization of national benevolent societies reflected the paradoxical nature of orthodox influence. In terms of material resources, organizational technologies, and a coordinated national plan, organized benevolence was without parallel and seemed poised for expansive influence.

In terms of influence over political institutions, it had the support of some of America's most distinguished politicians, but the country was entering a period of mass politics that would bring to an end the traditions of deferential politics. Market forces were generating tremendous resources for orthodoxy but at the same time challenging its moral influence over civic and market spaces. In terms of winning hearts in American churches, orthodoxy was only holding its own as support for Methodists and Baptists was exploding. In short, this radical innovation in the institutional workings of orthodoxy was part of a struggle to retain and regain religious authority in the face of serious political, religious, and economic challenges.

A Response to Political Change

The decline of the Federalist Party dealt a blow to orthodoxy's political influence. In New England, in particular, cooperation between leading Federalists and Congregationalists formed an effective political-religious bloc that governed public affairs for the first two decades after the Revolution. Continuing the close link between ministers and civil magistrates of the colonial era, Congregationalist ministers under Federalist rule retained considerable influence over civil as well as religious matters of New England communities. After Jefferson's "revolution of 1800," Federalist political power was confined to New England, and the first decade of the new century brought political defeats even to this stronghold. In 1807, Republicans gained control of the major political institutions in Massachusetts. In 1811, they elected the governor of Connecticut. In 1814, a major political blunder sealed the fate of the Federalists and undermined for good the political position of America's last established churches. At a convention in Hartford, leading Federalists discussed ways to put an end to a war with Britain that had devastated the mercantile economy of New England. Included in these discussions was talk of secession. Republicans seized the opportunity to paint Federalists as traitors, and the party struggled to recover from the charge. With the collapse of the Federalist Party, orthodoxy lost its representative in national political affairs and much of its political influence at the local level.[8]

This political blow was tightly coupled with an attack on the church-state tie Congregationalists had enjoyed, in one form or another, since the seventeenth century. As Jeffersonians publicly branded Federalists as a new aristocracy, Baptists and Methodists made similar charges against the established Calvinists in New England and the remnants of the Episcopal state-church tradition in Virginia. At the start of the nineteenth century, particularly outside of New England, Jeffersonians had translated the antinomian enthusiasm of populist sects into political activism against the Federalists. Idealized visions of the Revolution informed the antinomian spirit of populist preachers and their challenge to religious authorities and the privileged legal status of orthodox Calvinism. The Baptist John Leland exemplified this radical democratic thrust in religion and politics. A staunch supporter of Jefferson, Leland launched a blistering attack on the Standing Order in New England. The title of a 1791 pamphlet nicely captures the tone of his religious and political campaign: *The Rights of Conscience Inalienable. . .; . or, The High-flying Churchman, Stripped of his Legal Robe, Appears a Yaho.*[9]

Under the pressure of Baptists and Methodists and the ascendant power of Jeffersonian Republicans, disestablishment came gradually to New England. It came first to Connecticut in 1818, to New Hampshire the following year, and not until 1833 to Massachusetts.[10] Lyman Beecher—possibly America's most famous minister and leading light of organized benevolence—at first viewed the church's loss of public authority as a disaster. Decades later, Beecher recalled that when the success of the enemies of establishment became clear to him he thought it "was as dark a day as I ever saw."

> The odium thrown upon the ministry was inconceivable. The injury done to the cause of Christ, as we then supposed, was irreparable. For several days I suffered what no tongue can tell, *for the best thing that ever happened to the State of Connecticut.*[11]

In the end, he judged it "the best thing that ever happened" because it forced orthodoxy to develop a network of voluntary associations to recover and expand its influence. As Beecher correctly observed, disestablishment fueled the drive for organized benevolence. By the 1820s, interdenominational cooperation had convinced Beecher that with "voluntary efforts, societies, missions, and revivals" orthodoxy could "exert a deeper influence than ever they could by queues, and shoe-buckles, and cocked hats, and gold-headed canes"—in other words, by the offices of establishment.[12] For the first time in New England, orthodox Calvinism had to compete in an open religious market. Sociologists counting pews have concluded that they failed miserably in this contest, but missing in this accounting is the influence of the interdenominational voluntary associations of organized benevolence.

A Response to Religious Change

Roger Finke and Rodney Stark argue that the leaders of the Protestant mainline remained curiously unconcerned throughout the nineteenth century as they lost "market share" to upstart sects, but the efforts behind organized benevolence reflected a deep concern over the declining influence of orthodoxy.[13] Very early on, Presbyterians and Congregationalists recognized the threat of antinomian and heterodox sects. In New England, a Baptist minority had long resisted the institutional power of Congregationalism and was clearly growing. In urban centers of the East, many orthodox churches were taking a liberal, Unitarian turn against Calvinism. In the western reaches of the Middle Atlantic States, Presbyterian revivals prompted defections to the more enthusiastic Baptists, Methodists, and splinter groups like the Cumberland Presbyterians. While both denominations managed to hold their own in settled communities on the eastern seaboard, the expanding western frontier and rapid emigration from east to west posed new challenges—challenges the leading ministers were acutely aware of but did not fully understand.

From the outset, the leaders of organized benevolence saw the evangelization of the West as among their most important missions. They realized early in the century that political and religious power was shifting westward. As a missionary report argued just after the War of 1812, if the heirs of Calvinism were to influence the future direction of the republic, they would have to counter the enthusiasm of populist preachers with "intelligent and correct missionaries." The religion of uneducated backwoods exhorters caused "great injury to the cause of Christ" and posed a threat to the piety of their westerly brethren.[14]

Organized benevolence addressed these fears with two distinct approaches. First, they sought to address the problem of a dearth of Presbyterian and Congregationalist ministers. Unlike the upstart sects, the two mainline denominations relied on an educated clergy. Exclusive reliance on an educated ministry posed problems for the organization of churches in newly settled communities. In response, orthodoxy sought to organize efforts to swell the ranks of the ministry by subsidizing the education of poorer students and to sponsor missionaries in the regions of new settlements. Second, Presbyterians and Congregationalists sought to bring their message to Christians outside of their churches. In this second endeavor, they may have proved much more successful than sociologists counting pews can ever verify. Through broadcasts of print material and a curriculum for popular Sunday schools, organized benevolence "ministered" in regions and homes that its educated ministry could never reach. Taken together, Presbyterians and Congregationalists built a national plan that looked beyond their local regions of strength and sought to compete with the populist sects for souls in an expanding nation.

A Response to Economic Change

If westward expansion posed a challenge, the accumulation of wealth back east presented an opportunity. Commercial giants in Boston, New York, and Philadelphia financed the initial national efforts of organized benevolence. Both the westward expansion and the tremendous accumulation of wealth by elites in commercial centers were direct results of a market revolution, and organized benevolence was dependent in inconsistent ways on this revolution. The wealth of pious laymen provided the resources, the westward emigration of Congregationalists and Presbyterians provided the impetus, and the vices fueled by market practices provided the moral shock. Lastly, improved transportation through a network of turnpikes and canals, as well as new communication technologies, made religious broadcasts from commercial centers to the hinterland economically feasible. If educated ministers could not be enticed to settle in places like Indiana, at least tracts, Bibles, and materials for Sunday schools could make the trip.

Concerns for religious and economic control—sometimes at odds with each other—intertwined in organized benevolence. Many of the men and women of benevolence were genuinely disturbed by the effects of the market revolution on the piety of Americans. Orthodox dreams of a national missionary program were made possible by a willingness of a pious select to give away considerable portions of their wealth. As the great economic transition of the early nineteenth century filled the coffers of merchants, bankers, early industrialists, and professionals, concern for Christian virtue redirected some of this income to finance the national plans of organized benevolence. On the other hand, wealthy Protestants also sought discipline in the marketplace and workplace to ensure returns on their investments; religious control through benevolent societies was one way to get this.[15]

For the Baptist firebrand John Leland, this material interest was transparent in the elite work of benevolence:

> Religion has become the most fashionable thing among us. Moral societies, Sunday schools—tract societies—Bible societies—Missionary societies, and funds

to educate and make preachers, are now in the full tide of operation . . . In barbarous times, when men were in the dark, it was believed that the success of the gospel was according to the outpourings of the Holy Spirit, but in the age of light and improvement, it is estimated according to the pourings out of the purse.[16]

Unforgiving populist judgments like this failed to appreciate the extent to which the men of benevolence "served two masters" and were deeply disturbed by this. For some, anxiety over the temptations of wealth was as strong as the drive to succeed in their worldly calling. As they struggled for moral control over their own wealth, they financed a parallel public mission for moral control of society through benevolence societies.

Arthur Tappan was a model of this elite support for orthodox benevolence. Tappan was a silk merchant in New York City. As an importer of a foreign luxury, his business represented the high end of a consumer market buoyed by capitalist transformation. Tappan absolved himself from material gain by giving most of it away to organized benevolence. In spite of spectacular commercial success, he remained austere in lifestyle and even sought to avoid recognition in his charity by giving anonymously.[17] For orthodox Calvinists like him, benevolence defended Christian virtue in the midst of worldly treasures. Trying not to "sound trumpets," benevolence was Arthur's response to Jesus' disquieting words: "You cannot serve God and Mammon" (Matt. 6:24). It would also be a mistake to dismiss the prevalent feelings among evangelicals associated with organized benevolence of fear of and rage against the sinful indulgences of a market society as covers for material interests. The collapse of the covenanted community seemed to leave the temptations of taverns, theatres, lotteries, brothels, and frivolous entertainments unchecked. To orthodox evangelicals, the market revolution presented promise *and* peril.

The Spiritual Foundation and Practical Building of the Empire's Parachurch Institutions

To replace material interests with ideal interests in the explanation of the development of organized benevolence misses the tensions that emerged from the intertwining of material and ideal values, and these tensions were decisive in shaping the radical reforms of the 1830s. Drawing an analytical distinction between the spiritual foundation and the practical construction of organized benevolence helps explain how and why radicals used spiritual claims to impugn the "expediency" of conservatives and how they mobilized material resources by seizing spiritual leadership over special causes that developed within the institutions of organized benevolence.

Disinterested Benevolence

The theological foundations of benevolence are complex and not exclusively orthodox. Liberal denominations such as Quakers shared the understanding that disinterested benevolence was the highest expression of Christian virtue. Although their understandings of benevolence differed significantly, both liberal and orthodox could find missions to support under the wide umbrella of organized benevolence. The distribution of Bibles, for example, met wide and interdenominational acceptance as a mission beyond reproach. Insofar as Presbyterians and Congregationalists dominated organized benevolence, the theological roots of disinterested benevolence rested with Calvinist notions of trusteeship and social discipline and their "affectional" reformulation by Jonathan Edwards and his disciples. In the second half of the eighteenth century, the principles of Edwards's writings constituted the only American theology. Systematized by his disciples and dubbed the New Divinity, this theology reigned in the new seminaries of the late eighteenth and early nineteenth centuries. As a result, this articulation of Edwardsian principles dominated the theological training of most educated, orthodox ministers. It in turn provided a theological foundation for organized benevolence.[18]

The New Divinity was not universally accepted among the American heirs of Calvinism. From one side, it drew criticism from liberal Congregationalists (proto-Unitarians) who saw it as an unacceptable apology of a too-old and too-strict Calvinism. From the more conservative "Old Lights," it seemed a humanized corruption of Calvinism. In spite of these oppositions, the New Divinity successfully systematized the affectionate recasting of Calvinism that Jonathan Edwards taught and the majority of orthodox Calvinists were living. Ironically, as historians have noted, the New Divinity may very well have undermined the project it sought to redeem: a pious and honest Calvinism. Insofar as organized benevolence needed a theology, Samuel Hopkins's systematic articulation of Edwardsian principles provided it. Hopkins was a product of the First Great Awakening and a student of Edwards, but he lived long enough to see the dawn of the nineteenth century. His religious thought placed benevolence and humanistic values at the center of Calvinism. The Hopkinsian system provided a theodicy that became central to the orthodox vision that shaped the religious training of many of the men who committed themselves to the parachurch institutions of the united Presbyterian and Congregationalist front.[19]

For Hopkins sin was selfishness: the choosing of self over God. Virtue was disinterested benevolence: a selfless and holy affection for God and for being in general. According to Hopkins, "love to God, and love to our fellow-creatures, is of the same nature and kind."[20] Disinterested benevolence would will its own damnation or sacrifice out of love for God and out of love for fellow beings. Softening this doctrine, Hopkins believed that anyone capable of such self-denial had perforce received the gift of grace and could not be damned. Even more strongly, Hopkins conceptualized God *as* benevolence and redemption *as* reciprocal benevolence. In his theology, the older Calvinist themes of faith and consent were supplanted with love and practical benevolence. Hopkins had modified but not repudiated Calvinism. Humans were still depraved in that they chose the self over God, and grace was still a gift that they did not deserve. But he, like Edwards before him, wavered from a doctrine of total human depravity and suggested that the salvation of certain individuals and not others, by virtue of their position or attributes, served the purposes of God and the general good.

This God of benevolence was more humane than Calvin's sovereign judge and master. He saved every person he *could* while still furthering moral government. Hopkins was more optimistic than his Calvinist predecessors about the rate of salvation. He believed the vast majority of humanity would be saved. Hopkins's theodicy also gave sin a clearer purpose than early Calvinism had and elevated the role of humans in the divine plan. Redemption, that is, the reciprocity of benevolence, was made possible by the introduction of sin. Sin therefore worked for the greater glory of God and the fulfillment of human happiness. The redemption after the Fall was more glorious than dutiful obedience in the paradise lost. The practical impact of the New Divinity was to leaven Calvinist charity with a distinctly Reformed humanitarianism.[21]

If the theology of disinterested benevolence sought to make Calvinism more palatable to a humanistic age, it did so by threatening a crucial tenet. By intertwining benevolence and faith, good works competed with belief as the mark of sanctification. To many orthodox Calvinists this seemed like a retreat from the strong Calvinist reading of Paul that a remnant of humanity is chosen by grace alone. "But if it is by grace, it is no longer on the basis of works; otherwise grace would no longer be grace." [22] Earlier Calvinists had been very clear on this point: good works never led to salvation. Coupled with the softening of the doctrine of total depravity this opinion led more orthodox Calvinists, particularly conservative Presbyterians in the Middle Atlantic, to conclude that Hopkins's disciples had opened the door to the Arminian heresy of free will and salvation through works.

These opposing conservatives cleaved to a "covenant theology" that identified them as that remnant of humanity chosen by grace alone. The covenant or federal theology was a "complex nexus of person, church, and society." [23] Conservatives or Old Lights rejected the optimistic vision that the vast majority of humanity would be saved and the implicit valorization of works in the Hopkinsian schema of benevolence. For the agents driving organized benevolence, however, the Hopkinsian system legitimized what they felt in their commitment to evangelism—"faith without works is dead." [24]

By the 1830s, division between liberal heirs of Hopkins's New Divinity and conservatives would ultimately contribute to the demise of the Presbyterian and Congregationalist union in organized benevolence and even to schism within Presbyterianism in 1837. But in the first three decades of the nineteenth century, the New Divinity provided a theological framework for the practical work of organized benevolence that united more orthodox interests than it divided. It provided a theological ground for building institutions to spread the word of God's benevolence to a national audience beyond the corporate structures of a covenanted community of saints. For many of the most committed workers within organized benevolence, the theology of disinterested benevolence provided legitimacy to their pursuit of regeneration in good works. While expanding the ranks of the saved and recasting God as benevolent toward all, it still made ontological distinctions between saints and sinners and trusted the former with interpreting the order of God's moral government. This benevolent God was still a terror to sinners, and his chosen were still called to raise the alarm.[25]

The National Practice of Benevolence

With this shared theology, the national enterprise of organized benevolence grew together from similar but separate regional efforts. Simultaneously but independently, evangelical zeal in Connecticut, Massachusetts,

New York, New Jersey, and Pennsylvania led to regional benevolent societies for missionary work, Bible and tract distribution, and Sunday schools. After the War of 1812, regional societies began to cooperate, and by the mid-1820s they were incorporated into single, national societies with headquarters in Boston, Philadelphia, or New York. Cooperation was first made possible by the interdenominational framework of the 1801 Plan of Union between Presbyterians and Congregationalists that removed competition in missionary work, but an actual united front of benevolence was not accomplished until the 1820s. It developed in a piecemeal fashion with the two denominations taking the lead in different areas.

The first regional and national benevolent societies were missionary organizations. The American Board of Commissions for Foreign Missions, founded in 1810, may have been the first national benevolent society in the United States. The idea of the society was hatched four years earlier at a prayer meeting led by Samuel Mills at Williams College—the famous Haystack Prayer Meeting. Although the American Board was Congregationalist in origin, it enlisted Presbyterians in the cause of foreign missions. A decade after its formation, the society's annual report boasted:

> The A.B.C.F.M is not limited to any section of the country or to any denomination of Christians. Its members, chartered or corresponding, and its patrons, auxiliaries, and agents, are in all the States of the Union, and of nearly all considerable religious communions. In its form and spirit . . . it is a NATIONAL INSTITUTION.[26]

Domestic missionary societies formed on a regional basis earlier than the American Board but took longer to develop a joint national plan. In fact, the regional domestic missionary societies of New England provided a model for the American Board, but domestic competition slowed national union in home missions.

In 1797 Congregationalists in Connecticut formed a state missionary society to administer to the religious needs of emigrants moving west. The society was a cooperative effort between church and state. Lieutenant Governor John Treadwell headed the society. The Connecticut society became a model for a Massachusetts society organized in 1799. Founded in Boston by disciples of Hopkins and by Federalists already wary of their vulnerability to religious and political attacks, the Massachusetts society was careful to avoid formal ties with the state government. For the first quarter of the century, the missionary work of the two state societies remained separate because their emigrants moved to different regions. Particularly with the early emigration, Yankees moved as communities. Typically, large tracts of land were purchased by enterprising real estate capitalists and then sold in parcels within New England communities. Often entire communities would remove together to the cheaper and more abundant land.[27] The Bay State society focused primarily on emigrants to the north in Vermont, New Hampshire, and Maine, while the Connecticut society worked in New York, Pennsylvania, and Ohio.

In this early missionary work New Englanders cooperated with Presbyterians. As the Plan of Union designated New York and Ohio as officially Presbyterian, these missionary societies worked for the support of this denomination in these states.[28] As these emigrant communities expanded and intermingled, overlap in missionary work became more common and the need for a coordinated national society more urgent. An address in 1825 to supporters of domestic missionary societies gathered at the theological seminary in Andover outlined the need for a rationalization of missions:

> We want a system which shall be one; — one in purpose, one in action; — which shall be pervaded by one spirit, and palpitate with one heart; — a system, whose sentinel, stationed to survey our land in its whole extent, shall keep his eye alike on every part, — whose operations, though felt in every section of our country, shall still be as harmonious as the actions of a single man; — a system. . . which shall gather the resources of philanthropy, patriotism, and Christian sympathy, throughout our country, into one vast reservoir, from which shall flow to Georgia, to Louisiana, to Missouri, and to Maine, fertilizing every barren spot, and causing our whole country to flourish like the garden of the Lord, till the sun, and the moon, and the stars shall cease to roll over it. We want a Society that shall do all this; a society in which all who have the spirit of the Gospel, — all who love their country, — all whose bosoms ever glowed with philanthropy, may unite without one hesitating or discordant feeling; we want a National Domestic Missionary Society; *it* will do all this. . . . [L]et no sect raise its banner — no section stand alone — no party wake to strife — but blow the trumpet in Zion, and ALL SHALL COME.[29]

The next year the American Home Missionary Society was founded at Gardiner Spring's Presbyterian Church in New York.

This national domestic missionary society combined the two Congregationalist missionary societies with the missionary work of Presbyterianism and the Dutch Reformed Church. In a circular announcing the planned formation of the society, a letter from Alexander Archibald and his colleague from Princeton, Samuel Miller, appeared to welcome the news: "We rejoice to hear there is a plan in contemplation for forming a Domestic Missionary Society, on a much larger scale than has heretofore existed." Alexander and Miller then linked the fate of the nation with the success of orthodox missions.

> Our impression is, that, unless far more vigorous measures than we have hitherto witnessed shall be soon adopted, for sending the blessed Gospel and its ordinances to the widely extended and rapidly increasing New Settlements of our country, their active and enterprising population must, at no great distance of time, be abandoned to a state not much short of entire destitution of the means of grace. We would fain hope, that no Christian who loves the Redeemer's kingdom, and reflects on the value of immortal souls; no parent, who remembers that his own children, or children's children, may in due time, make a part of the population of those districts; no patriot, who desires to see the virtue, peace, union, and happiness of his country established, can possibly be indifferent to an object of such immense importance. Our prayer is, that the God of all grace may rouse the spirit of the Nation on this subject.[30]

Alexander would soon regret this endorsement of a rationalized national missionary society.

Missionary organizations were the earliest and most prized parachurch institutions of the separate denominations, but this coming together to remove redundancies and centralize the administrative work of home missions followed the lead of benevolent societies in the less sectarian areas of benevolence: Bible distribution, Sabbath schools, and religious tracts. Unlike missionary societies, Presbyterians took the lead in Bible distribution. One of the first Bible societies was established in Philadelphia in 1808. Societies modeled after it soon appeared in New York and New England. By 1815, there were over a hundred Bible societies in the United States. That same year organized efforts to form a national society commenced. Elias Boudinot, a Presbyterian from New Jersey, and Samuel Mills, founder of the American Board, helped form the national society in New York. Mills had done a survey of the state of religion in the West and advocated the establishment of a national society to ensure that the Holy Writ would reach the neglected frontier. Boudinot, head of the New Jersey Bible Society, impressed with Mills's vision, approached the leaders of the New York Bible Society and convinced them to join his society to expand their cause. Skeptical New Englanders were brought on board when the New York and New Jersey society appointed Lyman Beecher and Jedidiah Morse, prominent orthodox clergy in Connecticut and Massachusetts, to the executive committee. On May 10, 1816, a convention of the American Bible Society adopted its constitution.[31]

Other societies followed this pattern of electing prominent ministers to the executive committee in order to overcome interdenominational suspicion and competition. The centrality of the King James Bible among American Protestants made the Bible society the least sectarian of the national societies. So careful were the leaders of this society not to excite sectarian differences that they excluded opening prayers from their meetings.[32] This caution was representative of organized benevolence's wider attempt to restrain the divisiveness of confessionalism. Unlike the ecclesiastical structures of the participating denominations, these national societies did not require confessions of faith or tests of conversion. They were based on voluntary association requiring only contributions from members, but to coordinate massive publication campaigns like providing every white American on the other side of the Alleghenies with a Bible, they constructed efficient bureaucracies that depended on a staff of modestly paid professional managers.[33]

Present at the convention of the American Bible Society was the merchant Divie Bethune. With the model of the Bible society in mind, he set in motion a process that led to the founding of the American Sunday School Union. The first Sabbath school society had originated in Philadelphia, expanding first in the area around the city and then throughout Pennsylvania. By the 1820s, the society was national in everything but name. In 1824, it changed that too, calling itself the American Sunday School Union. Employing itinerant agents, the Union established schools with voluntary teachers in every state. These local Sunday schools, in turn, subscribed to the Union's published curriculum. In years when Presbyterian and Congregationalist churches lost considerable ground to Methodists and Baptists, the more general influence of orthodoxy may have expanded through the parachurch institution of the Sabbath school.[34]

The third of the three major publishing societies was the American Tract Society—possibly the best example of the pragmatic vision of interdenominational organized benevolence. With the use of stereotyping, steam presses, and depositories in regional cities, the publications of this print society could be found everywhere by the late 1820s. The tract society was the first American publishing enterprise to demonstrate the viability of a mass market of readers. It met an exploding demand for reading material—a demand that benevolence helped fuel with Sunday schools—with sentimental tales of sin and redemption. New Englanders took the lead in distributing popular religious tracts. In 1814, led by Justin Edwards of Andover, Congregationalist clergy in New England sought financial backing to publish popular messages of orthodox Christian wisdom. The New England Tract Society was the first to develop a national reach, with depositories in every state by 1823. It had published 167 different tracts with a circulation that extended well beyond the limits of its regional name. The New Englanders were not the first to form regional tract societies, only the most ambitious. In 1812, for instance, Presbyterian merchants and ministers formed the New York Religious Tract Society.[35]

In 1824, with the generous financial support of Arthur Tappan, the American Tract Society was formed in New York. At its first meeting, the society "invited all Evangelical Tract Societies to co-operate with us in the great objects of this Institution."[36] Congregationalists in New England were, at first, reluctant. They feared their denominational tracts would disappear in an interdenominational society that was based in Presbyterian and Dutch Reformed New York and that even included Baptists and Methodists in its operation. A delegation from New York was sent to Andover to allay these fears. The constitution of the new society provided for five or six ministers each from different denominations to approve all tracts. Any one of these ministers could block a tract from publication. "After considerable discussion, very amicably conducted, the [New England] Society voted that it was expedient to become a Branch of the Society formed at New York."[37] The organizational consensus among prominent Congregationalist, Presbyterian, and even some Methodist and Baptist ministers over the publication of popular tracts indicated the growing optimism among educated evangelicals that a loose doctrinal consensus among the denominations opened greater and greater opportunity for practical benevolence.

By mid-decade, when it came to the moral instruction of everyday Americans, the educated ministers of competing denominations had a lot to say in common. Possibly no single issue to appear in popular tracts received as wide and enthusiastic support as temperance and the fight against sexual sin. Popular tracts began to establish archetypal sinners like "the rake" and "the sot," sparing little detail in the description of their miserable lives and evil deeds. In 1829 the tract society launched a strategy of "general supply."[38] This campaign aimed to reach all Americans with the same tract at the same time. In this, America's first media blitz, the goal was to have the whole nation buzzing at once about the same moral lesson. In the United States, print evangelism prefigured the penny presses and pulp fiction of print capitalism in constructing a national audience. The popularity of and consensus over religious tracts demonstrated that the dangers of particular sins could support broad coalitions of evangelicals and engross a national audience. The relative comity among denominations evident in the tract enterprise was startling when compared to the interdenominational rancor of the first decade of the nineteenth century. Spearheaded by New Divinity Presbyterians and Congregationalists but legitimized by Methodist, Baptist, and Episcopalian elites attracted to the prestige and parts of the orthodox moral vision, the distribution of religious tracts represented an unprecedented civil-religious enterprise. Indeed, to the extent organized benevolence was successful, much of the credit belongs to its publishing campaigns. While Presbyterians and Congregationalists lost the battle of the pews, they still influenced the practice of religion in the pews they did not control by furnishing the reading material of most evangelicals.[39]

The least interdenominational society and, in terms of financial resources, the smallest was the American Education Society—the author of the survey of organized benevolence referred to at the start of this chapter. The society was founded in 1815 for the purpose of subsidizing the education of poor students who showed promise of adding to the ranks of orthodox Calvinist ministers, and, in particular, to find eligible students for the new Congregationalist seminary at Andover founded by Hopkinsians. As shown by the *Quarterly Register*'s survey of American benevolence, this predominantly Congregationalist society nonetheless considered itself an integral part of a united evangelical front of organized benevolence. For the New Divinity leaders of the American Education Society, fear of the popular ministries of uneducated preachers outweighed sectarian misgivings among the educated clergy in the Reformed tradition. "The tendency of every thing human is downward," the editor of the society's journal feared. "The great barrier against the deluge of impiety and ignorance and crime which is threatening our land, is an *educated and pious ministry*." [40] This high purpose extended well beyond denominational lines. The American Education Society furnished aid not just to students training at schools led by New Divinity Congregationalists but also to students at Presbyterian seminaries in New Jersey, New York and Virginia; at Baptist seminaries in Massachusetts and New York; at Episcopal seminaries in New York City and Virginia; and even at a Lutheran seminary in Pennsylvania.[41]

Colleges and seminaries provided a unique forum for Presbyterians, Congregationalists, and members of other Reformed denominations to come together in evangelical union. Yale, Princeton, and Andover—the principle colleges and seminaries of orthodoxy—were important supports for organized benevolence. National benevolent societies were first devised there. As organized benevolence expanded, presidents and professors of these schools conferred legitimacy on the Christian missions by sitting on their boards and addressing their conventions. These educational institutions also became recruitment centers for young soldiers for the causes. In the first quarter of the nineteenth century, Yale, for example, became a national institution drawing students from across the states, north and south, east and west. Organized benevolence paralleled this national development by enlisting support from these uniquely national institutions.[42]

Students for the ministry encountered representatives of a national community in these schools. Their world was immensely wider than that of their fathers, who typically had trained for the ministry through an apprenticeship with a settled minister. During breaks and after graduation, students brought national visions back home to their local communities. College students on summer breaks worked for tract societies and Sabbath schools across the nation. After graduation, many worked full-time for benevolent societies as they decided on careers. A select few even turned to benevolence as a vocation. Organized benevolence, in turn, helped establish a new generation of schools, many in the West. These new colleges and seminaries like Western Reserve, Hamilton, Lane, Oneida Institute, and Oberlin provided schooling to children from families of more modest means and became in the 1830s hotbeds of radical reform.

In short, organized benevolence emerged through creative and coordinated interaction between Presbyterians and Congregationalists. At the core of organized benevolence were national voluntary associations with broad evangelical tasks. These national societies removed redundancies and shared new print technology in a coordinated effort to bring religious products to a national audience. The American Home Missionary Society and the American Board, operating under the 1801 Plan of Union between Congregationalists and Presbyterians, subsidized and coordinated the placement of orthodox Calvinist clergy in congregations across the nation and in missions around the world. The Bible and tract societies supplied millions of copies of the scripture and popular religious tracts, reaching even the unchurched. The American Sunday School Union sponsored a network of religious schools for the newest generation of Americans, solicited its volunteer teachers, and drafted and published their curriculum. A growing network of colleges and seminaries developed alongside these societies. The directors of these societies and schools typically sat on the boards of multiple organizations forming a tight network of leaders of organized benevolence.

By 1830, organized benevolence had, according to a reliable accounting, raised $2.81 million since its beginning compared with the $3.59 million spent by the federal government on internal improvements since the end of the Revolution.[43] And the tide of support for benevolence appeared to be rapidly rising. Figure 1 shows the increase in income from 1811 to 1830 to the six core societies of organized benevolence. Much of this income came from the elite benefactors that helped form these national societies, but increasing financial support came from a growing national network of auxiliaries. For example, from 1825 to 1830 the percentage of receipts to the American Board coming from local auxiliaries grew steadily from 47 percent to 63 percent. In 1828, auxiliaries to the leading five benevolent societies operated in all of the states of the Union, and there were well over 2,000 societies nationwide. In a survey of voluntary associations listed in 23 city directories of the 1820s, only churches and Freemason

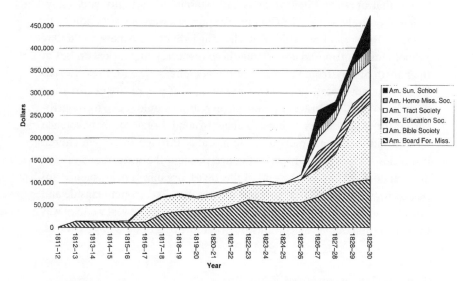

FIGURE 1. The Rising Tide of Orthodox Benevolence: Combined Receipts to the Leading Benevolent Societies, 1812–1830
SOURCE: American Education Society, *Quarterly Register*, 1825–1831.

lodges appeared more often than auxiliaries to organized benevolence.[44] The centralized efforts of orthodoxy were reaching Americans everywhere they lived.

Organized benevolence presented not only a new, rationalized system of evangelism but also a new national vision. In its effort to evangelize a rapidly expanding nation, it collected vast data on the country: data on its geographic dimensions, its expanding population, its religious institutions, its academic institutions, its publishing enterprises. As the 1829 report of American Education Society illustrated, organized benevolence had a penchant for numbers. From the early surveys of the religious conditions of the West to later accountings of the distribution of tracts and Bibles and reports on auxiliary societies, organized benevolence sought to project its influence over the nation through a correct and systematic accounting of its extensive features. In the imaginary of the leaders of benevolence, this rationalized impression of a diverse and immense nation mixed with an older vision of a community covenanted with God. As these evangelical leaders worked to extend their influence, the image of the nation they conjured was a peculiar mixture of this rationalized accounting and a mass variant of the covenanted community.[45]

From the outside looking in, the Unitarian William Ellery Channing feared that organized benevolence had established "a polity and a government entirely its own."[46] Channing's concerns were not groundless. In 1827, the Reverend Ezra Stiles Ely, a leading light of the American Sunday School Union, proposed converting these resources to political ends. On the Fourth of July, from the pulpit of Philadelphia's Seventh Presbyterian Church, he advocated "a new sort of union, or if you please, a Christian party in politics."[47] Direct intervention in politics would prove too controversial for most leaders of benevolence. Instead, organized benevolence made a bid to shape America's civic morality through these parachurch institutions. It sought national influence through the institutions of civil and religious society. By the end of the 1820s, organized benevolence appeared to be succeeding. It had built what looked like, from the inside and out, an empire of Christian benevolence. The empire's newest weapon was the society to combat special sins. It would prove a double-edged sword.

The Specialization of National Sins

In the late 1820s and early 1830s, the second week in May was designated "anniversary week" for these national benevolent societies. During this week, the leaders of the Bible, tract, and domestic missionary societies met in New York City to review the past year's work and devise plans for the year to come. Similar but smaller anniversaries were held for the societies based in Boston and Philadelphia. At these conventions new ideas for organized benevolence were hatched and acted upon. New benevolent societies planned meetings to coincide with the larger convention so as to harness the overflow of benevolence produced at such gatherings. In this fashion, by the late 1820s, as an adjunct to the general structure of organized benevolence, a host of societies emerged with special missions to combat particular worldly problems. Societies like the American Colonization Society (1819), the Prison Discipline Society (1825), the American Temperance Society (1826), the American Seamen's Friend Society (1826), the General Union for the Promotion of the Observance of the Sabbath (1828), the American Peace Society (1828), and the New York (1829) and Philadelphia (1826) Magdalen societies shared executive committee members with the big six, shared publishing houses and meeting halls, and coordinated efforts for the greater cause of benevolence.

Most of these adjunct societies emerged as specialized agencies within or closely associated with organized benevolence.[48] For example, the New York Magdalen Society—reborn as the American Society for Promoting the Seventh Commandment in 1833 and the American Moral Reform Society in 1836—grew out of the work of men and women associated with the American Tract Society.[49] While distributing tracts to prostitutes in the city's poorest neighborhoods, committed agents of the tract society developed a special calling to combat the sin that imprisoned these "fallen" women. The battle against an industry of violations of the seventh commandment soon attracted full-time champions and emerged as a relatively autonomous agency within the benevolence enterprise. The oldest of these special-purpose societies, the American Colonization Society, mixed a specialized mission to evangelize Africa with a nominal commitment to antislavery. The society launched colonies in Africa for freed American blacks under the moral standard of Christianizing a heathen continent and providing a means to gradually abolish the evil of slavery through expatriation. For the men and women of benevolence, colonization promised to be, in the words of the American Board's official publication, "at the same time the means of abolishing the slave trade, and of diffusing knowledge, civilization, and Christianity."[50] The Reverend Leonard Bacon, the chief advocate for the American Colonization Society in New England, promoted antislavery and African colonization as one mission.

[T]he civilized and enterprizing population of Africa shall send forth their pro-
ductions to compete in every market, with the sugar, and cotton, and coffee, of
the West Indies and Southern America, the planters will be compelled, by that
spirit of improvement which always springs from competition, to substitute the
cheaper process for the more expensive, to adopt the labour of freemen instead
of slaves; in a word, to convert their slaves into freemen.[51]

Efforts to rationalize and differentiate organized benevolence generated
widespread support for these special-purpose societies.

The founding of the American Temperance Society exemplified this
process of rationalization and differentiation within the parachurch institutions of organized benevolence.[52] When the wealthy merchant and
Congregationalist Arthur Tappan made clear his intentions to launch a
national tract society based in New York, Justin Edwards and other New
England leaders of organized benevolence moved to convert the resources
of the Massachusetts tract society to the cause of temperance. New York
and Boston leaders agreed that the two tract societies should not compete
with the new national association. Temperance had already become a special focus of religious tracts, the cause of a statewide organization, and
the most popular cause of local antivice societies. It had also garnered national attention in a series of sermons delivered by the Reverend Lyman
Beecher. Edward's new society, however, was the first to organize such
concerns on a national scale.[53]

In the late 1820s, under Edwards's leadership and the financial and
administrative support of stalwarts in organized benevolence, the new
American Temperance Society churned out thousands of tracts on intemperance, commissioned statistical studies on the nation's consumption of
alcohol, reported medical research on the deleterious effects of drink, and
printed theological and biblical discourses on the sin of drinking. The society also launched a campaign to spread temperance across the nation
through a coordinated network of auxiliary societies. Following the model
set down by the missionary and publication societies of organized benevolence, temperance took a national evangelical approach to the cause of
temperance. Linking these dispersed temperance societies were peripatetic agents, publications, and a standard public act of commitment, the
temperance pledge.[54]

Voluntary associations to combat the particular evils like drinking, sex,
or Sabbath violations were not exactly new, but the interdenominational
cooperation, the national scope, and the narrow specialization of associa-

tions like the American Temperance Society *were* new. Orthodox societies to counter vice were as old as the more general missionary societies. Organizing to enforce temperance, for example, antedated the emergence of organized benevolence, but a national organization dedicated to attacking this special sin came only after the coordination of the more general national societies. Early efforts to support temperance were typically one part of broader antivice campaigns. These campaigns were organized locally and sought to enforce morality through a partnership between church and local magistrates. The covenant theology of Calvinists informed these efforts to defend civic morality. Calvinists expected public sins to be punished in the here and now by God. They also expected this divine judgment to fall on the corporate body of the whole community. In this tradition, religious leaders, in league with civil magistrates, had a corporate duty to forestall these judgments by enforcing Christian discipline.[55]

Repentance during church trial was a typical social practice used to reintegrate communicants guilty of intemperance, economic deceit, licentious behavior, or other violations of Christian virtue. In the early nineteenth century, these parochial modes of moral control were failing. With sectarianism, disestablishment, and increased geographical mobility, individuals in the new century could ignore congregational discipline, rebuke the proceedings of church trials, or simply seek Christian fellowship elsewhere. Church trials declined as a mode of discipline, and local religious communities were increasingly unable to coerce individuals into observing their moral obligations.[56] The corporate structure of covenanted religious communities was collapsing. Orthodox interests in controlling public sins was not waning, but the institutional moorings of the means to realize these interests were giving way.

A host of local societies for "the suppression of vice" or "moral societies" emerged in the first two decades of the century to stand in for the failing modes of discipline of the eighteenth-century covenanted community. These short-lived societies existed in Calvinist-dominated towns, were tied to local churches, and assumed undifferentiated missions to combat sin. Although they responded to the decline of an eighteenth-century model of a covenanted community where family, church, and polis were roughly coterminous, they remained rooted in this model.[57]

Moral or antivice societies were not limited to the Congregationalist communities in New England or to Presbyterian communities in the Middle Atlantic. They appeared throughout the West where orthodox emigrants tried to reproduce the "steady" habits of the Calvinist way. For

example, in 1815, the *Weekly Recorder,* a newspaper published in Chilo-
cothe, Ohio, reprinted the following from a neighboring newspaper, the
Zanesville Express:

> That societies formed for the purpose of suppressing vice and immorality, by
> giving information to the magistrates, & aiding them in the execution of the
> laws, enacted for such purposes, have been, are, and may be highly beneficial
> to society, there can be no doubt, in the minds of those who have given the
> subject due consideration. The laws enacted against sabbath breaking, profane
> swearing, intoxication, &c. are of no service to the community unless they are
> enforced: they become a dead letter and serve to harden the vicious in their
> crimes. When the morals of the people have become so corrupt that the com-
> mission of such crimes excites little or no sensibility, and they will not give the
> necessary information to the magistrates; it is high time for the men that "fear
> God" and love righteousness, to associate for the benevolent purpose above
> mentioned. We therefore hope that such a society will be established in Zanes-
> ville and Springfield.[58]

A year earlier the *Utica Christian Magazine* reported on the formation of
the same type of moral society in the town of Westmoreland, New York:

> The object of this Society, is the promotion of good morals, particularly to sup-
> press Sabbath breaking, intemperance and profane language, and if necessary,
> to countenance and support Magistrates, and all other persons, in all prudent
> and lawful endeavors, to convict offenders against the statute laws of this state,
> for suppressing immorality; and that each member of the Society, shall so far
> as his example, advice or authority avail, discourage vice of every description.[59]

Like the national societies of organized benevolence, these societies exper-
imented with voluntary associations as a replacement for the eighteenth-
century social control that formally linked magistrate and pulpit. These
societies brought together pious local elites and sought to lead through
exemplary public behavior.

The third article of the constitution of one such society founded in
1817 in East Haddam, Connecticut, was typical of antivice societies
everywhere:

> The members of the Society shall by their conversation and example encour-
> age all virtuous conduct, and shall discount vice generally; and particularly the

vices of Sabbath-breaking—intemperance in the use of spirituous liquors—idleness—gaming and profane swearing.[60]

In the early 1820s, members of orthodoxy lamented that these moral societies and their ability to exercise control over the vices of their communities were diminishing. Their inability to curb intemperance was most glaring:

> Laws have been enacted in some of the states to post up in public, drinking persons, and to fine those who furnish them with spirits. In several cities the number and privileges of cellars, taverns and dram-shops have been restricted by the civil authority. Nothing comparatively is yet actually accomplished—Moral Societies, which sprung into being a few years ago, as by magic, at the alarming prevalence of vice, are [illegible] nearly all in oblivion. Their influence was gone, even sooner than their name. Intemperance now walks at large, aided rather than opposed by law. The sale of licenses has become a source of public revenue, at the expense of public virtue.[61]

As the following account of the development of a temperance movement in Mt. Carmel, Illinois, indicates, some of the earliest auxiliary societies to the American Temperance Society emerged within these undifferentiated, local, moral societies:

> In 1815 I belonged to an association, of different orders of the religious and moral persons that formed the first Temperance Society I ever heard of; this was, however, termed a society for the suppression of vice and immorality. The Temperance department was committed to the care of my inexperienced hands.[62]

Once independent and detached from the "whole counsel" of orthodoxy, societies devoted exclusively to fighting a particular sin like intemperance proved more popular than the undifferentiated moral societies.

The undifferentiated antivice societies represented the more settled interests of communities resisting social change. Auxiliaries to the American Temperance Society, in contrast, were national in character and represented a new idea in public influence. They attracted members of a mobile market society. They provided a form of association that helped newcomers to attach to a restless community. In a changing nation with weak national and public institutions and few political allies for evangelicals, these

special-purpose societies sought to stem the tide of sin through mass associations and media trumpeting Christian virtue. The specialization of
the campaigns against sin—the creation of national organizations, the differentiation of sinfulness into particular problems, and the emergence of
professional media campaigns and activism—sought to influence a nation
of individuals that had plowed under the covenanted communities of the
eighteenth century.

By affiliating with the national special-purpose societies, local groups
received the latest literature on the dangers and spread of the special sin,
epistles on how to counter it, and reports of progress elsewhere. In the
process, subtle but important changes to the orthodox notion of public sin
and the covenanted community took hold. In these campaigns, orthodoxy
was extending its battle against public sins by narrowing it—broadening its
appeal by focusing its message. In the rationalization of organized benevolence, evangelicals focused attention and alarm to particular problems
detached from the thick contexts of local interactions. They abstracted
from locally embedded experiences of evil by concentrating or distilling
the meaning and communication of sin. Temperance led the way in this.
By the late 1820s, the religious publications of orthodoxy were trumpeting
the moral claim that national destiny and divine favor depended on turning back the evil of alcohol.

A New Brand of Missionaries

The success of the American Temperance Society encouraged imitation.
In commercial centers, ministers like John McDowall, who headed the
New York Magdalen Society, Joshua Leavitt of the American Seamen's Society, and lay activists like Lewis Tappan, who directed the General Union
for the Promotion of the Observation of the Sabbath, were beginning to
make religious careers out of building organizations to combat special national sins. These men and their societies followed the early success of the
American Temperance Society and worked to reproduce it. Complement-
ing these central activists were the itinerant agents who sought to spread
and link the campaigns across the country. These two types of activists
brought together city and country sensibilities in coordinated and specialized missions. Both were rootless and professional missionaries freed
from the constraints of local concerns and community power structures.[63]

Many of these central officers and itinerant agents initially pursued vo-
cations as ministers but found a higher calling in these specialized organi-

zations. For young men in the 1820s, the ministry had become something quite different than it had been for their elders. At the turn of the century, an orthodox minister could still expect to hold one pulpit for his lifetime. His office was tightly linked to the structures of local congregations or presbyteries. He was most likely recruited at an early age by his local minister to train for the office, in an apprenticeship. He assumed the pulpit only after the careful scrutiny of a local congregation or presbytery. In contrast, by the 1820s, most candidates for the orthodox ministry trained in seminaries. Many more came from modest means and received support from national organizations like the American Education Society or directly from the seminaries. After graduation, they faced numerous options. Moving from congregation to congregation became a normal practice, and congregations and their ministers now severed relationships with greater ease. In short, the orthodox ministry had been transformed from a public office to a middle-class profession. For some, organized benevolence seemed to offer an opportunity to recover the public role that the pulpit had largely lost, but this role was considerably different not the least because the public was so different.[64]

The work of these men found strong support from a network of activist women. Evangelical women from the upper and middle classes, presiding over a domestic sphere that was emerging on the "private" side of a divide between home and market, turned their energies and moral commitments to the missionary enterprise of benevolence. With the active participation of women in fund-raising, administrative support, and the day-to-day activity of distributing tracts and praying for and with sinners, benevolence admitted a dissenting moral voice into its patriarchal affairs.[65]

In general, the distribution of power within the societies did not favor the career officers, itinerant agents, or the women's auxiliaries. In most societies, the executive committee, comprised of wealthy laymen and prominent ministers, held most of the discretionary power. Most decisions were made at the annual convention in May or at smaller seasonal meetings. The professional managers—the corresponding secretaries, book custodians, agents—and female foot soldiers carried out this agenda and reported back to the committees on their progress. They were afforded little leeway in directing affairs. During most of the 1820s, this relationship worked with little dispute; the professional men of benevolence, the female auxiliaries, and their benefactors on the boards of the societies enjoyed relative comity. The conservative agenda of executive committees, however, did not always sit well with the young men and women who had devoted their lives to benevolence. In the 1830s, the executive boards of most societies would prove wary of contentious issues, and some professional managers would grow impatient with the conservative dilettantes and luminaries sitting on the committees.

As these societies grew in size and responsibilities, financial support from middle-class evangelicals across the north swelled. While based in the commercial centers of the North and headed by prominent Calvinists who expected deferential treatment, the growth of organized benevolence, with its expanding distribution network of tracts and Bibles and educational organizations of Sunday schools and seminaries, increasingly depended on the evangelical farmers and shopkeepers spread out along the rivers of New England and natural and manmade waterways of New York and Ohio. In the 1820s, the work of professional managers, agents, and female auxiliaries broadened the financial base of the societies to include a wider cross-section of evangelicals. Religious newspapers in towns like Utica ran letters from the corresponding secretaries of the national societies asking for support.[66] With increased support from large numbers of evangelicals across the North, the potential for managers to exercise greater independence from the wealthy board members emerged.

While auxiliary societies had little influence on the national agenda, national societies also had little control over their subsidiaries. As resources mobilized on the periphery became more important for the general working of benevolence, a precarious relationship developed. Executive committees out of touch with their auxiliary societies were poorly equipped to defend themselves against the dissension of professional managers and female activists. When radicals within benevolence pursued matters against the will of the elite leadership, executive committees found it difficult to cut them off from the flow of resources along the social networks organized benevolence had built. In short, with these special-purpose societies, powerful institutional resources with national reach became tied to moral agendas built on precarious class, regional, and gender divides.

Organized Benevolence on the Brink

Conservative forces within orthodoxy had brought this about, but they did not intend to grant the managers, itinerant agents, and women's auxiliaries any initiative in the operation of organized benevolence. The executive committees of the largest parachurch institutions expected polite deference from the consumers of their religious products; they were not courting contentious collective action. In the 1820s, although this network of national societies dominated an emerging public arena of issue-oriented discourse on civic morality, it lacked the collective action form of a mass movement. Compared to the explosion of public participation in electoral politics marked by the successes of Jacksonian Democrats and the growth in church attendance spearheaded by Methodists and Baptists, organized benevolence of the 1820s was still an elite affair. And yet, while many and probably most Americans ignored or derided these moralists and their causes, campaigns against particular sins were beginning to show signs of mass appeal by the end of the decade. Driving some of this appeal was the greater interest shown by members of the populist sects. Many more Methodists and Baptists were willing to cooperate with orthodoxy in its combat against particular worldly problems like intemperance than they were in more general missionary campaigns. As well as broadening interest beyond the traditional constituency of orthodox Calvinism, organized benevolence's calls to combat specific sins had deepened the significance of these sins within diverse evangelical communities.

The call to combat special sins signaled the emergence of a new unorthodox leadership and constituency. By calling into existence a new brand of religious activist, organized benevolence had developed communities of missionaries increasingly unwilling to compromise in the battle against these sins. For example, William Lloyd Garrison, a young Baptist newspaper editor in Boston, saw in the temperance cause a new and effective means to redeem the nation. In 1828, Garrison became the editor of the *Philanthropist*, a Boston newspaper devoted mainly to the cause of temperance. In his first address to the readers of this novel special-purpose paper, Garrison reflected on what the newspaper and the cause of temperance had already achieved:

> By extraordinary efforts, and under appalling disadvantages, the first number [of this paper] was presented to the public; and since that time it has gradually expanded in size, and increased in circulation, till doubt, and prejudice, and ridicule, have been swept away.
>
> Nor is this all. The change which has taken place in public sentiment is indeed remarkable—almost without a parallel in the history of moral exertions—incorporated as intemperance *was,* and still *is,* into our very existence. . . . A regenerating spirit is everywhere seen.[67]

Garrison's letter to his readers reflected a growing optimism among evangelical men and women that the new methods of organized benevolence were making *unparalleled* gains for the kingdom of Christ against the evils of this world.

Closer to orthodoxy, the response to the work of the ministers John Mc-Dowall and Joshua Leavitt to combat the interwoven vices of sailors and prostitutes pointed to the challenge this new brand of missionary posed to the elite leadership of benevolence. In his 1829 letter published in the American Education Society's *Quarterly Register,* the Reverend Archibald Alexander of Princeton warned against the public activities of young ministers susceptible to the excitements and delusions of "great service" peddled by "hot-headed men" and animated by "spiritual pride." Placing the vitriol aside, Alexander's alarm rang true. He was describing young men like McDowall and Leavitt. In 1830, McDowall headed up the New York Magdalen Society and Leavitt the American Seaman Friends Society. McDowall was a recent graduate from Alexander's Princeton and a Presbyterian; Leavitt was a graduate of Yale and a Congregationalist. Both had turned down the life of a settled minister for activist careers within organized benevolence. Their work brought them together in the poorest neighborhoods of New York City, where they distributed religious tracts and fought the vices of prostitutes and sailors. Within a year, both of these career officers in benevolence were at the center of contentious disputes resulting in public attacks on their integrity, angry repudiations by former supporters, a radical reorientation of their religious callings, and the emergence of single-issue social movements.[68]

In 1831, McDowall, with the support of Leavitt, released his *Magdalen Report.* The report was commissioned but later rejected by the American Tract Society. It sought to alarm the public with an exposé of the extent of licentiousness in the city. It claimed that there were no less than ten thousand prostitutes in the city and spared few details in relating stories of their activities. The report, along with the newspaper that followed, argued that men from the best Christian families frequented the brothels, that the pulpit, in its silence, was guilty of complicity, and that both had to be exposed. Conservatives within orthodoxy were shocked by McDowall's "indelicate" handling of sexual sin and alarmed at the controversy it was stirring within prestigious congregations and the secular press. They moved quickly to silence him. The Reverend Alexander, president of McDowall's alma mater, advised him to step down from the Magdalen Society. His early benefactors withdrew their support and charged him with misappropriating funds for the publication of his scandalous newspaper. The Third Presbyterian Church in New York proffered charges against him for unministerial conduct. In the mid-1820s, if McDowall had been denied the institutional support of the leaders of organized benevolence, his crusade would have come to an abrupt end. By 1830, a movement to trigger mass confessions had made its way from unorthodox and western sources to the commercial cities on the eastern seaboard. There, western revival met with special-purpose benevolent societies, and would-be radical reformers seized on a way to replace the constraints of elite institutional support with a popular evangelical constituency. McDowall's own efforts for "moral reform" would meet modest success, but crusaders against intemperance and slavery would spark national social movements.

CHAPTER FOUR

Rise Up and Repent

Among its central purposes, organized benevolence tried to counter a populist form of religious revivalism driving the success of upstart sects. In the 1830s, as reformers within or closely associated with organized benevolence began to press for stronger stands against special sins, they used a variation of this revivalism to attract new support and counter conservative resistance within orthodoxy. Men like McDowall, Leavitt, and Garrison challenged the conservative leaders of organized benevolence to live up to their moral calling to combat special sins. When organized benevolence balked, these men and the activist women that supported them threatened to overrun the conservatives with the popular appeal of public confessions. This move to combine the orthodox schema of special sins with the populist schema of public confession was startling and radical because it depended on bridging a contentious divide between evangelicals.

In a context of broad religious controversies among evangelicals over doctrine, liturgy, and church government, the issue of revivalism became something of a capsule of the differences that divided. This controversy over revivals divided orthodoxy from the populist sects in the first two decades of the nineteenth century. Later, in the 1820s, it came to divide factions within orthodoxy. In these conflicts, the fight was not over whether revivals were liturgically or doctrinally sanctioned, but rather over what was the nature of a genuine revival. The controversies over revivals pitted opposing modes of piety shaped by regional, class, and sectarian differences.

A standard claim in the historiography of antebellum America is that the religious revivals of the Second Great Awakening fueled the drive for organized benevolence *and* social reform. Most instances of this general claim do not specify important differences among contentious traditions of revivalism within evangelical Christianity *and* between organized benevolence and the later radical reform movements. Over the first three decades of the nineteenth century, there were three different forms of revivalism that shaped the religious institutions of different regions and social classes. One form of revivalism was made famous by the spectacular revivals in Kentucky and Tennessee, another form took shape in the settled communities of New England and the Middle Atlantic, and a third in a region populated predominantly by Yankee emigrants extending from western and northern New England across upstate New York and further west into Ohio.[1] Each of these three forms of revivalism had influence on the religious practices of a wider area, but it was in these separate regions that the different types of collective action developed their characteristic shape and also remained most popular. The second form shaped organized benevolence and the third form, borrowing from the first, disrupted orthodoxy's benevolent enterprise unleashing radical reform movements.

The many different evangelical movements of the early nineteenth century all agreed that salvation was accompanied by a transformative religious experience, a new birth.[2] Revivals of religion occurred when significant numbers of people, gathered together, experienced these saving transformations. Great differences surrounded the nature of this regeneration and what measures, if any, were available to promote such experiences. These differences in the nature and practice of religious revivals were as much liturgical as doctrinal and separated evangelicals along lines of experiences and practices of the conviction of sin, repentance, and conversion. These differences in religious experience and practice conformed roughly to class and denominational distinctions. In the first two decades of the century, the populist revivals of frontier Methodists, Baptists, Cumberland Presbyterians, "Christians," and other upstart sects experiencing breathtaking growth differed greatly from the more genteel revivals of Congregationalists and Presbyterians back east.[3]

Populist and orthodox clashed over revivals and standards of piety for the first two decades of the century, but in the 1820s a third type of revivalism stirred evangelicals in both camps. It grew particularly popular with an emerging middle class. The *New York Evangelist*—a newspaper designed "to promote Revivals of Religion, and to disseminate those doctrines of the Bible embraced generally by those who are denominated

Calvinists"—became the mouthpiece for the new form of revivalism among orthodox evangelicals.[4] In one of its earliest editions, it provided a definition of revivals that bridged important differences that had brought the populists and orthodox into conflict:

> A REVIVAL of *religion* is the *renewal* of those affections which were exercised by man in his *primeval state;* and which, since the fall, are totally extinct in every soul, until renewed by the grace of God.
>
> In the more ordinary use of the term, a *revival* is the first excitement of holy affections and holy actions in sinners; and the increase of those affections and actions in saints. This excitement, which constitutes a revival, is effected *invariably* by the Holy Spirit, through the instrumentality of gospel motives. . . .
>
> A great revival in one heart, is the excitement of *high* and *holy* affections. A *great* and *general* revival is the excitement of *high* and *holy* affections throughout a community. . . Religion is *revived* in any and every heart, so far as holy affections are excited or revived; and it is self-evident, from the very nature of the case, that there can be no revival in any heart any further than there is an excitement of holy feeling.

The article concluded with the observation that "some churches never have revivals of religion" because the "*fear* of excitement deters them from using those means which are absolutely necessary for producing a revival."[5]

The *Evangelist* promoted "new school" Calvinism—the liberal outgrowth of the Hopkinsian system best articulated by the theology of Yale's Nathaniel Taylor. The paper's champion in the field of revivals was the controversial Charles Grandison Finney. The *Evangelist*'s stand on revivals compromised orthodox practices and doctrines in two significant respects: it encouraged "the excitement of affections" against the restrained traditions of orthodoxy, and it argued for the effectiveness of human "instrumentality" or "means" in "producing" revivals (albeit maintaining somewhat inconsistently that regeneration was "invariably" effected by the Holy Spirit). These concessions to enthusiastic or experiential religion and Arminian theology attested to the impact of populist forms of evangelism on orthodox religious culture.

In the hands of heirs of orthodoxy, populist revival techniques were adjusted. As the *Evangelist* described revivals, they could be "*great*" and "*general*" exciting an entire community; and, in the orthodox cosmology, this community could encompass the nation as a whole. Populist revivals, though attracting mass audiences, were decidedly local in their scope, individualistic in their message, and centrifugal in their impact on religious institutions. A surprising consequence of smuggling this populist mode of piety into orthodoxy was the explosion of radical reform and the rise of extensive social movements with a coherent national agenda. Through the creative combination of populist and orthodox religious schemas, radical reformers triggered these events. The surprising popular resonance of this cultural fusion depended on the coming together of disparate evangelicals on the matter of revivals. This coming together was decades in the making.

Populist Revivals of the Early Nineteenth Century

At the turn of the nineteenth century, Presbyterians in Kentucky and Tennessee initiated revivals of religion that quickly spun out of their control. The role of Presbyterian ministers in initiating these revivals is important. Although these revivals came to be associated with the meteoric rise of the upstart sects, they stemmed from the work of orthodox missionaries. Over the first two decades of the nineteenth century, the defenders of orthodoxy would draw a sharp divide between their authentic revivals and the shallow enthusiasm of the upstarts, but the two forms were initially tied together.

In 1787, there was a modest revival among Baptists and Methodists in Virginia. Although historians have typically treated the period immediately after the Revolution as one of religious declension, Finke and Stark convincingly argue that Baptists and Methodists were enjoying gains during these years with an unorthodox variety of practices and beliefs, and, at least in Virginia, some orthodox Calvinists took note.[6] At the Presbyterian college of Hampden-Sidney, students impressed by the apparent regeneration among their sectarian neighbors experienced their own awakening. The revival was somber and orderly. It did not imitate the conspicuous display of emotion that characterized Methodist and Baptist worship, but for some of those moved by the event it shaped a vocational commitment to promote an "experiential" religion—a religion of the heart over the head. This Presbyterian revival spread west to Washington College (formerly Liberty Hall) and south to congregations in North Carolina.[7]

The Reverend James McGready was instrumental in its spread south. A decade later, he revived the excitement in Kentucky where it took on a new form. Originally from western Pennsylvania, McGready visited

Hampden-Sidney during the revival. He adapted the revival techniques used at the school first to North Carolina and then to the frontier setting of southern Kentucky and northern Tennessee. In North Carolina, he won many enemies by directing the revival spirit against the materialism of elite families of the Piedmont. These enemies forced him out of North Carolina, tearing up his pews and burning down his pulpit, but he also won the support of young ministers like Barton Stone who would join him on the other side of the Alleghenies.[8]

In 1800, events surrounding his ministry in Kentucky showed the first signs of a "work of God." This work spread over the next few years throughout the backwoods of the West and even reverberated back east. In southern Kentucky, McGready enlisted four other ministers in the revival: three Presbyterians and one Methodist, John McGee. McGee injected an excitement into the preaching. Describing his own role in the revival, he said, "I went through the house with all possible ecstasy and energy, and the floor was soon covered with the slain." The religious excitement could not be contained. Barton Stone applied what he learned from McGready to his ministry at Cane Ridge in Bourbon County, a more densely populated region north of Lexington. The Cane Ridge Revival was the most spectacular of the Kentucky revivals, both in size and excitement. It was also a harbinger of things to come.[9]

The Cane Ridge Revival began in August of 1801, when Stone and another Presbyterian, Richard McNemar, called for a traditional Presbyterian communion service—a highly ritualized sacramental supper brought to America from Scotland and Ulster. The sacramental service was to be held at the Cane Ridge meeting house, but as the gathering became a countywide event it was moved outdoors to a large clearing in the woods. The gathering numbered somewhere between ten and twenty-five thousand. Inundated with wagonloads of people who arrived over six days, the organizers opened their meeting to the ministers and lay exhorters of other denominations, the sacramental structure of the communion service broke down, and a nonsacramental and nonsectarian revival took place.[10]

Eighteen Presbyterian ministers presided over the gathering, which probably included many more Baptist and Methodist ministers and exhorters. Traditionalists were ambivalent about the development. As one Presbyterian minister wrote of the revival,

> There are many irregularities among us: so it was in 1776 among the whigs, in their enthusiasm for liberty; and so in human nature every where. Sitting up

whole nights is extravagant, but you cannot bid them quit, or you need not. We may be too indulgent to the Methodists; to this I only say, they appear friendly, and are very anxious to do good; and for my part, I should be sorry to forbid them, or even discourage them. I see several things I do disapprove, but I can say, if only the tenth person convicted is truly converted, it is a great work.[11]

The ecumenical spirit—the indulging of the Methodists—worked against Presbyterian authority. The prepared sermon was supplanted by passionate extempore preaching; the uneducated exhorter proved a most successful revival rouser. Calvinist doctrines of election and inability were overwhelmed by popular messages of individual freedom and the conscious employment of techniques to exacerbate the frenzy and push sinners to the brink of conversion. There were also reports of unusual "exercises": swooning, catalepsy, the "jerks," uncontrolled laughing and singing, even barking.[12]

Most alarming to orthodox Calvinists was the outcome of the revivals. Populist preachers were not friendly to orthodox doctrine and liturgy, and they raided the Presbyterian flock without remorse. Methodists and Baptists reaped the lion's share of the harvest of souls, and revival within Presbyterian ranks led to schism. Methodists seized on the camp meeting idea and made it into a denominational institution even as Presbyterians began to repudiate it as promoting disorder. By 1804, Barton Stone, Richard McNemar, and their followers had moved so far from orthodoxy that they dissolved their association with Presbyterians and established a new denomination that avoided labels and took the simple name of "Christian." In a parting blow to the Kentucky Synod preparing to put him on trial for heresy, McNemar and his brethren presented a paper charging that Presbyterian doctrines were "in a measure darkened by some expression in the confession of Faith which are used as means of strengthening sinners in their unbelief and subjecting many of the pious to a spirit of bondage."[13] The populist revivals had turned orthodox ministers into insurgents rebelling against the stultifying effects of a confession of faith centered on principles of human inability and partial election.

In the same year as Cane Ridge, the Kentucky Synod established a new presbytery to accommodate expansion along the southwestern frontier. Under the leadership of McGready, this Cumberland Presbytery, in a significant departure from the traditions of orthodox Calvinism, licensed ministers without formal training. Known as exhorters, these new ministers were ardent promoters of revivals and attracted great controversy within

Presbyterianism over their ministerial practices. The ruling body of the Kentucky Synod quickly declared the proceeding of the new presbytery "irregular" and the new ministers "destitute of any authority to administer sealing ordinances, preach or exhort in the Presbyterian Church."[14] In 1809, the Presbyterian National Congress moved to dissolve the new presbytery. In further evidence of the splintering power of enthusiastic revivals, the Cumberland Presbyterians responded by formally dissolving its bonds with the Presbyterian Church.[15]

These events exhibited a dynamic that would recur over the next four decades. Emotional and public confessions of sin and faith expanded and revitalized the ranks of the converted but only at the expense of challenging the ecclesiastical and liturgical order of established denominations and splintering evangelical Christianity. The populist approach proved attractive to yeomen farmers across the nation and particularly to commoners resentful of the privileges enjoyed by elites and their churches headed by doctors of divinity. These democratic and deliberately engineered revivals were not unique to the frontier. Although they proved particularly popular on the periphery of the new republic and it is there that they reached new emotional heights, populist revivals were not exclusively western. Baptist and Methodist revivals before the events at Cane Ridge displayed many of the same features, if on a smaller scale. Effective revivalists like the Methodist Lorenzo Dow and the Baptist John Leland challenged orthodoxy in its strongholds of New England and the Middle Atlantic. In the early nineteenth century, throughout the United States, ordinary people seeking more egalitarian and freer expressions of piety sent evangelical Christianity "cascading in many creative directions."[16]

A demystification of theological orthodoxy and a commonsense confidence in the individual's conscience and spiritual impulses united these many directions. Across the considerable differences among the upstart sects, religious enthusiasm challenged the authority of an educated clergy and its mediation of grace as it empowered the individual's spiritual quest. In the history of American Christianity, populist revivals were noteworthy for their acceleration of the conversion process, their public and conspicuous displays of convictions of sin and confession, and their melting of social and denominational distinctions in the heat of religious fervor. As they opposed liturgical and doctrinal formalism and ecclesiastical hierarchy with experiential piety, populist preachers espoused a belief in the efficacy of human action to promote regeneration and an egalitarian faith in the power of conversion. They devised new collective action techniques and a vernacular homiletics to reach mass audiences. They solicited impromptu, public testimonials from ordinary converts; encouraged physical displays of religious ecstasy; and borrowed folk music and other forms of popular recreation for the service of the Gospel.

Populist revivals stoked religious excitement with lower-class resentment of the conceit of wealth. At the extreme end of this leveling ethos, they even transgressed racial and gender distinctions. Well before the more genteel communities of orthodoxy would face the issue of women praying and speaking in public, churches of the upstart sects allowed women a leading role. As early as 1808, in a pamphlet titled "Christianity Defended Against the Cavils of Infidels and the Weakness of Enthusiasts," an orthodox minister in Whitestown, New York, warned against the preaching of Martha Howell in Baptist churches: "They suffer that woman Jezebel which called herself a prophetess, to teach and to seduce the servants of the Lord." Before 1825 at least two women preached regularly in the Methodist and Freewill Baptist churches of western New York.[17]

Populist piety also demonstrated a power to overcome racial prejudice. In McGready's account of the Kentucky revival published in a missionary magazine, he observed that "children, young men and women, and old grey-headed people, persons of every description, white and black, were to be found in every part of the multitude, pricked to the heart."[18] Where the cold and formal religion of Anglicans and Presbyterians failed to convert blacks, free or enslaved, the experiential religion of populist revivals triumphed. The genteel and orthodox religions, generally squeamish of emotional displays in worship, were particularly fearful of what such excitement would mean among African Americans, but populist preachers encouraged rapturous experiences of saving grace and promised instantaneous grace without the demeaning instruction and preparation insisted on by Presbyterians and Anglicans. As a result, in many Methodist and Baptist meetinghouses of the turn of the nineteenth century, whites and blacks sat in the pews together and even shared the pulpit. From the Revolution to the War of 1812, African Americans joined the churches of the upstart sects by the tens of thousands. At the turn of the century, the public messages of many Baptist and Methodist preachers attacked slavery. In accepting and attracting African Americans to Christian fellowship, the populist religion of the upstarts proved capable of melting the deepest social divisions.

As early as 1804, the Methodists began to back away from their antislavery pronouncements. By the 1830s, the vast majority of evangelical churches in the South had rejected the turn-of-the-century message of racial equality before God and nation. This repudiation was not completed before a tradition of black preachers and black churches was firmly established in the United States. In the early nineteenth century, African American Methodists and Baptists established their own denominations. In Philadelphia alone, their churches could boast nearly four thousand confessors by the 1830s. Overtly, as they did in Philadelphia, or in secret as they did across the South, preachers and congregants defended these public institutions in the face of mounting repression.[19]

The explosion of church membership within the upstart sects in the first half of the nineteenth century was a testament to the effectiveness of the populist techniques of religious persuasion. Although drawing mass appeal, these revivals remained local or regional phenomena and mostly worked to disrupt the interregional coordination of religious institutions—such as the control of presbyteries, synods, and associations or conferences of churches. Their mass message was individualistic and their impact on American Christianity centrifugal. With their mobile legions of uneducated clergy and lay exhorters, the upstarts swamped orthodox Calvinist missionary attempts in the West, where the upstarts clearly won the battle to pack the pews. And it was the emotional, mass revivals of the West, for good or bad, that came to represent their new form of evangelical Christianity. From 1800 to 1804, salacious accounts of the Kentucky revivals reached orthodox Calvinists back east, who saw them as a populist threat. The threat was familiar to orthodox Calvinists. In many aspects, it recreated events that had agitated New England and the Middle Atlantic a little over a half a century earlier.

Echoes of the Great Awakening

These events in Kentucky and Tennessee echoed the divisions precipitated by the eighteenth-century revivals of the Great Awakening. The Cumberland schism, although smaller and on the periphery of the denominational polity, resembled the 1741 split between "New Side" and "Old Side" Presbyterians. In this eighteenth-century conflict, "converted" or New Side ministers employed enthusiastic revivals and itinerant preachers as a means to challenge the authority of "educated" ministers. The revivals, by rallying popular support behind ministers who justified their office on the grounds of their spiritual regeneration and not their higher education, caused deep divisions not only within Presbyterianism but also within the Dutch Reformed Church and New England Congregationalism.

Similar to events in Kentucky, the eighteenth-century controversy over revivals pitched popular piety against elite training. William Tennent spread the revival spirit among Scotch-Irish Presbyterians in the middle colonies. He turned out "converted ministers" from his "Log College" to rail against the cold formality of the educated ministry and its Philadelphia Synod. His son, Gilbert, became a leader in this Presbyterian insurgency. He captured the angry spirit of the New Side in his famous 1740 sermon, "Dangers of an Unconverted Ministry," a sermon Archibald Alexander termed "one of the most severely abusive sermons which was ever penned."[20] Likening the educated ministry of the Old Side to Pharisees in the time of Jesus, he expressed a "mendicant turn" in the Calvinist ministry that sought to knit itself to the laity's demand for a passionate and common religion. Tennent charged that the Old Side opponents of the revival were spiritually dead, attached to filthy lucre, and not fit for the ministry. Like "the old Pharisees" they were "proud and conceity" and "look'd down upon . . . common People, with an Air of Disdain."[21]

Tennent echoed and radicalized sentiments first voiced by the New England Congregationalist Jonathan Edwards. Revivals in Edwards's hometown of Northampton, Massachusetts, in 1734 were the first publicized events of what came to be known as the Great Awakening. Edwards's account of these events influenced a generation of Calvinist ministers across denominational lines. In a chronicle of frontier revivals from 1734 to 1736 in the Connecticut River Valley, Edwards advocated emotional revivals against the contemplative and increasingly Arminianized Calvinism (proto-Unitarianism) of wealthy congregations in and around Boston.[22] In 1739 and 1740, George Whitefield momentarily linked these disparate regional revivals—Presbyterian revivals in the middle colonies and Congregationalist revivals in New England—as he traveled up and down the American strand.[23] Apart from Whitefield's tour, the revivals were mainly local events and often tied to one or two congregations at a time. The converted or prorevivalist ministry—New Side Presbyterians and New Light or Edwardsian Congregationalists—won a qualified victory. The revivals were also a triumph for the common laity in its demands for a more egalitarian religion of "holy affection."[24]

In a battle to control churches, schools, and doctrine, the New Side and New Light ministers mobilized the laity as a weapon for seizing pulpits from Old Side and Old Light ministers and raiding their congregations for followers. Through these means, the converted ministry came to dominate American Calvinism. Like the populist revivals of the nineteenth century, there was a strong class dimension to this struggle, particularly evident in western New England where farmers and converted ministers combined to usurp religious authority from wealthy mercantilists and their highbrow preachers.[25]

While the events of the Great Awakening and the populist revivals of the turn of century both defended the "existential fact of the conversion experience" as the "hinge" to "the evangelical scheme," challenged the authority and station of an educated ministry, and valorized enthusiastic revivals and itinerant revivalists, they differed significantly in doctrine. Whitefield, who had worked with John Wesley in England to promote Methodism, espoused an orthodox Calvinist doctrine in America. He rejected the Methodist notions of free will and human instrumentality in his promotion of American revivals. Writing to Wesley about the American revivals, Whitefield relayed that the "work of God is carried on here (and that in a most glorious manner) by doctrines quite opposite to those you hold. . . . There are many worthy experienced ministers, who would oppose your principles to the utmost."[26] Jonathan Edwards in his defense of experiential religion sought to shore up the doctrines of Calvinism against the Arminian tendencies of the advocates of reason. In the eighteenth century, in pitching piety against reason, reason was associated with doctrines of free will, emotional piety with the inscrutable dynamics of grace. As Edwards described eighteenth-century revivals, they were the surprising work of the Holy Spirit. Even the Baptist separatists who emerged in the wake of the Great Awakening held to Calvinistic principles of human inability to affect salvation through works. In contrast, the upstart sects that were so successful in the Kentucky revivals presented a doctrine of free will and saw human measures as decisive in bringing men and women to a conviction of sin and salvation.

Another significant difference was over the experience of conversion itself. Growing out of a Puritan tradition of conversion that worked "by degrees, from preparation through calling, faith, justification, adoption, sanctification, up to, at the end of the long process, assurance," the eighteenth-century revivals did not promise the accelerated and almost instantaneous conversions of the later populist revivals on the frontier.[27] Conviction of sin could be torturously long, so too regeneration. The revivals of the turn of the century, on the other hand, spread the popular message of a "short cut to heaven"—they promised immediate repentance and conversion. The basic unit of regeneration also distinguished these two awakenings separated by sixty years. In the eighteenth century, awakenings came by degrees to communities or covenanted societies as a whole. The populist revivals at the turn of the century, on the other hand, did not recognize this corporate subject. The upstart sects made individuals the subject of their work and converted them quickly. The distinction was one between a gradual process of revival coming to a community of saints and the rapid conversion of a mass of individuals.[28]

The eighteenth-century revivals led to excesses that even the defenders of an emotional religion decried. Chief among the offenders was James Davenport, whose attack against "priestcraft" betrayed a love for the popular spectacle. Not even Gilbert Tennent would follow Davenport in burning his vestment. By the early 1740s, the prorevivalist side began to consolidate their gains in pulpits and pews and rein in some of the more enthusiastic promoters and their "excesses." A short two years after his sermon attacking unconverted ministers, Tennent wrote in a letter published in the *Boston Evening Post* that "the practice of openly exposing ministers, who are supposed to be unconverted in public discourses serves only to provoke them." His message was directed at the likes of Davenport who were inclined to give no quarter to the Old Lights and to publicly expose every unconverted minister by name. As the revivals died down in the 1740s, the revivalist camp made concessions to their opponents, admonished prorevivalists who continued with the hostilities, and generally sought to heal divisions. The loose agreement arrived at defended the authenticity of revivals as the work of the Holy Spirit and affirmed them as a central purpose of religion. The backers of enthusiastic piety conceded to charges of emotional excesses and the undermining of ministerial authority by itinerant raiders. This peace gesture was in the interest of New Lights concerned with institutionalizing their gains. They sought to limit the enthusiasm they had started, particularly as it displayed the unfortunate tendency of eating its own.[29]

As orthodoxy settled back into the routine workings of grace in the second half of the eighteenth century, it sought to protect congregations from outside movements that might challenge ministerial authority and undermine orthodox Calvinism, and the revival spirit slumbered under a colder, more formal liturgy. One important outcome of the revival movement was to bring prorevivalists within New England Congregationalism and within Middle Atlantic Presbyterianism closer together. This set the foundation for the religious bloc that united behind organized benevolence in the nineteenth century. This eighteenth-century rapprochement between the two Calvinist denominations anticipated the 1801 Plan of Union. In 1757, in a move that symbolized both the success and the institutionalization of the Awakening, the New-Side trustees of the Presbyterian College of New Jersey at Princeton appointed Jonathan Edwards president of their school.

At the end of the eighteenth century, an enthusiastic revival spirit remained latent within orthodox Calvinism. Although it slumbered, it remained part of the collective memory of orthodoxy. Most Presbyterians and Congregationalists still considered themselves the authentic representatives of revival religion—and no one ever spoke against the need for revival. After all, most of them were the heirs of the Great Awakening. This made them vulnerable to popular appeals for a more emotional faith freed from ecclesiastical constraints. It was difficult to deny the legitimacy of such movements if only because they had been so decisive in the rise of the present ecclesiastical order. Moreover, central aspects of the liturgy and doctrine of these two churches could be mobilized in support of disruptive revivals. Indeed, this is what McGready and Stone did in Kentucky at the turn of the century, and what Charles Grandison Finney would do again in western and upstate New York in the 1820s.

In the first years of the new century, when word of frontier excitements reached settled orthodox congregations back east, it was met first with ambivalence and soon with rejection. Although the religious movement was initiated by Presbyterians who revived pietistic strains evident in the New Side and New Light revivals of the Great Awakening, orthodoxy dismissed the Kentucky revivals as "Methodist enthusiasm" and Arminian heresy.[30] And there was good cause for orthodox repudiation: in these religious enthusiasms an ascendant populist movement threatened the authority structures of orthodox denominations.

The Orthodox Response to Populist Enthusiasm

As populist revivals started to flourish, the orthodox in New England and the Middle Atlantic experienced heartfelt, if somewhat defensive, renewals in their own congregations. In sharp contrast to the enthusiastic revivals of the populists, these orthodox revivals occurred within settled communities, congregations, and Calvinist schools. They also fell under the auspices of learned ministers and followed a liturgy that valued slower, more contemplative, often solitary conversions.[31]

Starting with the first year of the nineteenth century and continuing for fifteen years, the *Connecticut Evangelical Magazine* published "religious intelligence" on revivals throughout the country. From these accounts, it is clear that on the eastern coast and particularly in the Northeast a revival code developed among the orthodox that opposed the more remarkable features of the Kentucky revivals and repudiated in no small part the legacy of Edwards and the Tennents. In the process, many powerful heirs of the New Side and New Light adopted and adapted Old Side and Old Light arguments to condemn the enthusiasm of populist revivals. This repudiation did not come immediately and it could not entirely cover up the more enthusiastic roots of orthodoxy.

A young Archibald Alexander, for example, received the earliest reports from Kentucky with optimism. As president of Hampden-Sidney College, an institution tied to the Presbyterian missionaries laboring on the other side of the Alleghenies, Alexander was invested in the authenticity of the revivals. In a letter published in the March 1802 edition of the *Connecticut Evangelical Magazine,* Alexander passed on the firsthand account of the Kentucky revivals by the president of Washington Academy in Virginia, George Baxter. As a prefatory remark endorsing the credibility of Baxter, Alexander writes:

> In this inquiry [Baxter] obtained complete satisfaction, and now entertains no doubt about [the revival] being a glorious work of God, as you will see by the contents of his letter. I scarcely know a man on whose judgement, in a matter of this kind, I could more confidently rely on than upon his. Possessing a clear, discriminating mind, and rational piety, he was in as little danger of being deceived by delusive appearances as any other person with whom I am acquainted.[32]

Alexander's comments reflected an awareness that orthodox readers of the magazine were uneasy with reports of the emotional excess of the revivals. In Baxter's otherwise favorable account, there were disturbing details. At Cane Ridge, he reported:

> The largeness of these congregations was a considerable inconvenience. They were too numerous to be addressed by any one speaker. Different ministers were obliged to officiate at the same time at different stands. This afforded an opportunity to those who were but slightly impressed with religion, to wander

backwards and forwards between different places of worship, which created an appearance of confusion and gave ground to such as were unfriendly to the work, to charge it with disorder. There was also another cause which conduced to the same effect. About this time the people began to fall down in great numbers under serious impressions. This was a new thing among Presbyterians. It excited universal astonishment, and created a degree of curiosity which could not be restrained.[33]

Baxter was quick to add that the disorders were removed and defended the falling as the genuine work of the spirit. In time, both Baxter and Alexander would back away from their endorsements of the Kentucky revivals. Indeed, thirty years later, faced with another wave of popular revivals, Alexander and Baxter led a rearguard action to defend doctrinal consistency and ecclesiastical authority against itinerant insurgents and revival enthusiasts.[34]

In spite of this early endorsement from leading lights, orthodoxy disowned the Kentucky revivals. Apart from the odd eighteenth-century phrases, the following words of "protestation" presented at a 1741 meeting of the Philadelphia Synod by Old-Side Presbyterians, could have just as easily come from the mouths of nineteenth-century defenders of orthodoxy against populist revivals:

> Their Preaching the Terrors of the Law in such a Manner and Dialect as has no Precedent in the word of God, but rather appears to be borrowed from a worse Dialect; and so industriously working on the Passions and affections of weak Minds, as to cause them to cry out in a hideous Manner, and fall down in Convulsion-like fits, to the marring of the Profiting both of themselves and others . . . and then after all, boasting of these Things as the work of God.[35]

In 1808, for example, at the opening of Andover Theological Seminary, Timothy Dwight, president of Yale, defended the role of educated clergy in true religion. In an ironic twist, Dwight, the grandson of Jonathon Edwards, argued for theological training against the enthusiastic religion of the populist sects.

> While they demand a seven-years apprenticeship, for the purpose of learning to make a shoe, or an axe; they suppose the system of Providence, together with the numerous, and frequently abstruse, doctrines and precepts, contained in the Scriptures, may be comprehended without learning labour or time. While

they insist, equally with others, that their property shall be managed by skillful agents, their judicial causes directed by learned advocates, and their children, when sick, attended by able physicians; they were satisfied to place their Religion, their souls, and their salvation, under the guidance of quackery.[36]

To be fair, this was not an outright repudiation of the legacy of his grandfather. In defending enthusiastic religion and the New-Light movement of converted versus educated clergy, Edwards had never argued that ministers should not be learned. Nonetheless, the great American theologian held a much deeper and abiding faith in the emotional compass of the common worshiper than his grandson's generation of New England Calvinists. Disorder was too much feared by the nineteenth-century Calvinists to endorse the emotional testaments of commoners, and the *Connecticut Evangelical Magazine* took care to report on the staid decorum that attended the "glorious workings of God" in orthodox revivals. In many respects, the heirs of the New Side turned "old" in the face of popular enthusiasm.

A Gentle Rain of Grace

In the *Connecticut Evangelical Magazine*'s running accounts, "genuine" or orthodox revivals were consistently described as involving deep anguish over sin and heartfelt regenerations, but conspicuous displays of emotions rarely exceeded weeping and regeneration came slowly. The falling and other extravagant exercises associated with Methodist, Baptist, and western revivals did not take hold (or were suppressed) in orthodox Calvinist settings back east, and immediate conversions were suspect. As a counter to the populists, orthodoxy developed a revival critique in which the size of the gathering, conspicuous displays of emotion, and the speed of reformation worked against the revival's authenticity. Speaking of the uneducated clergy and their ministerial works, a New England clergyman observed with contempt: "They measure the progress of religion by the number who flock to their standards, not by the prevalence of faith and piety, justice and charity and the public virtues in society in general."[37] In the battle to pack pews, this was a losing position. Orthodox revivals where "the word of God distils upon the mind like the gentle rain" could not compete with religion that encouraged "the strong commotion of animal feelings."[38]

In the November 1803 edition of the magazine, Silas Churchil wrote a letter reporting a revival in his congregation in New Lebanon, New York, located right on the border with Massachusetts. His letter, like so many others reporting on revivals, commenced with a description of declension: "The church continued to decrease in numbers, so that in September 1801, but eleven members remained. Our prospect was exceedingly dark." On the first Sabbath of October "prospect" changed and the work of God began. That day two "courses" on the "miseries of hell" were delivered and "several persons were . . . much impressed." That evening Churchil called for a conference in his home. "This was a solemn meeting, and gave some encouragement to hope that God was about to cause a shaking among the dry bones of this valley."

> Conferences were continued, and the numbers and solemnity gradually increased, until the solemnity became general and until the awakening arose to a great height. There was no uncommon providence, nor any new means made use of in the beginning of the revival, but the same kind of providences with which the people were before visited, and the same truths which they before heard made a very different impression. None can, therefore, rationally attribute the awakening to anything short of the power of him who worketh all things according to the counsel of his own will.[39]

The revival did not occur suddenly in October but only started its gradual work in that month. Extending through the winter, attendance at conferences and Sabbath worship mounted until gatherings of four and five hundred, "it was supposed," were held. During this time, numerous individual conversions occurred. Churchil included in his letter a number of accounts of individual conversions. One man pondered his sins after his wife joined the church. "At length he obtained a humble hope in the mercy of a sovereign God."

> Another person was much opposed to the sovereignty of God and other doctrines connected with it . . . He was however brought under conviction. He then saw the doctrines to be true, but hated them . . . At length his heart became hopefully changed, and then he realized those doctrines which he had opposed to be not only reasonable, but inexpressibly amiable and precious.[40]

Still another "openly opposed to the doctrines of grace" became a subject of the work. "At length, he also became hopefully reconciled to God; and those doctrines which he hated, are exceedingly delightful."

After five months of steady increase in inquiry and individual cases of regeneration, something closer to a collective awakening took hold. The awakening was triggered by the illness and death of a woman in the community. Before her death, it seems she made quite a stir by publicly anguishing over her fate as an unrepentant sinner.

> She expressed herself in the following manner. "O! wretched sinner that I am! I have lived in sin all my life. I have resisted the holy spirit and crucified the Lord Jesus Christ by my sins. Christ called me, but I have refused: he had stretched out his hand, but I have disregarded, and now too late, I see my error: my probation state is ended: the door of heaven is shut against me. I know it is just in God to sentence me to eternal misery. . . ."[41]

When this woman, who had met the Reverend Samuel Hopkins's most exacting standard of a disinterested love that would will its own damnation to please God, died without apparent relief, the community was moved as a whole. At her funeral and at communion the next day, worshipers were in tears. Rather than being dismayed at the doctrine of election, the residents of New Lebanon deepened their heartfelt inquiry, and the revival intensified. Churchil knew of no one who "obtained hopes in this awakening, who have not embraced the Calvinistic system of doctrines." According to the letter, 110 were added to the church.

Churchil concluded by making sure that the temperament and the impact of the revival was not misconstrued.

> Perhaps some, when reading the foregoing narrative, may suppose there was much enthusiasm among the people. But this is a wrong supposition; for instead of noise and enthusiasm, even when there was the greatest engagedness, there was remarkable regularity and order. I have never heard any outcries in any public meeting, and the appearance of people was more like rational creatures, who realized they were soon to enter the eternal world, than like boisterous enthusiasts.[42]

Not only the absence of enthusiasm marked this revival as genuine but also its positive impact on the community as a whole:

> A great alteration has taken place in the society, as to family prayer. The scriptures are more generally read, and all divine ordinances are apparently much more reverenced. Church discipline is reviving and the Sabbath is visibly kept in more suitable manner. There appears to be a remarkable friendship among the subjects of this work. This is more observable on account of the former disagreements arising from political opinions. It was pleasing to see those who

had been at variance in political matters, unite in joining the church, in love and harmony.[43]

It may be that Churchil suspected that the events surrounding the woman's death and the size of the gatherings might have the hint of a collective hysteria and wanted to defend the events from critics of enthusiasm. There was no better way to do this than to highlight the moral discipline of the community as a whole.

In 1809, a young Lyman Beecher also stood fast against enthusiasm. Writing in the preface to a sermon to be published as a pamphlet, Beecher described the solemn revival radiating out from his home, and first pulpit, of East Hampton, Long Island:

> From the village it extended to the body of the town and it is now about six weeks since it has pleased God to extend the work to every village and in two of them especially, with power and great glory. About seventy persons have obtained hope of deliverance from death, by Jesus Christ, and it is hoped, that the work is but just begun.
>
> The consolations of the people of God, are abundant, and a spirit of supplication is copiously poured forth. The work is unusually *silent, deep, and apparently genuine.*[44]

In the pamphlet wars of the time, Beecher was by implication claiming that loud and conspicuous displays of regeneration were suspect. The Reverend Joel Byington, relating the events surrounding a revival in Chazy, New York, went a step further denouncing them as evil: "There have been no instances discovered of delusion, wildness, or of enthusiastic ardour. Great care has been taken to guard against all these evils as much as possible."[45]

A quarter of a century after the first revival in New Lebanon, Silas Churchil appeared to change his view on excitements and revival and invited Charles Grandison Finney to preside over another revival from his pulpit. Finney's preaching in and around New Lebanon in 1827 brought him further east than he had been before as a revivalist—right to the border with New England. He brought with him the enthusiasm of the populist revival. There and then, he was met by an opposing camp of orthodox clergy and was forced to defend his so-called new measure revivals. At the debate in New Lebanon, sitting with the anti-Finney camp was Lyman Beecher. Seeing in Finney the popular means to compete with upstart sects, Beecher tried to find a compromise between the warring parties over enthusiastic revivals. In the early years of the nineteenth century, however, separate revivals, populist and orthodox, affecting separate religious communities were structured around opposing modes of piety, religious practice, and authority.

The Waning Influence of Settled Ministers and Covenanted Communities

Drawn into competition with legions of mobile and heterodox preachers, the orthodox clergy was forced to change, and with this change came divisions in orthodoxy over enthusiastic revivals. Organized benevolence emerged out of the orthodox tradition that viewed revivals as "the gentle rain" of the Holy Spirit—a rain that came to a covenanted community as a whole, as a consolation to "the people of God" as one body. While orthodoxy cleaved to the leadership of an educated clergy and defended the order of the covenanted community, competition forced it to change its evangelism. Some of the orthodox revivals of the first two decades did not occur in settled communities but within the leading colleges and seminaries of Presbyterians and Congregationalists. For example, in 1795, Timothy Dwight became president of Yale College and initiated a series of revivals among the students there. Although these revivals exhibited none of the enthusiasm of Cane Ridge or even mid-eighteenth-century Northampton, their institutional setting distinguished them from traditional orthodox revivals. As the elite colleges of orthodoxy became national in mission, revivals among their students assumed a likewise national character. If southerners, northerners, and westerners could experience regeneration together within the halls of Yale, then a national revival outside these walls was also possible. Through the national institutions of seminaries and organized benevolence, orthodoxy transformed the focus of its ministry from the settled communities of saints based on the corporate structure of the eighteenth century to a national audience of a market society. For some within these institutions, as the call to evangelize turned to a national community of increasingly heterodox believers, their understanding of revivals also changed.[46]

Among the most influential itinerant revivalists of orthodoxy, Asahel Nettleton represented the restraint and deference that structured orthodox revivals of the first two decades of the century. His preaching was plain and solemn and his appearance austere. He scorned excitement and stuck to intellectually demanding and doctrinally strict preaching. In his travels he always deferred to the authority of settled ministers, working to bolster not undermine their authority. He worked mostly in the close-knit small towns of rural New England and bordering regions of New York where the settled minister still knew the spiritual state of many of his congregants. There was nothing in Nettleton's work of the mass phenomenon present at Cane Ridge or the later revivals of Finney in western New York. He stuck to a traditional homiletics of written and carefully scriptural sermons. In keeping with his own slow and torturous conversion, he saw no shortcut to heaven. All the same, in a period and place that remained dominated by settled ministry, when and where the vast majority of Calvinist clergy could expect to hold just one pulpit in their life, the itinerant Nettleton was a novelty and an early example of the specialized ministry that flourished within orthodoxy in the 1820s.[47]

In eighteenth-century New England, ordination established a bond between minister and community that was generally assumed to hold for life. For example, from 1702 to 1794, 550 graduates from Yale went on to become Congregationalist ministers. Of these, 392 spent their entire career with one congregation and only 21 held more than three different pulpits.[48] This record of commitment speaks to the stability of the public culture of religious communities in the eighteenth century. Bonds between minister and community were not easily severed. The three decades following the Revolution slowly abrogated the localistic and settled character of the ministry and its public function—a process that accelerated after 1815. As democratic processes and the disestablishment of Congregationalist churches robbed the clergy of its public role—undermining its official ties with magistrates—necessity and invention yielded a new brand of minister more attuned to popular and shifting sentiments. Because this new brand of minister was less attached to the church of a settled community, he was less afraid of the enthusiasm of mass revivals and less concerned with their disruption of established ways.

The New Measure Revivals

By the mid-1820s, factions within Presbyterianism and Congregationalism, particularly the heirs of the New Light split who had moved westward away from orthodox centers and into the circuits of backwoods upstarts, started to imitate the populist revivals. These events on the periphery of orthodoxy's sphere of influence would rebound on the core with dramatic impact. This influence was in no small part due to the fact that the core institutions of orthodoxy had trumpeted the importance of the western regions to the future of the nation and Christian religion. The early orthodox leaders of the Second Great Awakening, ministers like Samuel Mills and Lyman Beecher, had pointed to the religious fate of the West as inextricably linked to the future prospects of orthodoxy. When religious developments in this region proved out of their control, they were in a weak position to ignore or diminish their significance.

In the newly opened religious market of the West, the mass movement of upstarts competed against the missions and resources of orthodoxy. The competition was heated and acknowledged by both sides. Nowhere was this more true than in Vermont, upstate New York and the Western Reserve of Ohio. In these regions, still frontier lands at the turn of the century, emigrants from New England were exposed to the egalitarian ethos of the upstart sects. Many of the emigrant families came from the western hills of Massachusetts and Connecticut where the Edwardsian revivals of the 1740s had led to popular revolt. As the availability of arable land declined and real estate values soared, many farmers moved with the receding frontier. Some traveled north along the Connecticut River Valley into Vermont. Many more went west through the Mohawk Valley into the fertile Ontario plain north of the Finger Lakes and still further west into Genesee country and the Western Reserve. As they moved from the overpopulated farmland of western Massachusetts and Connecticut, they quickly outpaced the reach and influence of orthodox institutions.[49]

Although Congregationalists from Connecticut and Massachusetts established missionary societies and Presbyterians new synods to minister to the westward emigrants, in the early years of the migration, orthodox institutions were weak and the devout settled with what religion they could find. As a result, there was considerable joint worship among denominations. The following 1817 account of a Baptist minister from Ontario County, New York, was representative of the experiences of many others:

> I do not administer to a church in this Neighborhood where I live, for there is none—my congregation has . . . some nominal Baptists, presbyterians, congregationalists; and some of them have been . . . deeply tinctured with Arminianism; several Universalists; and there are a number of nothingarians, and profane vulgarists . . . that sometimes attend my preaching.[50]

Finney described a similar setting as late as the early 1820s in the northern counties of New York.[51] In these years and regions of ministerial dearth, Christians attended the nearest meetinghouse regardless of the denomination of the preacher or lay leader.

This is not to suggest that sectarian competition and tension was absent. As areas became more densely settled, one or two denominations might work to keep out competitors. Under the Plan of Union, Presbyterians and Congregationalists worked to keep the emigrants faithful to orthodoxy, but they could not protect them from exposure to the emotional religion of the upstarts. The mobile ranks of lightly educated ministers reached many an orthodox Calvinist where no doctor of divinity could yet be enticed to go. In a pamphlet published in 1812, descriptively entitled *Christianity Defended Against the Cavil of Infidels and the Weakness of Enthusiasts,* Elijah Norton, a Presbyterian minister in Oneida County, New York, imagined orthodoxy succumbing to Methodists "swarming out like the locusts, out of the pit, and like grievous wolves and roaring lions, with deadly poison among our lambs render our families, societies, and churches in pieces."[52] After the War of 1812, Presbyterians and Congregationalists stepped up their commitment of resources to defend true religion. By 1826, the first report of the American Home Missionary Society reported that 101 of its 169 missionaries were working in western New York.[53]

Ministering to a Population and Economic Boom

The need for ministers was tremendous because population growth in the West was phenomenal. In western New York, Albany grew by 96 percent during the 1820s, Utica by 183, Syracuse by 282, Buffalo by 314, and Rochester by 512. These "instant cities" were supported by the only slightly slower growth of population in neighboring agricultural areas. The population in the counties along the western half of the Erie Canal more than doubled in size during the decade. Buffeted by the rapid expansion of agrarian capitalism in areas opened up by the canal and an improved network of turnpikes, this growth transformed the region from a hinterland of subsistence farmers to a breadbasket for the northern states. Emerging cities along the canal became hubs for the booming agrarian economy. Agricultural goods flowed into them and on to commercial centers farther east, and manufactured goods flowed west back to the farmland. As market penetration and demographic explosion combined, a new class emerged in these cities and the neighboring farmland. Shopkeepers, millers, mechanics, and wage laborers populated the towns as subsistence farmers gave way to agrarian capitalists. Early on, Utica established itself as a center for cultural enterprises for the canal region, as well as for political and religious assemblies and a regional print revolution. The early printers in Utica were Presbyterian and their tracts, newspapers, and magazines traveled with the manufactured goods flowing out of the city along the canal and turnpikes into the villages and homes of the neighboring farmland. In the 1820s, the mill town of Rochester rivaled and eventually surpassed Utica in cultural production. Rochester evangelicals also exercised great influence over the print media. Together, the two cities, one on the eastern and the other on the western side of the canal, sent broadcasts to the rich agricultural communities north and south of the 341-mile Erie ditch and still further west into northern Ohio.[54] It was in this media and market conduit that the advocates of new measure revivals thrived and first gained national attention.

A New Brand of Preacher

Chief among the advocates of the "new measure" revivals was the controversial but wildly popular Finney. A nominal Presbyterian, Finney did not train at a seminary. His applications to Princeton and Andover were rejected. He learned theology and homiletics as an apprentice to a small town Presbyterian minister, the Reverend George W. Gale of Adams, New York. Finney came late to the ministry, working through his twenties as a lawyer. He brought his experiences in court to the pulpit, treating matters of salvation and damnation as similar to proving innocence and guilt to a jury. From his earliest days as an apprentice under Gale, Finney chafed at Calvinist doctrines of partial election and human inability in the work of grace. Finney's understanding of his own conversion to Christ was deeply Arminian. According to his memoirs, at the age of twenty-nine he had a revelation:

> I think I then saw, as clearly as I ever have in my life, the reality and fulness of the atonement of Christ. I saw that his work was a *finished* work; and that instead of having, or needing, any righteousness of my own to recommend me to God, I had to *submit myself* to the *righteousness of God through Christ.* Indeed the offer of Gospel salvation seemed to me an offer of *something to be accepted,* and that it was complete; and that all that was necessary on my part, was to get my own consent to give up my sins, and give myself to Christ.[55]

As Finney described it, an "inward voice seemed to arrest me . . . 'Will you accept it *now, to-day?'* I replied, 'Yes; I will accept it to-day, or I will die in the attempt.'" "Will you accept Christ" became something of a refrain in Finney's preaching.[56] He rejected the Calvinist doctrine that election was limited to only a part of humankind. Although only some were willing to accept it, he insisted that salvation was open to all. Also in contradiction of orthodoxy, he argued that grace could come *now,* immediately, without the arduous work of saintly preparation.

Licensing an individual with heterodox views like Finney as a Presbyterian minister and granting him a commission as an itinerant would have been highly unlikely even a decade or two earlier (except for in the Cumberland Presbytery). Under the pressure of keeping pace with an expanding frontier, ministering to an exploding population, and competing with upstart sects, the guardians of orthodoxy sponsored, in Finney, a minister with questionable doctrinal views and only the loosest commitment to his own denomination. If recruits for the ministry had still been selected locally through congregations, sponsored by their elders, and elected by settled congregations or placed under rigorous examinations by the synod, as they had been in the eighteenth century, it is unlikely Finney would have ever donned Presbyterian or Congregationalist cloth. But he did. A presbytery—one that barely knew him—licensed him, and a female missionary society sponsored him as an itinerant. He did not have to woo a congregation led by conservative elders or compromise his convictions to keep them satisfied. Finney was cut loose of the ties to local and regional institutions that had defined the orthodox ministry. And he was not alone but part of a group of new ministers with weak institutional ties to the ecclesiastical structures of orthodoxy. In its race to keep pace with upstart sects, orthodoxy set up a system of recruitment and support for ministers that could not ensure the faithfulness of its new leaders and converts.

The Female Missionary Society of Utica sponsored Finney's itinerancy, and his first exploits came in rural communities east of Lake Ontario and south of the St. Lawrence River. In these rough backwoods of Jefferson and St. Lawrence counties, New York, a region thick with Baptists and Methodists, he developed a "denunciatory" style peppered with vulgar colloquialism and exaggerated physical gestures. Finney rejected formulaic sermons that displayed "great eloquence" but rarely spoke to the worshipers in the pews. He preached extemporaneously and always plainly, repeating his emotional messages to impress his audience. He addressed congregants directly and never hesitated to identify them as sinners and torture them with their suffering to come as a convict in hell. Following the advice of a judge, he expected "to get a *verdict,* and to get it *upon the spot.*"[57]

Finney's revival meetings and those of his fellow western revivalists were more emotionally contained than the events in Kentucky at the turn of the century, but their focused intensity and sense of spectacle made them as controversial. A letter from C. C. Sears of Hamilton College, written in the spring of 1825, when Finney was still laboring in St. Lawrence County, reveals the kind of controversies Finney's early work raised. Finney knew Sears from his days in Adams, when he first found Christ.

> Brother Maynard showed me a l[etter] from you, with which I can not but find some little fault. I know not how you derived your impressions but I have no hesitation in saying that you have either been misinformed, or that you have changed your maxim since I knew you. If there are any Christians among us, I believe Brother Maynard is one. You charge him at least by implication with "a cold heart[,]" "endless theories[,]" [and] "baptizing ungodly and carnal policies into the sacred name of prudence." I am inclined to think that your ear has been foully polluted by some designing person or that you wrote without much consideration, and intended merely for counsel what you expressed in the language of very severe reproof. I confidently presume that . . . you did not mean that everything in a revival was right, and that no degree of rant and passion could be wrong . . . [I] shall also take the liberty of expressing a very serious doubt of the genuineness of that revival which is conducted upon the principle that no degree of animal feeling is too great, and that every excitement however raised, is to be cultivated and cherished . . . I have written as a friend to a friend.[58]

Finney, like the upstarts and the converted ministers of the mid-eighteenth century, challenged settled, educated ministers with accusations that their religion had grown cold, and he used the instruments of enthusiasm to overwhelm them with popular and insurgent revivals.

In the fall of 1825, Finney moved his ministry from the backcountry of Jefferson and St. Lawrence counties to the booming towns along the Erie Canal in Oneida County. Here he achieved national fame and refined his revival preaching. Distancing himself from the backwoods in steps, his first revival was staged in Western, New York, a small town within the cultural orbit of the bustling Erie Canal. Success in Western brought renown in Rome, New York, and an invitation. Utica followed. Success in Utica brought fame throughout the Northeast. In Utica, Finney began to build bridges to a broader evangelical community of considerable influence. His work brought together the Methodist, Baptist, Presbyterian, and Congregationalist churches of the city, increasing the membership of all four. It was also his work in Utica that first attracted the attention of a formidable opposition.

Although his style owed much to the Methodist circuit riders and yeomen Baptist preachers, Finney was no populist. He used the vernacular in his sermons, but it was the language of a rising middle class. He held the fashionably rich in contempt, but he wanted nothing more than to convert "those of the higher class in society" and to win their regard.[59] In courting the educated and more refined residents of Oneida County, Finney toned down his style, relying less on inflammatory exhortations to trigger paroxysms of enthusiasm. With the educated middle class of Utica he was an immediate success, and he proceeded by making trophies out of converts from the ranks of the most influential. He prided himself in reaching the lawyer, doctor, clerk, and shopkeeper. His plain talk, sober but urgent arguments, and message of the individual's control over his or her salvation resonated with those that had left the farm for white-collar jobs and urban living.

In Utica, he and the band of revivalists that flocked to him staged protracted meetings lasting for days. He extended the excitement by traveling to neighboring towns. Many ministers welcomed his work and celebrated the gains in church membership. Others felt threatened and started to attack Finney's methods. The opposition focused on six objectionable practices: public praying by women in mixed or "promiscuous" audiences, protracted prayer meetings, the practice of publicly praying for people by name, the colloquial and vulgar language of his sermons, the anxious seat or bench, and granting immediate church membership to converts.[60] A few years later, the list of complaints also included invasions of towns without invitation from the local clergy and public abuse of ministers opposed to the revivals. Although Finney denied that he engaged in some of these practices, his work was correctly associated with them. If Finney did not engage in each one of these, his "holy band" of adjuncts did. Behind these methods and these objections lay a more serious source of contention: with their new measure revivals, Finney and his band were fighting for the control of churches and presbyteries.[61]

The first three objections can be grouped together as aspects of the same practice: social prayer. The new measure revivals made prayer open and public. One of Finney's adjuncts, the Reverend Daniel Nash, was renowned for praying publicly for sinners by name. This public "outing" of sinners placed them under considerable social pressure to repent and violated an unwritten code that prayer and wrestling with sin was best done in private—as Alexander put it, in the individual's "closet." The protracted meetings during the week also rendered prayer social. Women played a central role in these gatherings, hosting them in the parlors of their middle-class homes. Here the revivalist could meet with the community's most devout members and gather intelligence on the spiritual state of the most influential residents. In Utica in 1825, for example, Finney worked on the young Theodore Weld, a student leader at Hamilton College, through these means. Weld's aunt, a founding member of the benevolent society that first commissioned Finney, informed the preacher that the student was a detractor of his. They conspired to trick Weld into attending a meeting at which Finney would unexpectedly assume the pulpit. When he did, Weld recalled feeling that Finney's sermon was directed exclusively at him: "He just held me up on his toasting-fork before that audience." [62] The next day, confronting Weld in a store on Genesee Street, Finney is reported to have said: "Puke it up, Mr. W—, puke it up!" [63] These public outings were as controversial as they were popular. Finney enlisted women directly in his cause, allowing them to pray in public with men and encouraging them to confront their male counterparts with their sins. From the beginning, Finney owed his ministry to the beneficence of women, and as he gained fame and fought for influence over churches women remained his staunchest supporters. Finney reciprocated and gave them a central role in his revival work. This arrangement gave Finney independence from the male-dominated ecclesiastical structure.

In the 1820s in western New York, Finney encouraged the excitement and even hysteria that attended his revivals. His language was blunt and threatening. He viewed anxious energy as instrumental in "breaking down" sinners and used it as a catalyst for conversion. Conspicuous displays of anxiety also attracted a crowd and made a name for him. All through his career, he favored public recognition of people under conviction. This developed into institutionalizing the practice of the anxious bench. On this bench, Finney liked to display in front of the assembly a line of the community's most influential residents struggling under the conviction of sin. Finney insisted conversion could come instantly and advocated immediate church membership for converts. In this fashion, western revivalists could quickly gain control of local churches as they swelled their membership with their devotees. Obviously, this practice undermined the power of many settled ministers and established elders, and quite naturally many of them resisted. The new measure advocates often responded by attacking these ministers as coldhearted enemies of the work of grace. As in the revivals of the 1740s and the contemporaneous populist revivals, Finneyites used the support of the laity to challenge antirevival ministers and capture pulpits.[64]

Finney's success alarmed conservative Presbyterians and Congrega- tionalists. Asahel Nettleton witnessed Finney's work in Utica and sought to mobilize orthodox ministers against the new measure revivals. He en- listed Lyman Beecher and the Reverend Justin Edwards of Andover in his campaign to defang Finney before he moved further east. In the sum- mer of 1827, leading ministers from the East and West met in the town of New Lebanon, New York, to settle the controversy that was brewing over Finney's new measure revivals. The Reverend Silas Churchil, under the pressure of leading women in his congregation, had invited Finney to New Lebanon to preach revival. The meeting shaped up as an interregional debate on the nature of authentic revivals. Finney and the westerners de- fended enthusiasm, instrumentalities, and promiscuous assemblies. The westerners gave little ground on their revival techniques and the eastern- ers, save Nettleton, came away feeling Finney was less a threat than they had supposed. In one sense they were right: the movement threatening the ecclesiastical order of orthodoxy extended well beyond the work of Finney.

In 1827, the religious press reported on more than two hundred reli- gious revivals in New York State (see fig. 2 below).[65] These revivals oc- curred in almost every county, but the majority took place in the north- ern and western reaches of the state. They involved Methodists, Baptists, Presbyterians, and Congregationalists, often joined together, and in gen- eral they worked to undermine the ecclesiastical authority of orthodoxy. Respected ministers like Lyman Beecher and Leonard Bacon still enjoyed a measure of control in Connecticut, but they no longer directed the re- ligious affairs of their orthodox brothers and sisters outside their New England strongholds.

The Rochester Revival and Reform

In 1828, Finney moved his revival work to Philadelphia, where he con- fronted the conservative forces of Presbyterianism in their capital. His work raised the ire of some, but on the whole his favorable reception in Philadelphia was a mark of Finney's increasing respectability. Reports from Philadelphia on the lack of controversy that attended his revivals reached the city of New York. Only a year earlier, friends of Finney had been wary to bring him to that city because they thought its conservative congregations would reject his measures. The peaceful news from Philadelphia caused them to reconsider. After Philadelphia, Finney paid a short visit to New York; there his revival met the special purposes of organized benevolence, and his work took a decided turn toward social reform. The powerful effects of this turn were evidenced the following year in Rochester, the winter of 1830–31, when he enjoyed his greatest triumph as he set the canal city ablaze with a movement that was part revival and part social reform campaign. The most famous description of Finney's revivals comes from Henry B. Stanton's account of the Rochester revival.

> While depicting the glories or the terrors of the world to come, he trod the pulpit like a giant. His action was dramatic. He painted in vivid colors . . . His gestures were appropriate, forcible, and graceful. As he would stand with his face towards the side gallery, and then involuntarily wheel around, the audience in that part of the house towards which he threw his arm would dodge as if he were hurling something at them. In describing the sliding of a sinner to perdition, he would lift his long finger towards the ceiling and slowly bring it down till it pointed to the area in front of the pulpit, when half his hearers in the rear of the house would rise unconsciously to their feet to see him descend into the pit below.[66]

What was new in Rochester was a period of meetings and sermons devoted exclusively to temperance reform. Finney discovered in temperance an issue that united evangelicals from the middle and upper classes, mobilizing their faith around combating the most prominent vice of the Erie Canal's transient culture. Finney called on Theodore Weld to assist in the lecturing. Starting on New Year's Eve, 1830, Weld delivered a series of lectures on the sin of intemperance to great success. In front of benevolent societies and congregations, Weld urged the evangelicals to cut all ties with the liquor trade. Merchants of alcohol responded by pledging to abstain from the business. The Smith brothers, Albert and Elijah, owners of the largest grocery store in Rochester, emptied their entire stock into the city's gutter to the delight of Christians under the sway of the revival spirit.[67]

On February 1, 1831, the *Western Recorder* reported on this joining of social reform and revival:

> [W]e have been informed that a large number of wholesale grocers and others, have had a meeting with reference to abandoning the sale of ardent spirits, and we have no doubt they will generally do so. . . . We wish Mr. Weld could visit

every town in this region with reference to the promotion of temperance. Should we say what we might anticipate from such a visit, we should be charged with enthusiasm.[68]

In Rochester the joining of revival and temperance met little resistance. In New York City, the *Evangelist,* under the leadership of its newly appointed editor, Joshua Leavitt, spread the word: "Temperance and the cause of Revival go hand in hand, and mutually sustain each other . . . the cause of Temperance and the cause of revivals are only two branches of one cause—the cause of patriotism, of philanthropy, of religion—*The cause of Triune God.*"[69]

The Rochester revival was the beginning of an eventful year of religious enthusiasm. Throughout New York, notices for no less than six hundred revivals appeared in the religious press during 1831 (see fig. 2). As new measure revivals challenged orthodox ministers and congregations with popular, accelerated, and promiscuous spectacles of confession and conversion, they opened the way for activists to use mass support to challenge the elite direction and control of resources within organized benevolence. When Finney encountered resistance to his revivals and measures, he excoriated his opposition as accommodating sin and prayed for them in public. "If you don't set about this work immediately, I shall take for granted that you don't mean to be revived."[70]

This same challenging disposition informed the break from elite benevolence by radical reformers. The central role of women, the very public

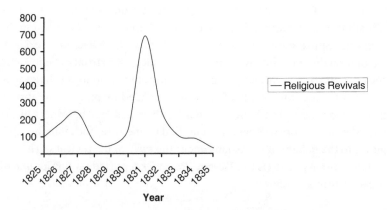

FIGURE 2. Total Number of Religious Revivals in New York State, 1825–1835
SOURCE: Hammond ICPSR data set 7754.

methods of raising a conviction of sin, calling the repentant to stand forth and proclaim their conversion, and charging detractors with accommodating sin became the standard measures of radical reform in the 1830s. The "new measures" provided radical reformers with a form of collective action to mobilize popular support against the conservative inclinations of the directors and institutions of benevolence and to move reform away from dependence on ecclesiastical structures and toward a public forum of popular religious sentiments.[71] The success of these revivals also pointed out the natural constituency of single-issue reforms: evangelicals of the middle class and especially the women of that class. But unlike Finney, radical reformers sought Christian fellowship and national redemption in campaigns against special sins; they stirred up the fervor of revivals for single issues.

The competition between populist and orthodox evangelicals had unwittingly combined opposing configurations of attitudes toward personal religious experiences and commitments to civic morality. The orthodox tradition of public intervention in matters of civic order and its new national parachurch institutions mixed with the populist practice of public testimonies to produce a new form of collective action. In the process, the orthodox concern for private conversions and the populist resistance to religious interventions in civic life were overwhelmed in the public morality of an emerging middle class. In the words of the sociologist George Thomas, the new revivalism of the 1820s had "radicalized mainstream Protestantism" by demanding that "a moral citizenry must actively construct the Kingdom of God" in America. It had syncretized the wildly popular Arminian revivals of the populists with the emerging nationalism of orthodoxy. This fusion harnessed the "irresistible power" of the revival while countering its centrifugal nature. It gave rise to national social movements.[72]

CHAPTER FIVE

A National Wave of Confessional Protests, 1829–1839

In 1831, conservative Presbyterians drafted a "Secret Circular" distributed to committees of several synods "believed to be friendly to their views, and disposed to co-operate in giving efficiency to their plans." The circular warned that Presbyterian seminaries were being "perverted," church property and endowments were falling into the hands of people who had "contributed little," doctrinal standards were in danger of "total disregard," and the ecclesiastical judicatory included delegates with no "legal claim to membership." Concluding this list of threats, the circular stated,

> our Boards of Education and of Missions, are in danger of being wrested from the hands of those who wish to make them the sources of supply to the wants of our church in an uncorrupted state, and of being rendered subsidiary to the plans and purpose of *voluntary associations, subject to no ecclesiastical responsibility, and adopting no formula of faith by with their religious tenets may be ascertained.* ... The voluntary associations that seek to engross the patronage of our church, and have already engrossed a large part of it, have taken the start of us in the all important concerns of education and of missions. They now labor to get the whole of these into their hands; well knowing, that if this be effected, they will infallibly, in a very short time govern the church.[1]

Believing it had "been credulous and hoodwinked too long already," this conservative wing of orthodoxy, led by Archibald Alexander and like-minded men, began to withdraw its support from organized benevolence and set in motion a process that would lead to a schism within Presbyterianism in 1837.[2]

This withdrawal of conservative support began just as resources flowing into organized benevolence from middle-class auxiliaries swelled and western revivals agitated orthodox churches. At the same time, a radical wing within organized benevolence was bending the ears of leading patrons like Arthur Tappan on particular causes like temperance, antislavery, and moral reform (a campaign against sexual sin). As the elite partnership within orthodoxy began to fall apart over revivals and benevolent societies, reformers harnessed middle-class and western enthusiasm for the eradication of special sins to unleash national social movements independent from orthodox institutions but taking with them considerable resources.

This historical moment of radical insurgency within organized benevolence depended on two religious processes coming together to mix a popular mode of personal piety with public commitments to moral order. The revival in Rochester was a spectacular instance of the power of this combination of populist and orthodox sentiments, but the mix appealed to evangelicals across the North and even into the South. The populist appeal of public displays of personal confession and conversion countered orthodox suspicion of conspicuous and emotional piety. The orthodox campaign for public control of *particular* sins countered the populist suspicion of hypocritical saints claiming rights to enforce moral order. This combination reconfigured these opposing sentiments into a form of collective action that fused the reform of society and the self. Cut loose by the more conservative wing of orthodoxy as it withdrew from the Presbyterian and Congregationalist union, relatively detached from the leadership of moderates like Beecher and Bacon within organized benevolence, and drawing significant support from members of the upstart sects and women disenfranchised from orthodox power structures, reform movements cut across traditional religious lines and forged new, extensive, and *un*orthodox religious commitments. Almost as soon as movements for causes like temperance, moral reform, and antislavery appeared, they were met with significant resistance. Opposition was in part religious, coming from within orthodoxy and from without. It also came, most furiously, from the *un*churched—the majority of Americans.

Bearing Witness against Intemperance

In this wave of moral protests that broke out across America, advocates of temperance took the lead. Temperance emerged at the center of organized benevolence, and as a cause it remained dear even to many of the conservatives within orthodoxy. Among evangelicals, it never became as controversial as immediate abolition or other causes like moral reform. Nonetheless, it took a radical turn at the end of the 1820s that spread the cause well beyond its orthodox origins and escaped the control of the men who had founded the first temperance organizations.

The American Temperance Society emerged firmly within the orthodox fold of organized benevolence. The society was modeled after core associations like the American Tract Society and the American Bible Society. Its first leaders, men like Justin Edwards and Leonard Woods, were distinguished Congregationalist ministers and leaders of benevolence. The temperance society was an extension of organized benevolence but it departed from the benevolence mold in two important ways: its focus on a particular sin and the innovation of the temperance pledge. The specific cause of temperance provided a degree of freedom from the sectarian image of organized benevolence, and the temperance pledge was the first commingling of the programmatic focus and resources of organized benevolence with a public display of commitment. At the outset, the pledge did not pretend to any spiritual significance; it was simply a public display of membership and commitment to temperance principles. It was not solicited as a sign of personal reform.[3] It was a gesture from the already temperate of their resolve to stay that way and to encourage others to join them in formal association. The pledge provided publicity for the temperance cause, but for the pledged it also deepened the personal significance of not drinking. It proved a powerful draw and motivator. Whereas benevolent societies had only required dues for membership, temperance inched toward a commitment of behavior and belief that the individual was duty bound to acknowledge in public.

In the antivice campaigns of the moral societies of the earlier part of the century, intemperance was viewed and dealt with as a public sin easily disassociated from the personal lives of visible saints or the supposed elect. What orthodox leaders like the young Lyman Beecher who advocated antivice societies took as their moral imperative was to protect their communities from the dangers of public sin. The imagery used in the battle against these sins was of an external force flooding the land. In his widely publicized sermons on intemperance Beecher described the threat this way:

> Intemperance is the sin of our land, and, with our boundless prosperity, is coming in upon us like a flood; and if anything shall defeat the hopes of the world,

which hang upon our experiment of civil liberty, it is that river of fire, which is rolling through the land, destroying the vital air and extending around an atmosphere of death.[4]

The personal grace of those called on to do battle was not the heart of the matter. Personal sin was something to wrestle with in the closet or through the counsel of a minister. In these moral campaigns, what was at risk was the covenanted community, now understood as the nation.

In 1826, the fledgling American Temperance Society promoted a pledge that opened with a comparatively weak statement that the drinking of alcohol was "not only unnecessary but injurious, and . . . while it is continued the evils of intemperance can never be prevented."[5] This early pledge was compatible with the orthodox dissociation of public and personal sin. Whether drinking itself was sinful was not entirely agreed upon, but few thought everyone who consumed or did business in alcohol was a sinner. The focus was on preventing the "evils" of widespread and excessive drinking. The method seized upon was voluntary associations of men pledged to lead the nation out of intemperance by providing the example of "abstaining" from the use of "ardent spirits." In the fall of 1826, the work of building a network of auxiliaries to the American Temperance Society started in earnest. For two years, Edwards and Nathaniel Hewitt, a Connecticut minister, traveled throughout the Northeast and the Middle Atlantic to build support, traveling the well-worn path of the agents of organized benevolence and working to generate support through the churches and larger ecclesiastical institutions of orthodoxy. They also, maybe to their surprise, found many Baptist and Methodist institutions open to their cause. By the spring of 1829, they had affiliated 229 temperance societies to the national organization, many of them revived antivice societies based in orthodox churches. At this point, support for the American Temperance Society was almost as large as for some of the core societies of organized benevolence. The success cheered the men of benevolence, but it was nothing compared to what was about to happen.[6]

Over the next few years, support for temperance exploded. In 1829 alone, almost eight hundred auxiliaries were added, and in 1830 more than a thousand (see table 3). In two years, the American Temperance Society added more than twice the total number of auxiliaries of the largest benevolent societies in orthodoxy's united front. In the winter and spring of 1831, the American Temperance Society published the name of every auxiliary that had formally affiliated with the national society.

TABLE 3 **Number of Auxiliary Societies to the American Temperance and American Anti-Slavery Societies, 1829–1838**

Year	American Temperance Society	American Anti-Slavery Society
1829	222	—
1830	1015	—
1831	2,203	—
1832	>4,000*	—
1833	NA	32
1834	NA	75
1835	NA	229
1836	NA	525
1837	NA	1005
1838	NA	1348

SOURCE: American Temperance Society (1828–1832); American Temperance Union (1852); Goodman (1998); American Anti-Slavery Society (1837–1838).
*In 1832, the American Temperance Society stopped keeping track of the exact number of auxiliary societies. The society's estimates for subsequent years are unreliable, but growth was probably strong and steady through 1837 but falling off toward the end of the decade.

The movement, particularly strong in New England and New York, was also well represented in the South and even on the western frontier (see table 4). Four years after its launch, the temperance movement was already national. After 1831, growth was so great that the parent organization was unable to keep an accurate accounting. The records kept in the earlier years, however, provide sample snapshots of the year-by-year formation of the early movement as 30 percent of the auxiliaries reporting to the parent society indicated the year in which they were formed. Map 3 shows this geographic spread. A higher proportion of New England societies can be located than societies elsewhere, so these maps represent something of an undercount of temperance outside of that region. Nonetheless, the data show that the temperance field was, from the very beginning, extensive, and growth in western New York was at least as significant to the early formation of a mass movement as growth in New England. This was not a New England movement that then spread across the nation.

During these years of exploding support, the moral dimensions of both the temperance pledge and the problem of drinking shifted. For temperance advocates, drinking alcohol shifted from a practice that encouraged an array of social problems understood as public sins to an inherently sinful act that brought the nation and the individual under divine judgment. Drinking alcohol in any form and amount became a sin, the temperance pledge became a confession of sin and faith, and the trafficker of spirits emerged as the arch sinner because he encouraged others to sin. This innovation came from the periphery not the core. Activists leading the local societies promoted the moral claim that any part in the consumption, production, or distribution of alcohol was sinful. The parent organization followed their lead.

In this early phase of the movement, the temperance pledge and the revival testimonial fused. The work of Theodore Weld, Finney's assistant, reflected this shift. During these early years as temperance became a national movement, 1829 through 1831, Weld lectured on temperance throughout New York, soliciting emotional testimonials from repentant drinkers and merchants of liquor, but the temperance revival extended well beyond Weld's efforts. Reports from auxiliaries to the New York Temperance Society in the early 1830s reveal that the revival spirit was turning the pledge into a confession across the state. This public act of commitment

TABLE 4 **Auxiliaries to the American Temperance Society by State and Territory, 1831, Sorted in Descending Order by Proportion of Total Population**

State	Temperance Societies
Connecticut	202
Vermont	132
New York	727
New Hampshire	96
Maine	140
Massachusetts	209
Michigan Terr.	13
Rhode Island	21
New Jersey	61
Mississippi	19
Georgia	60
Ohio	104
Virginia	113
Pennsylvania	124
Maryland	38
Indiana	25
Delaware	5
Illinois	12
North Carolina	31
Kentucky	23
Alabama	10
South Carolina	16
Missouri Terr.	4
Tennessee	15
Louisiana	3
Total	2203

SOURCE: American Temperance Union (1852).

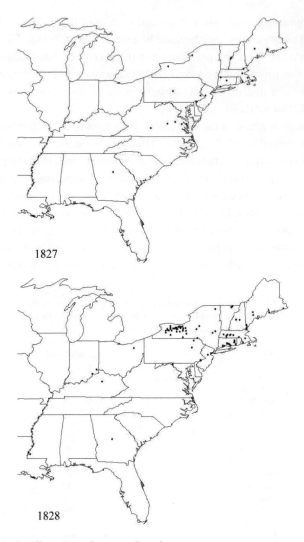

MAP 3. Growth of Temperance Support, 1827–1830.
SOURCE: *Journal of Humanity* (1831).
NOTE: Each dot represents a society formed in that year. There are some missing data because not all societies could be located. Most of the missing data comes from the western states.

shifted from an open claim to abstemiousness—the exemplary behavior of an elect—to a testimony of a transforming experience and a new personal covenant. For example, these reports are filled with claims of penitent merchants, reformed tipplers, even some reclaimed sots. The editor of the magazine of that state society did not blush in comparing the temperance

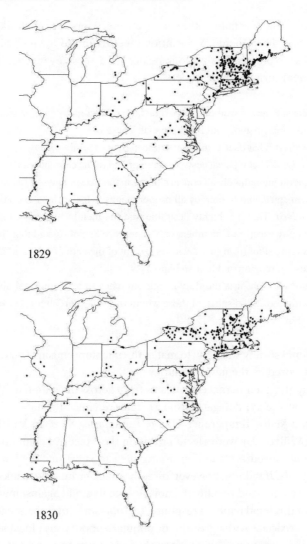

pledge to "the Sabbath, circumcision, baptism, the Lord's supper." In his eyes, they were "all pledges or covenants." The society exhorted the individual "to *deny himself,* to abandon his prejudices and error, and become a firm, active, and a *pledged* friend of TEMPERANCE."[7] Temperance was becoming a salvific ideal tied to a special sin.

This was shocking to many conservatives. One influential Presbyterian termed it "Protestant Jesuitism."[8] For the conservative wing that bolted from the united front of evangelicals in the early 1830s, that particular sins could demand particular covenants had the feel of a counter-reformation. For many other evangelicals, temperance felt like a *new* reformation. The Oneida Association meeting in the town of Marshall, New York, expressed the zealous response of these evangelicals to the confessional turn in temperance:

> Whereas it is now a well established fact, that the common use of ardent spirit not only does no good, but immense evil: Therefore,
>
> *Resolved,* That its use, and the traffic in it, are morally wrong.
>
> *Resolved,* That it be earnestly recommended to the churches under our care, to abandon immediately all concern in the manufacture and sale, as well as use of ardent spirit, and to employ all proper means to lead others to do the same.
>
> *Resolved,* That it is highly desirable that the members of our churches be, without any exception, members of Temperance Societies; and that those who are standing aloof from such societies are out of the path of duty, and hindering the cause of religion and human happiness.
>
> *Resolved,* That it is the duty of our churches to insist on total abstinence from ardent distilled spirit, in those whom they may hereafter receive to their fellowship.[9]

The national society was slow to match the uncompromising stand against alcohol favored by the new auxiliaries.

In May 1833, temperance advocates from across the nation met in Philadelphia, where 371 delegates from 21 states renamed the national society the United States Temperance Union. Luminaries Stephen Van Rensselaer and William Jay were elected to sit on the executive committee. The convention passed a resolution urging men to substitute cold water for ardent spirits. It did not, however, directly attack fermented drinks—beer, wine, and cider—and remained ambivalent in its stand against merchants. In spite of this tepid national response, teetotalism—total abstinence from all that intoxicates—was growing in popular support, and local societies and temperance presses were increasingly identifying merchants as arch sinners. The following for teetotalism was particularly strong in New York. Edward Delavan, the director of the state society and a former wine merchant, spent a good portion of his fortune to circulate four million copies of the New York State Temperance Society's publications.[10]

In 1834, national leadership followed the lead of local associations and tried to make clear the movement's moral claim against alcohol and its distribution. At its anniversary meeting it announced its stand on "a controversy which has long agitated us, but which must end this night. Strong prejudices have been aroused; by attaching an idea of vileness to the phrase immorality, as here used. The [annual] report places the subject where it should be; as wrong in itself, in the sight of heaven." [11] Two years later, in Saratoga, New York, the national society followed the lead of its auxiliaries and formally supported the teetotal pledge, renaming itself the American Temperance Union.

The national society was slow to change because of a contentious divide between its original constituency and its new popular base. Among wealthy supporters wine was still a drink of choice. Also, many older members advocated moderation, not abstinence. These longstanding members of the society resisted the "ultraism" of teetotalism and defended respected merchants of fermented alcohol. The teetotal pledge also raised biblical and doctrinal disputes over the use of sacramental wine. National leadership was wary of taking sides on an issue that would lead to conflict within churches and denominations, but teetotalism overwhelmed the ranks of temperance, and national leadership was left with little choice if it wanted to retain some control of the movement. In Massachusetts, where the battle against alcohol had a long history, the Temperance Union and the Temperance Society remained distinct networks of auxiliaries divided along the lines of the teetotal pledge.[12]

Of the various special-purpose societies within organized benevolence, temperance was a favorite among conservative supporters. As such, they worked hard to accommodate the revival spirit of immediate and public renunciation. The attack on alcohol was never as controversial as abolitionism or women's attacks on the sexual license of men. Prominent figures in organized benevolence like Justin Edwards and Lyman Beecher accepted the public demand for an uncompromising stand toward alcohol while resisting a similar stand against slavery. With teetotalism, unlike the "ultraisms" of abolition and "moral reform," organized benevolence adjusted (albeit reluctantly) to the popular appeal of public confessions to special sins. In this, the first confessional phase of temperance, merchants were targeted as greater sinners than drunkards. Although it was plain to all teetotalers that "no drunkard shall inherit the kingdom of heaven," many doubted his capacity for reform. Some societies, many of them in the state of New York, reported the reclamation of drunks, but as had been the case in the Rochester revival the sin of making drunkards by making drink was the prime focus of temperance for most of the decade. Advocates like Justin Edwards chillingly claimed that all the sots would "soon be dead," so that if subsequent generations could be raised to only drink cold water, intemperance could be eradicated by midcentury.[13]

In the late 1830s, advocates of temperance flirted with legislative action.
The outcome was disastrous for the national coordination of the movement. In Massachusetts in 1837, temperance advocates pushed through a
piece of legislation outlawing the sale of small amounts of alcohol (anything under fifteen gallons). The law singled out drinking by men of modest means for criminalization. This departure from "moral suasion" was
met by disaffection within the lower ranks of teetotalism. One response
was yet another confessional turn in the temperance movement.[14]

This second mass phase of temperance was so close to the populist temperament of the religious revivals that it almost withdrew all public claims
on civic morality for a purely personal movement of reform. In May of
1840, a small group of drinkers in Baltimore founded the Washingtonian
Temperance Society, and by New Year, Washingtonians were orchestrat-
ing the largest revivals against special sins of the period.[15] The *Baltimore
Clipper* boasted that "never since the establishment of our city has there
been so great an excitement, relative to the cause of temperance, as at the
present. New societies are being formed almost daily, and immediately
swelling in numbers to hundreds."[16] The *Baltimore Sun* marveled, "How
many will date their declaration of independence from King Alcohol,
from January 1st, 1841?"[17]

News of the movement spread quickly from city to city. In March 1841,
the *Clipper* reported that the Washingtonians had sent deputies to New
York, who were said to have produced great impressions.[18] Another Baltimore newspaper reprinted a report from the *New York Commercial Advertiser* detailing what happened at a meeting there:

> All addresses were made by four delegates from the Washingtonian Temperance
> Society of Baltimore, and by Captain Wisdom, of this city. These gentlemen
> have all been reclaimed from intemperance within a short time, and the delega-
> tion from Baltimore declared themselves "reformed drunkards." . . .
>
> During the first speech, a young man arose in the gallery, and though intoxi-
> cated, begged to know whether there was hope for him, declaring his readiness
> to bind himself from that hour to drink no more. He was invited to come down
> and sign the pledge, which he did forthwith in the presence of the audience,
> under deep emotion, which seemed to be contagious, for others followed, and
> during each of the speeches they continued to come forward and sign, until
> more than a hundred pledges were obtained.[19]

Among the Washingtonians, the teetotal message reached down into the
lower classes and the legions of heavy drinkers. Drunkards, frequently

vilified and dismissed as lost, were exhorted to be touched by the regenerating power of confession and enlisted as agents. With reformed drunkards relating tales of the evils of alcohol and encouraging public displays of signing the pledge, Washingtonians mobilized men by the hundreds of thousands to expose the tyranny of alcohol in their lives and to convert to total abstinence. Washingtonians were, in effect, a secular band of temperance revivalists. They distanced themselves from the ministers who led the national temperance society, believing that too much God talk would ward off the intemperate. Their practices, however, were pure populist revival. The reformed drunk was encouraged to recant his past depravation through coarse "experience speeches." These public confessions, in turn, triggered emotional testimony from the audience.[20]

The emotional conversion of drunks during Washingtonian revivals shocked the more restrained and decorous in the ranks of temperance. Washingtonians, even more than teetotalers, split the ranks of temperance. At first, the national temperance society supported the enthusiasm but withdrew its support when it realized that it could not control the revival and would soon be overwhelmed by its popularity. From the beginning, Washingtonians were not especially gracious in their acceptance of the parent society's help. Washingtonians drew their support from the lower classes and counted more members of the upstart sects than the teetotalers of the mid-1830s. They resented attempts at central control from a national society led by educated ministers and wealthy laymen. In kind, many established temperance reformers saw a dangerous antinomian force in Washingtonianism. Supporters of the American Temperance Union and organized benevolence criticized the Washingtonians for acting as if conversion to abstinence was the same as achieving a state of grace. The same stand that the teetotalers of the middle class had made appeared unacceptable when independently asserted by an unchurched working class.

The national society for temperance did not survive the Washingtonian revival. In the 1840s, this confessional challenge from below expanded the ranks of temperance but was met with attempts from above to squash the enthusiasm. As a result of the conflict, temperance shattered. Elements of the movement withdrew into local, secular, secret societies scattered across the nation.[21] Other elements resurfaced in the next decade initiating a political and legal battle for prohibition, a battle closely associated with the nativist campaigns against Irish and German Catholics. The effects of Washingtonianism and the move for prohibition are instructive of more general trends across the range of movements launched by confessional protests: as personal confessionalism deepened it threatened to undermine the public campaign of social reform. Something similar would occur with Garrisonian abolitionists and women's activism for moral reform. As the personal dimensions of bearing witness diminished, temperance veered into prohibition and vilification of outside or foreign troubles and troublemakers. Again something similar would occur with moral reform or antivice campaigns toward the end of the nineteenth century.[22] The balance between personal confession and public commitment that fueled popular mobilization in the 1830s could prove quite delicate. Greater weight placed on either side threatened to push the movement out of moral protest within civil society into either deeply personal movements of salvation or more instrumentally political movements for social power. Temperance as a national social movement emerged and flourished as it held the personal and the public in creative balance.

Bearing Witness against Slavery

A new form of American antislavery emerged at roughly the same time as temperance's first confessional phase: a form of activism so different in tone, method, and membership as to constitute a new movement. With it, calls for immediate abolition challenged the gradualism, colonization schemes, and racism of earlier antislavery. Unlike temperance, activists at the center of organized benevolence in Boston and New York initiated this confessional break. Whereas western supporters of temperance took the lead in spreading public confessions against the special sin of marketing and consuming alcohol, it was eastern urban activists, attentive to the popular spread of temperance, who launched immediate abolitionism.

William Lloyd Garrison was the first to herald the new movement by publicizing the *immediate* duty of Christians to renounce the sin of slavery and the gradual antislavery schemes of the American Colonization Society. Odd as it might seem to twenty-first century students of protest, Garrison's message of liberation was first and foremost directed at white, nonslaveholding supporters of organized benevolence. Immediate abolitionism emerged as a conflict within the parachurch institutions of benevolence over a Christian's duty to renounce the special sin of slavery and racism. It centered on the guilt of complicity as much as the guilt of slaveholding.

On the Fourth of July, 1829, Garrison, gave a controversial address to a Boston gathering of supporters of the American Colonization Society. In the North, the reputed mission of the society was to set the groundwork for the safe and gradual abolition of slavery through the expatriation of Americans of African descent. Reverend Simeon Jocelyn, Reverend Joshua Leavitt, Lewis and Arthur Tappan, Elizur Wright, Reverend Beriah Green, Gerrit Smith, James Birney, and many other famous abolitionists were members of the society in the 1820s. Garrison had also supported the society, but his 1829 address shocked his audience by publicly declaring their guilt. "We are all alike guilty," Garrison exhorted. "Slavery is strictly a national sin. New-England money has been expended in buying human flesh; New-England ships have been freighted with sable victims; New-England men have assisted in forging the fetters of those who groan in bondage. I call upon the ambassadors of Christ everywhere to make known this proclamation: 'Thus saith the Lord God of the Africans, Let this people go, that they may serve me.'"[23] That slavery was a source of evil was not disputed by Garrison's New England audience. Garrison's simple equation of slavery and sin, though not an entirely new claim, was generally discounted. More shocking was his charge of the collective guilt of nonslaveholding Americans, a guilt no less shared by the advocates of Christian benevolence because of their failure to fearlessly testify against the sin.

On that day in 1829, from the pulpit of the Park Street Church in Boston, Garrison did not renounce the gradualism and expatriation plans of the American Colonization Society, but his confessional stand was headed in that direction. By 1830, contact with African American activists resisting the society's plans to expatriate freed slaves convinced him that the colonization scheme assumed the degradation of blacks and served only to lessen concerns about the sin of slaveholding and the moral complicity of northerners. Colonization countenanced sin because it preached that America's problem rested not so much with slaveholding and racism as with the presence of 2 million individuals of an unequal race. Garrison's conversion to immediatism and his awakening to the sinfulness of colonization were inextricably linked. The unprecedented mobilization of free African Americans in the late 1820s exposing the racism and hypocrisy of white Christians involved in colonization made the sin pressing. David Walker's pamphlet, *Appeal to the Colored Citizens of the World,* published in 1829, rubbed salt into Garrison's wounded conscience. In the *Appeal,* Walker, a free African American living in Boston, argued that slavery amounted to a divine trial of whites and openly called for insurrection and retribution. The redemption of whites depended on the emancipation of the slaves and the realization of racial equality; failure to reform would result in judgment from an angry God in the form of a bloody slave rebellion.[24]

On January 1, 1831—while Weld was attacking liquor merchants in Rochester—Garrison launched the *Liberator*. The opening editorial for the newspaper employed the argot of the revivals calling for the immediate emancipation of the slave. This demand was followed with a personal confession:

> In Park-street Church, on the Fourth of July, 1829, in an address on slavery, I unreflectingly assented to the popular but pernicious doctrine of *gradual* abolition. I seize this opportunity to make full and unequivocal recantation, and thus publicly to ask pardon of my God, of my country, and of my brethren the poor slaves, for having uttered a sentiment so full of timidity, injustice and absurdity.[25]

In subsequent editions, he predicted national calamity if Americans did not follow him in repentance. In August of 1831, only months after the first edition of the *Liberator,* Nat Turner's revolt added weight to this prophecy of imminent judgment and the urgency of immediate confession. Garrison saw the insurrection as confirmation of his role as America's Jeremiah:

> We shall cry, in trumpet tones, night and day,—Wo to this guilty land, unless she speedily repent of her doings! The blood of millions of her sons cries aloud for redress! IMMEDIATE EMANCIPATION can alone save her from the vengeance of Heaven, and cancel the debt of ages![26]

He found guilt not only with the South, but also with pious New England and the agents of benevolence. He wanted to awake their slumbering consciences and disabuse them of the notion that the problem was not theirs. "But what if it should appear on candid examination, that we are as guilty as the slaveowners?" Candid examination exposed ties of business, politics, consanguinity, and religious fellowship implicating all: "We are all guilty—all guilty—horribly guilty."[27]

In the first year, Garrison garnered little support beyond a small New England community of African Americans and a handful of leaders within benevolence. These early white converts were influential: Arthur Tappan, premier patron of organized benevolence, and the Reverend Simeon Jocelyn joined Garrison in his call for immediate abolition and renounced their support of the American Colonization Society. In a move that showed how knotted the various special sins were in the minds of the radical advocates of benevolence, Tappan used reports that the ships commissioned by the Colonization Society to Liberia were also selling rum in West Africa to legitimate the renunciation of his membership and financial support. Within a year of its first edition, Reverend Beriah Green and Elizur Wright—faculty members of Western Reserve College, an orthodox school founded by Connecticut emigrants to Hamilton, Ohio—laid their hands on a copy of the *Liberator*. Green, writing in 1832, described the impact:

> A great change has, within a few months, been wrought in the view and move-ments of some the gentlemen connected with this College, both as instructors and students, respecting the ground occupied by the American Colonization Society, and the tendency of the principles avowed, and the course pursued, by that institution. . . . They had been ardent friends and prompt patrons of the American Colonization Society; had labored to sustain its claims to public patronage by their authority, their eloquence, and their purses. They now feel, and feel very deeply too, that they have been blinded by a strange prejudice, which had the effect of infatuation on their minds. They have opened their eyes upon an object which has taken fast hold of their whole souls. They feel them-selves impelled by motives which they cannot and would not resist, to give "arm and soul" to the cause of African emancipation.[28]

Wright described the event as "a revolution of the soul."[29] The itinerating temperance lecturer Theodore Weld converted to the cause after a short stay with Green and Wright. Linking up Garrison's clique in Boston, Tap-pan's clique in New York, and a loose collection of western Evangelicals, immediate abolition developed as an insurgency within the parachurch in-stitutions of organized benevolence to renounce expatriation, racism, and gradualism in favor of the immediate emancipation of whites *and* blacks from the sin of slavery.

In his newspaper, Garrison directly attacked the Colonization Society as a libel upon Christianity. In a pamphlet of 1832, he outlined an exhaus-tive list of charges against colonization, arguments that would be echoed by immediate abolitionists for the duration of the decade. By 1833, defec-tions were large enough to consider a new national society. In December, a racially mixed assembly of men and women in Philadelphia established a national organization for the immediate emancipation of slaves, the American Anti-Slavery Society. Fittingly, Garrison penned the society's "Declaration of Sentiments," dedicating the society to "the destruction of error by the potency of truth—the overthrow of prejudice by the power of love—and the abolition of slavery by the spirit of repentance."[30]

The call for immediate abolition reverberated throughout organized benevolence. An early and widely publicized example of this fallout oc-curred in a nationally prominent seminary in Ohio on the border of the slave state of Kentucky. Only a few months after the first national anti-slavery convention, a protest at Lane Seminary—a school near Cincinnati with students sponsored by the American Education Society and under the leadership of the Reverend Lyman Beecher—led to expulsion and withdrawal of almost the entire student body and the emergence of a "holy band" of itinerant abolitionist agents. The event, which came to be known as the Lane Rebellion, started as a formal debate on the merits of the American Colonization Society but quickly triggered emotional and collective confessions from students for their association with the society and slavery. Led by Theodore Weld, the rebellion took the form of a collective awakening to the sin of slavery and the moral complicity of organized benevolence. These conversions to immediatism included a number of southern heirs to slaveholding families and suggested to the leaders of abolition that slavery could be ended through a movement that pressed the guilty conscience of the Christian South.[31]

In a speech to the second annual meeting of the American Antislavery Society held in New York and published by Garrison in an antislavery pamphlet, a student from Lane Seminary described the influence of the "debate" on his conscience. James A. Thome started with a description of his initial state of depravity:

> The associations of youth and the attachments of growing years; prejudices, opinions and habits forming and fixing during my whole life, conspire to make me a Kentuckian indeed. More than this; I breathed my first breath in the atmosphere of slavery; I was suckled at its breast and dandled on its knee.

Thome's guilt did not stop with being a southerner and a slaveholder:

> Permit me to say, sir, I was for several years a member of the Colonization Society. I contributed to its funds and eulogized its measures . . . yet duty bids me state, solemnly and deliberately, that its direct influence upon my mind was to lessen my conviction of the evil of slavery, and to deepen and sanctify my prejudices against the colored race.
>
> But, sir, far otherwise with abolition. Within a few months residence at Lane Seminary, and by means of discussion unparalleled in the brotherly feeling and fairness which characterized it, and the results which it brought out, the great principles of duty stood forth, sin revived, and I died.

To that same 1834 national convention, Thome offered the following resolution: "That our principles commend themselves to the consciences and interest of slave-holders; and that recent developments indicate the speedy triumph of our cause."[32] Although subsequent years would witness few other southerners born again as abolitionists—James Gillespie Birney and Angelina and Sarah Grimké being the most notable exceptions—there remained plenty of guilt to expose and sin to reform in the complicity of northerners.

From 1833 to 1838, auxiliary societies appeared across the North affiliating themselves with the principles of immediatism and renouncing colonization. During these years, the national total of auxiliary societies grew from 75 to 1348, with the strongest representation among evangelicals in northern and western New England, upstate New York, and Ohio (see table 3 above and table 5). Maps of the year-by-year growth of societies reveal that the movement was from the very beginning an interregional phenomenon (see map 4). A most striking feature of the geographic spread of the movements is that the basic footprint of the movement's

TABLE 5 **Auxiliaries to the American Anti-Slavery Society by State and Territory, 1838, Sorted in Descending Order by Proportion of Total Population**

State	Anti-Slavery Societies
Vermont	104
Massachusetts	246
New Hampshire	79
Rhode Island	26
Ohio	251
New York	369
Connecticut	46
Michigan Terr.	19
Maine	48
Pennsylvania	126
New Jersey	14
Illinois	13
Delaware	1
Indiana	6
Virginia	0
Alabama	0
Georgia	0
Louisiana	0
Mississippi	0
North Carolina	0
South Carolina	0
Kentucky	0
Maryland	0
Tennessee	0
Missouri Terr.	0
Total	1348

SOURCE: American Anti-Slavery Society (1838).

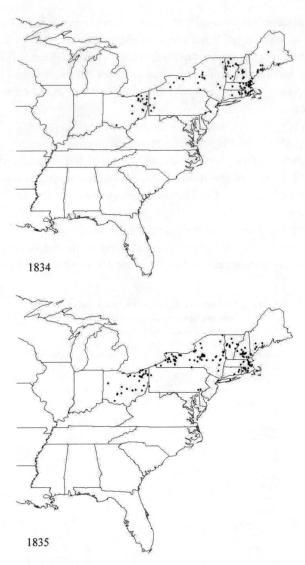

1834

1835

MAP 4. Growth of Antislavery Support, 1834–37.
SOURCE: American Anti-Slavery Society, 1834–1837.
NOTE: Each dot represents a society formed in that year and still operating in 1838. There are
some missing data because not all societies could be located. Most of the missing data comes
from the western states.

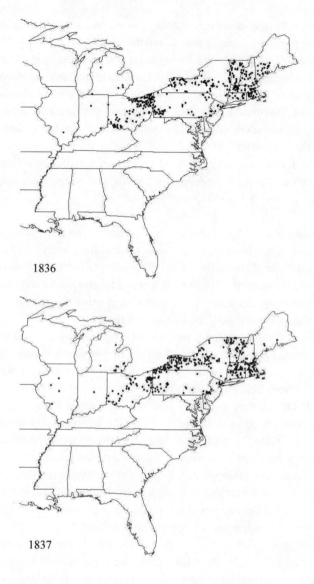

1836

1837

scope was established in the first few years. Antislavery did not emerge in New England and spread west. The antislavery field was from the start national (or at least sectional).

The reports from these antislavery societies reveal that the form of collective action employed across the North among disparate evangelical sects was remarkably standard. The following notice from the French Creek Association of Pennsylvania Baptists was typical:

1. Resolved, That we deem slavery a sin of most cruel and dangerous character, making war upon the rights of man, and the laws of God.
2. Resolved, That like other sins, slavery ought to be immediately abandoned; that like all other sins, it ought to be driven from the church; and like all other sins, the whole energies of the church should be concentrated for its extermination.
3. Resolved, That this Association refuse fellowship with slave holding Baptist Associations, and advise all our churches to adopt rules excluding slave holders from their communion tables.
4. Resolved, That we sympathize with the American Anti-Slavery Society in their noble efforts for the emancipation of our enslaved countrymen, and that we pledge them our prayers to God for their success.[33]

Resolutions placed before Presbyterian synods, Congregational associations, Methodist conventions, and independent local antislavery societies varied little from those of the French Creek Baptists.[34] For the duration of the decade, immediate abolitionists worked to usurp the moral authority of the American Colonization Society and to bring the nation to repentance through confessional associations of this type.

At the end of the decade, two related issues disrupted national unity among immediate abolitionists: the role of women and party politics. In 1837, Angelina and Sarah Grimké, sisters of a prominent slaveholding family from South Carolina, began a lecturing tour throughout New England. During this tour, men and women gathered together to hear the sisters testify against slavery. Their public lectures violated orthodox norms that women should not speak or testify to mixed audiences and generated a religious controversy which contained strong echoes of the disagreements that emerged over Finney's new measure revivals. The large crowds drawn to their talks also made the question of female leadership within the movement unavoidable. Divisions over this issue would drive a wedge between supporters of immediate abolition.

Linked to this controversy was the issue of whether immediatists should enter party politics. In 1837, the American Anti-Slavery Society began to question electoral candidates to determine their positions on slavery in order to provide a voter guide for abolitionists. By 1839, there was a strong movement within the national organization to enter electoral politics more directly as an organized party. The followers of Garrison, in general, supported the leading role of women in the national society and opposed this political action. They saw denying women the right to testify against slavery in order to placate public sentiment as a corruption of their moral calling. They saw entering the corrupt sphere of electoral politics in similar terms. Through the 1840s and 1850s, Garrisonians recoiled from the politics of antislavery, operating mostly as a loud but marginal voice of conscience. They continued to bear witness against the sin of slavery and refused to compromise with people and institutions unwilling to do likewise.[35]

In contrast, a political wing of immediatists, for the most part reject-ing the leading role of women, formed the Liberty Party in 1840 to force antislavery as a political issue. The party was short-lived, but it led to new alliances and moral compromises instrumental in the formation of the Free-Soil Party and later the Republican Party. These abolitionists kept antislavery on the political agenda of northerners for the next two de-cades. The immediatists that took this more pragmatic assault on chat-tel slavery played a central role in political processes that led ultimately to the coming of the Civil War and to emancipation.[36] Both sides—the Garrisonians and the men of the Liberty Party—thought the other had compromised the cause.

Beyond Temperance and Antislavery

Temperance and antislavery became mass, interregional movements as they turned confessional. Other causes made the same turn, but with less success. The Sabbath observance movement showed signs of a similar dy-namic in the late 1820s, but the movement collapsed very quickly after a misguided venture into federal politics. Activism against sexual sin fol-lowed a similar path as temperance and antislavery. In spite of the contro-versy swirling around Rev. John McDowall's 1831 *Magdalen Report* (see chapter 4), his newspaper continued reporting detailed accounts of preda-tory men and defiled women. The paper expressed sympathy for prosti-tutes and questioned why women alone should suffer for the guilt of both sexes. It directed blame at libertines, the double standards of men, and Christian indifference as much as at prostitutes. Orthodoxy responded with excommunication, and less pious men threatened violence. And yet, McDowall was not without support.

In spite of church trial, slander in the press, and the loss of elite sponsors, McDowall's campaign evolved into a broader movement. His newspaper was eagerly received in rural northern and western New England, upstate New York, and Ohio, and moral reform societies led by women emerged as his staunchest advocates. Although never as popular as abolitionism, let alone temperance, moral reform developed as an interregional movement on the unprecedented mobilization of women. Following the model of temperance societies, McDowall encouraged the development of "moral societies everywhere and irrespective of sect or party, on the principle implied in the pledge—*I bind myself to the observance and promotion of moral purity*." [37] Women, more than men, responded to McDowall's call to pledge moral purity and to hold men equally guilty for violations of the seventh commandment. Like all other benevolent and reform societies, an army of women stood behind and empowered the leadership of this minister. Unlike these other campaigns, in the case of moral reform, women came forth to lead the cause because the men proved wanting. They publicly challenged Christian institutions to rouse themselves from their slumber and men to confess and pledge themselves to moral purity. The constitutions of these societies were similar in form to abolitionist and temperance societies. In Ohio, the Female Moral Reform Society of Gustavus, "impressed with the conviction that licentiousness and vice have become so prevalent and desolating in cities and are extending their evils into the country," adopted the following article in their 1834 constitution: "We engage to do all we can to prevent vice and immorality, to be chaste and moral ourselves, and to consider vicious men equally guilty, and treat them with the same scorn and contempt that we do females of the same character." [38]

In 1834, bitter at the seeming complicity of "good" Christian men in sexual sin, McDowall turned his newspaper over to his supporters in the New York Women's Moral Reform Society and assumed the role as their itinerant agent. [39] Under new leadership, the paper was renamed the *Advocate of Moral Reform*, and its first edition announced the purpose of the paper: "to warn the innocent and the unwary of their danger, and to arouse and alarm the guilty." As the institutions of benevolence—their publications, societies, and pulpits—had been silent about licentiousness, the paper sought to spark a conviction of the widespread sin of complicity among Christians in the country's "violations of the seventh commandment."

> The necessity for such a paper as the one now contemplated, arises first from the fact that other papers will not expose this vice. . . . They are willing to the evils of intemperance, of lotteries, of theaters, and of dueling, and they will not hesitate, in connexion with these vices to publish names and places. . . . But as to the vice of licentiousness, it is a question settled in our minds, that even religious editors will not bring the subject before the public in such a manner as to warrant much hope of good. [40]

Through publications, prayer raids on brothels, and above all else, moral associations, the women of moral reform sounded a call to awaken the men of benevolence to the guilt of licentiousness.

The women of moral reform would not be silenced by admonitions to a false delicacy. Although men joined the movement, women in the country who converted their prayer meetings, sewing circles, and benevolent societies into moral reform associations made up its core constituency. As women took control of the movement, they made claims to control the sexual behavior of men. With this challenge, evangelical women stepped out of their "proper sphere" and into the affairs of men.

These societies took the familiar form of temperance and antislavery societies. The women of the Walton, New York, moral reform auxiliary, for example, resolved in 1835,

1. That lewdness abounds most fearfully in this and other nations.
2. That it will continue to prevail until proper measures are adopted.
3. And that the virtuous alone, can be expected to make the disclosures and put forth the efforts necessary to reform the abandoned and prevent the ruin of the unwary.

This state of moral degradation authorized an unprecedented assertiveness by this association of women in the affairs of men:

We associate to aid friends of purity, and God, in exterminating this evil from the earth.

We pledge ourselves to avoid all social intercourse and otherwise treat with merited abhorrence, those men and women who are known to have been guilty of a single violation of the seventh commandment.

The banishment of the vile from our social intercourse is not to be regarded as equivalent to an excision from the commiseration, counsel and kind offices which their miseries and reform may demand, and purity itself may prompt. So far from neglecting them, like our blessed Saviour, whom we would always imitate, we will encourage their return to the paths of virtue, and restore them when penitent to the favor and privileges which they forfeited by transgression.[41]

In 1837 the American Moral Reform Society claimed 226 auxiliaries, 108 of them formed in the prior year alone, and embracing an estimated 15,000 women.[42] By the end of the decade, moral reform societies were commonplace across the northern states. The *Advocate* boasted 16,500 subscribers and auxiliary societies had doubled since 1837, now numbering 445. The leading role of women in public campaigns against sexual sin threatened to undermine male prerogatives, and arguably, by sowing the seeds of a more genuinely feminist activism, it did.[43] The justification for this aggressive and novel public action was the same as with abolition and temperance: the threat of a special sin and the duty to call the nation to confession.

By the 1840s moral reform declined. Little is known of this demobilization, but historian Mary Ryan suggests that for the women of moral reform in Utica the increasingly exacting demands of moral purity began to run counter to public exposures of vice. Moral reform, she argues, withdrew into a more private sphere of child rearing and housekeeping manuals that sought to defend sexual purity through maternal instruction. As with Washingtonians and some Garrisonians, answering the morally intensive demands of confessional protest led many activists away from public engagement. Public antivice campaigns would resurface in the late nineteenth century, but they would lack the confessional dimensions of the antebellum period focusing on protecting children from immigrants peddling obscene literature.[44]

In summary, during the fourth decade of the nineteenth century, participants within the national institutions of organized benevolence were at war. In all these events, the challengers exhibited a shared form and orientation of collective action. With demands for the immediate confession of particular sins, radicals within organized benevolence challenged the leaders of the parachurch institutions and solicited the confessions of all: Methodists, Baptists, women, African Americans, even drunks. Antislavery, moral reform, and temperance did not originate or terminate in confessional protest. However, in the 1830s these causes emerged as popular and interregional movements precisely when they turned confessional.

Common Dimensions of Confessional Protest

Antebellum reforms emerged as popular movements through confessional breaks with or within organized benevolence. In these breaks, they shared a similar form of collective action in their popular and radical moment. Across very different issues—slavery, alcohol, and sexual sin—common dimensions appeared in the formation and operation of the thousands of reform societies driving the movements.

As in the examples quoted above of the Walton Moral Reform Association's resolutions, the Oneida Association's temperance resolutions, the

French Creek Baptists's antislavery resolutions, and in the resolutions of countless other reform associations, Americans joined these movements through a modular form of association. Special purposes were integral to this form. The central intention of the reform societies was to bear witness against a special sin. They passed resolutions to this effect. For example, the New York State Temperance Society passed this resolution in 1833: "That the traffic in ardent spirit as a drink, is an immorality, and should be abandoned throughout the world."[45] The Baptist Association in Bowdoinham, Maine, in 1834 resolved, "That we consider slavery, as understood in this nation, as a great *moral evil*."[46] And, at the Alleghany County Moral Reform meeting in 1836, the assembly passed the following resolution: "That the sin of licentiousness suggests a more destructive influence upon body and soul than any other in the catalogue of human crime."[47]

Calling out particular social problems as special sins automatically demanded confession. These public testimonies against sin were preludes to reforming individual sinners and the nation as a whole. The Taunton Anti-Slavery Convention of Rhode Island expressed faith in this method of social pressure with the following resolution:

> That those who retain in vassalage their fellow men, and use their neighbor's service without wages, because unjust and inhuman laws give them power, are nevertheless guilty of the highest species of robbery and oppression, and therefore guilty of a sin against both God, and man, which demands immediate repentance.[48]

This pressure to repent led to conversions, a centerpiece of reform meetings. At an 1836 meeting of the Vermont Anti-Slavery Society a clergyman "arose and spoke in substance as follows":

> I have heretofore been opposed to the movements of the abolitionists. I have been prejudiced against them. But I thank God, that prejudice is beginning to be removed! I have formerly supported the Colonization Society, and taken an active part in its operations. But a ray of light has burst in upon my mind. I am satisfied that the Colonization scheme is *wrong*.[49]

Through public testimonies, moral associations sought to lead other sinners to repentance. They saw these public confessions as powerful beacons, diffusing a light leading others to conversion. This is what had happened at Lane Seminary, as Thome testified: "Sin revived and I died!"

These testimonies against sin were inextricably linked to public commitments to resist the sin. As the Moral Reform Society of Hallowell, Maine, resolved,

> All who join this society pledge themselves to discountenance all men who are guilty of entrapping innocent females, and leading them from the paths of rectitude and virtue and of visiting houses of ill fame.[50]

Cleansing the American Church and its benevolent societies of special sins was the primary goal of all reformers, as in the case of the Oneida Association's resolution on the use of alcohol: "That it is the duty of our churches to insist on total abstinence from ardent distilled spirit, in those whom they may hereafter receive to their fellowship," or the French Creek Baptists's resolutions with regard to slavery: "That this Association refuse fellowship with slave holding Baptist Associations, and advise all our churches to adopt rules excluding slave holders from their communion tables."[51] While some reformers would eventually consider the nation irredeemable and confess themselves "come-outers" after the biblical injunction of Revelation 18:4 to "come out" of Babylon, "lest you take part in her sins," most reformers saw their practices of denying fellowship to special sinners as "clapping and whistling" sinners out of *their* place (Job 27:23).

This national wave of movements emerged as reformers sought to purify the associations within American Christianity of the failure to testify against particular sins. Frustrated with the silence of the pulpit, for example, the New York Female Moral Reform Society resolved, "That it is the duty of ministers of the gospel to preach God's word faithfully on the subject of licentiousness, as it is on any other vice or sin."[52] An Alleghany County Moral Reform meeting in New York joined the parent society and resolved: "That the ministers of the gospel of every name in the county, be requested to preach on the 7th commandment the last Sabbath in Oct. int."[53] If churches and benevolent societies failed to act, reformers called on Christians to leave these institutions. As Ralph Waldo Emerson noted,

> it was directly in the spirit and genius of the age, what happened in one instance when a church censured and threatened to excommunicate one of its members on account of the somewhat hostile part to the church which his conscience led him to take in the anti-slavery business; the threatened individual immediately excommunicated the church, in a public and formal process.[54]

Reformers across the nation moved to dissolve Christian bonds with unrepentant institutions. For example in Pittsburgh, Presbyterians resolved

> [t]hat the colonization society, in making expatriation a condition of emancipation, in fostering and not suppressing prejudice against the colored man, in extorting the consent of the enslaved to banishment as if by a *cart whip,* does not merit, but has forfeited the patronage of the Christian community, and cannot have the probation of the Reformed Presbyterian Church.[55]

John Rankin encouraged similar action in the *Evangelist:*

> Our benevolent societies ought to hear testimony against slavery. If it is a duty to bear such testimony as individuals, it is equally so in our associated capacity. If all our benevolent societies would withdraw their agents from the slave states, and say, We cannot receive the proceeds of slavery into the treasury of the Lord; it is the price of blood, the blood both of the souls and bodies of men; we cannot receive it—the system of slavery would tremble to its centre, its very foundations would give way, and it would soon sink into ruins.[56]

The work of exhorting repentance engaged the movements not only in a struggle with the churches and benevolent societies but also in the streets, taverns, boardinghouses, and homes of the nation. The Connecticut State Temperance Society of Colored People resolved: "That it is the duty of all Parents to instruct their children, by precept and example, in the principles of total abstinence, and discountenance those shops kept by *colored men* where intoxicating liquors are sold."[57] The New-Garden Anti-Slavery Society in Columbia County, Ohio, set down in its constitution that "[o]ne of the most important means employed by this association, for effecting [its] design, shall be the influence of moral example, in abstaining, as far as practicable, from the use of the *products of slavery,* and by appeals to the understandings and consciences of others, endeavoring to dissuade them from its use."[58] Article 3 of the New York City Young Men's Moral Reform Society constitution defined the character of the society as one of pure moral relationships extending to all social contacts:

> This society shall be composed of such young men as subscribe to this Constitution, and discountenance the sin of lewdness in thought, word, and deed; and who will use their influence to raise the standard of moral purity, both by reclaiming the guilty, and preventing the virtuous from habits of licentiousness;

but who will wholly exclude from their social intercourse all such as persist in the practice of this sin.[59]

Article 2 of the 1834 Constitution of the Ladies' Moral Reform Society in New York also sought to purify all social intercourse of the sin of licentiousness:

> This Society shall have for its object the prevention of licentiousness, by diffusing light in regard to the existence and great extent of this sin; by showing its fearfully immoral, and soul-destroying influence; by pointing out the numberless lures and arts practiced by the unprincipled destroyer, to seduce and ruin the unsuspecting; by excluding from social intercourse with us all persons of both sexes, who are known to be licentious in habits; and by such other means as the Society shall, from time to time, deem expedient.[60]

These organized sanctions against the unrepentant led to something of a parallel society of reform institutions.

Evangelical and reform publications of the period were littered with advertisements for temperance eating houses, hotels, steamboats, and grocery shops. Moral reformers ran boardinghouses for chaste young men and women. Abolitionists launched a free-produce movement selling goods untainted by the filthy lucre of a slave economy, generating funds for the cause, and strengthening bonds of sociability.[61] Reform societies provided networks for sociability, collective identities, recreation, and employment opportunities. As evangelical members of an emerging middle class and especially the women among them became the core constituency of this subculture of reform, the parlor in the private home became a center for reform activity. The increasingly private sphere of women had also become increasingly pious. The mix of revivals and benevolence offered women a way to influence public affairs that resonated with their deepening moral commitments—at once eluding private confinement and actualizing personal piety. This turned their private homes into places for social prayer and reform organizing.[62]

These pledges against sin were not only directed at others and their institutions, but also at the self—as specified in a resolution of the Female Moral Reform Society of Gaustavus, Ohio: "to be chaste and moral ourselves, and to consider vicious men equally guilty."[63] The purpose of testifying against special sins was to publicly commit to social *and* personal reform. In the presidential address to the 1836 convention of the

New England Temperance Society of Colored Persons, J. W. Lewis asked his delegates, "[W]hy do we give [a teetotal] pledge?" He answered for them: "It is that we may deliver our own souls, and that our example and testimony may save others."[64] The duty to bear witness linked the personal and the public in practice and principle. This link held not only for drinking and sexual vice. Abolition and temperance advocates frequently expressed how these seemingly different sins of slavery and drinking were parallel. J. W. Lewis spoke again for his fellow temperance delegates when he explained why they must pledge total abstinence:

> Nor do we oppose simply what is called drinking in excess, but also the moderate and occasional use of alcoholic liquors, because it is the latter which begets the excess. It is as absurd and deceitful to talk of the abuse of dram-drinking, as it is to talk of the abuses of slaveholding. Total abstinence alone can cure the former; immediate emancipation . . . alone can remedy the latter.[65]

While for African Americans the battle against slavery illuminated their struggle against intemperance, for white Americans, the logic predominantly flowed in the other direction. As the Reverend Phelps discussing the first principle of abolition to a Philadelphia convention in 1834 explained,

> by slave holding, is meant the usurped authority of holding man as *property*. This is a *sin*, which nothing can make *right*. The fact that the law sanctions it, is no excuse, nor does it make it right, any more than selling liquor is *right*, because it is not unlawful. *How are you to reform?* The remedy is simple, *total abstinence from holding man in slavery;* in other words, *immediate emancipation.*[66]

Phelps's formulation of antislavery as personal abstinence had wide currency.

Immediatists knowingly conflated the individual's total renunciation of all ties to slavery and the social reform program of freeing two million Americans from bondage. For evangelicals mixing the orthodox concern with public morals and the populist experience of mass confessions, this did not appear as faulty logic. Religious revivals and popular democracy taught together that there was no qualitative split between individual and national redemption, only a difference in number. As they saw it, the reform of social problems required that particular sins be made immediate to a critical mass of individuals. In the eyes of these reform evangelicals, licentiousness, intemperance, and chattel slavery thwarted moral self-control, blocked personal redemption, and undermined national destiny. The idea of a covenanted community mediated by an ecclesiastical order of ministers and deacons was reconfigured into a democratic constitution of individual and nation mediated by voluntary associations brought together over special sins. This was an astonishing transformation in the structure of the worldviews of orthodox and populist evangelicals. Through the public confession of special sins, an individualist and associational ethos overcame the antithesis of the corporate but exclusive commitments of orthodoxy and the popular but centrifugal appeal of upstart sects.

Typically reform societies acknowledged that the sin obligated individuals and associations to confess. The latter was construed at varying degrees of abstraction: from a congregation to the Church, from a local auxiliary to organized benevolence as a whole, from a village to the nation. In West Bloomfield, New York, the First Church resolved "that we view it our duty, by all Christian means, to advocate the immediate emancipation of the enslaved. . . . And to this we pledge ourselves as individuals and as a church." [67] Abolitionists relentlessly pressed the idea of individual duty and national guilt. This was often expressed as a responsibility incurred by the democratic constitution and union of slaveholding and free states. The Vermont State Anti-Slavery Convention resolved "[t]hat slavery being recognized by the Constitution of the United States, its evils and its sins are national, for the continuance of which the whole people of the United States are responsible." [68] The Topfield Anti-Slavery Convention in Massachusetts did not run away from this guilt: "*Resolved.* That the people of the *Free States* are involved in the guilt, the shame and the danger of slavery, and are consequently bound to use all constitutional and christian means for its utter and immediate extinction." [69]

Many historians have seen in the *personal* character of the abolitionist movement its greatest weakness: From their perspective white abolitionists were self-absorbed eccentrics more concerned with personal perfection than practical solutions to a complex social problem. [70] From the perspective of reformers, the national sin of slavery was embedded deep in the hearts of white Americans. To condemn slavery as an unjust institution was to touch only the surface. But to redeem America—and that is what most evangelical immediatists wanted to do—required rooting out racial prejudice in the hearts of white Christians.

This explains the seemingly impractical methods of certain reformers. The American Anti-Slavery Society commissioned H. C. Wright as its official agent to children. In this capacity, he sought access to Sunday schools, churches, and homes to work on the consciences of children. Reporting on his work in Paterson, New Jersey, Wright wrote to the *Evangelist* that

> [c]hildren's prayer meetings are held—children take the anxious seat, asking the prayers of God's people—children love to converse about Christ, and his dying love for them and the poor slaves—children pray for souls in Paterson, and for the slave, in their closets, and in the prayer-meetings. One little girl of four years said, "Ma, I want to go and pray for the poor slaves." "Go then my dear." She did. Soon she said, again, "Ma, I want to pray for Mr. Wright, the children's agent." Such is the spirit that pervades many tender little hearts in Paterson.[71]

Abolitionists like Wright viewed the sin of slavery and racism as one and the same, and in redeeming the nation they envisioned a generation nurtured without racial hatred. Temperance also sought to influence impressionable youth. At an Eighth Ward temperance meeting in New York, a Baptist minister instructed the women in the audience that

> [s]hould they banish all intoxicating drink from the nursery, the kitchen and the sideboard, and from their social parties, teach their children that to drink was a sin, beg their husbands and brothers to abstain, and with the pledge in their hands go as angels of mercy from door to door, to influence their neighbors also to join them, the world might soon be purified from the curse of the drunkard.[72]

The revival technique of playing on the anxieties of the young and of employing women for the service of salvation had been converted to special and national purposes.

The concern these reform movements showed for all souls—irrespective of their age, color, sex, and standing as citizens—speaks to their radical populism but also to a disregard for what antebellum reformers would have termed political expediency. The movements sought a pervasive and permanent reformation of public sentiments, not short-term gain. In so doing, they threatened to short-circuit traditional patterns of deference by bringing their message directly to individuals without regard to formal or informal relations of familial, ecclesiastical, and civic authority. Whether in preaching to and praying with prostitutes, blacks, children, or women, they engaged broad categories of Americans that were excluded from political and civic discourse.

If individual and nation did not repent, Topfield abolitionists predicted, "the just judgment of God will deprive them of that liberty which they have denied to others, and give them over to the reign of tyranny and despotism." Warnings of impending divine judgment on individual and nation were widespread. The women of Mercer and Wayne, Maine, testified to this:

> Whereas immorality, as forbidden in the seventh commandment, and expounded by our Saviour in Matt. V. 28 has become exceedingly prevalent in our land, and believing the false delicacy, which has prohibited the exposing and using proper means to prevent this vice, wholly at variance with the scriptures of the Old and New Testament, and believing it to be the duty of every individual in the country to arise, and by united prayer and effort, avert the judgements of insulted heaven, we form ourselves into a Society.[73]

Leading the calls for personal and public reform, broadcasting the campaigns to bring individual and nation to repentance, and organizing the challenge to American churches and civil society was a new brand of activist. The thousands of modular reform associations dedicated to special purposes were responding to the agitation of a new type of protestor. Radical newspaper editors and itinerant agents spread the calls for public confessions against special sins and worked to coordinate a national response.

Print evangelism was crucial in articulating special sins as problems that bridged the levels of abstraction from self to nation. Following the American Tract Society's plan of general supply, advocates of these reform movements sought to inundate the reading public with shocking tales of moral degradation tied to special sins. The cultural archetypes of the pitiful drunkard and the devilish rum merchant, the suffering slave and the barbaric slaveholder, the defiled woman and the scurrilous rake—a victim paired with a villain—furnished an imagined concreteness to the immense social problems they represented. These sins were at once felt as immediate threats to the individual and also as endangering the nation as a whole. By publicizing the threat of special sins, editors like William Lloyd Garrison, Joshua Leavitt, and John McDowall facilitated the leap from individual to nation in the calls for repentance and reform. As individuals and associations answered these calls, these activist editors heralded the good news bringing together readers and reformers across the nation in a common feeling of movement.

As editors flooded the mails with reform print, agents traveled from town to town holding meetings in churches, town halls, barns, and converted theaters, lecturing to lyceums and matching wits with opponents in debating societies. Theodore Weld was an exemplar of the peripatetic reform agent. Newspaper accounts of his work in the early 1830s open a window into this world of reform. The *Baptist Register* reported how in his lectures in Rochester he mustered the army of two hundred thousand victims of intemperance

> picked from the gutters and sewers, the groceries and grog-shops, poor houses, prisons, and asylums, and marshalled with their bloated and shocking visages, their staggering gait, their filthy and tattered habiliments, their fettered limbs, and clanking chains. . . . [W]e cannot think that any vendor of the poison, who loves his country, and has any belief in a future judgement, heard the address, and then returned back and drew off the poisonous liquor for his customers, with an untrembling hand.[74]

At the Rochester Young Men's Society, Weld used Finney's technique of soliciting public avowals from those under the conviction of sin:

> At a late meeting of the Society, (says the *Observer*), an address was delivered by Mr. Weld, a young gentleman of the Oneida Institute, who is spending a few days in this village. We can only say of the address that it was one of surpassing excellence; occupied two hours and a half in the delivery; and yet we can say for ourselves, that we could have listened, not only with patience, but pleasure, had it been much longer. The fixed attention paid by the audience showed that they felt themselves participating in a rare mental treat, and the friends of temperance that the cause could not have found an abler advocate. The effects produced by it cannot be more than partially known; but after Mr. Weld sat down, Rev. Mr. Penney arose and requested those present, who were now in the habit of using, manufacturing, or vending ardent spirits and who were willing then to give a public pledge, that from that time they would cease to do so, should rise, when some eight or ten gentlemen arose in token of such determination.[75]

It is impossible to know what proportion of the moral associations had revival beginnings like this, but all reform movements considered itinerant agents indispensable to the cause. All three movements aimed to impress individuals with the immediacy of specific social problems to personal as well as national reform.

In the early 1830s, Weld worked as a temperance agent, and by mid-decade his well-publicized exploits for that cause placed him in high demand. McDowall sought his service as a moral reform agent, but Weld committed himself to an itinerant agency for immediate abolitionism. In the autumn of 1836, he trained the "seventy"—named after the seventy apostles of Christ—in the measures of immediatism. Letters like this one from Geneva, New York, calling for the service of Weld and other agents reveal some of what Americans expected of them:

> The spirit of inquiry is increasing here every day. . . . Come my Bro. because the voice of my poor brothers cries up from the ground, and his distressed and abject condition, and the principles of the eternal throne violated in his subjection demand the influence,—the intelligent well directed influence of this learned village. . . . Come because we need light! light! Come and we will pray that God the Eternal spirit of Truth and wisdom and Grace may come with you.[76]

The *Evangelist* published the following letter from Tompkins County, New York:

> We very much want one of the Anti-Slavery agents with us to lecture for one week. The good cause is gaining ground with us as fast as could be expected. We have some noble blood in this village, devoted to that cause. We are waiting for some agent to visit us, and then with to form a County Anti-Slavery Society and go ahead. Trusting in the God of freedom and friend of the oppressed, I am yours, in the bonds with those that are bound.[77]

Like the revival spirit, the light of reform—and its holy train of conviction, confession, and conversion—seemed to follow some agents more than others. With the Washingtonians the role of itinerant agents was most central. The movement spread from Baltimore to cities as far away as Pittsburgh and Cincinnati through the travels of its "apostles" and the spectacle of their public confessions.

Leaders of all three movements spoke of the *light* of reform and its unmediated capacity to transform public sentiment. At the 1834 convention of the American Seventh Commandment Society (the male counterpart to the Female Moral Reform Society), Rev. S. L. Pomeroy offered the following resolution:

> That the first step to be taken in the great work of Moral Reform, is the diffusion of light. Yes sir, *light,* light, is what we want. "Let there be LIGHT." In the

work of redemption, the first thing is to give light—to convince the world of sin comes first, *then* show the remedy. "Arise, shine, for thy *light* is come." Christ himself is "the light of the world." Why has it pleased God to uncover the pit of wo, and almost cause her to hear its groans and lamentations? To warn us—to stop us in our course of sin. . . . How was it with the slavetrade. Clarkson traveled thousands of miles gathering *light* on the subject, and then he scattered it far and wide. . . . How was it with intemperance. . . . [Dr. Hewitt] scattered light, and where is the monster now? . . . And just so must it be with this evil which we have met here today to consider. This is the *great* evil.[78]

The reform editor and itinerant agent were called to scatter light, to uncover woe, and to stop Americans in their course of sin. This separated them and often set them against local communities and religious traditions. Through confessional protest, these reformers and their most committed supporters avowed a new collective identity. Public confessions against special sins created detached protest identities. Personally identified with particular but extensive social problems, these "ultraists" were at once hated and revered, marginal and cosmopolitan. It also made them intensely vigilant of personal guilt with regard to specific problems *and* extensively concerned with regard to particular sins. It made them modern activists.

CHAPTER SIX

"To Bear Witness to the Horrors of the Southern Prison House"

The new evangelical schema of bearing witness against special sins was not only essential to the impressive breadth of this wave of protests, it also tightly controlled the moral commitments of reformers. Intensive personal projects underpinned the extensive support for this national wave of movements. Personal assertions of moral reform and claims to new collective identities shaped the modular declarations of reform associations and their special purposes. These public declarations were the collective expressions of detached, mobile individuals seizing on specialized, broadcast problems and projecting themselves anew by publicly confessing to particular but extensive sins. The announcements of new auxiliary societies and the testimonies of their members revealed this dynamic mix of personal confessions and public evils. In the formation of reform societies, evangelicals avowed new identities through the particular but nationally pivotal causes of immediate abolition or the total renunciation of all that intoxicates.

The skeptical reader might think this social-psychological account reads too much into the announcements reform societies published in the press. Much of the intimate workings of these associations are lost to history, but detailed community studies have uncovered the guilt, the anxious personal transformations, and the new moral assertions of self that animated the formation of some reform societies.[1] This social-psychological account also accords with the understanding of orthodox leaders opposed to the reform movements. At the very beginning of this wave of confessional protests, Archibald Alexander disparaged this moral assertion of self through extensive causes as the work of "weak, hot-headed men, who *push themselves forward* when there is any excitement, from a belief that they can be of *great service.*" Leonard Bacon decried the leaders of these movements as revivalists of "one ideas" and as "flaming enthusiasts."[2] The evaluations of Alexander and Bacon, fair or not, appreciated the motive force behind the reform movements taking shape: the confessional projection of the self in a great yet specialized cause.

Leading abolitionists acknowledged the personal hinge to the extensive cause of immediate emancipation. A good example of this is found in James Gillespie Birney's widely published letter entitled "Vindication of the Abolitionists." In the fall of 1835, Birney—a former slaveholder and agent of the American Colonization Society, and new convert to immediate abolitionism—received in the mail a circular announcing the formation of a "vigilance committee" in Athens, Alabama. Birney had recently worked as a lawyer in the county where the vigilance committee was formed. As a southerner, a slaveholder, and a leader of the American Colonization Society, his conversion to abolitionism garnered national attention. Abolitionists like Theodore Weld and William Lloyd Garrison viewed Birney's conversion as a singular achievement of the nascent movement. The circular he received publicized the committee's formal resolutions to seize, whip, or execute "gamblers," "blacklegs," and "abolition fanatics." The committee identified Birney by name as a leader of these fanatics and among the targets of its vigilante justice. In his letter, Birney responded to this committee and defended the character of advocates of immediate abolition. He focused primarily on the religious character, personal lifestyle, and moral choices of the abolitionists he had recently met in a tour of Ohio and New England. Birney discussed the practicality of abolition and the destructive nature of slavery; however, he started with the personal moral commitments of the abolitionists. To be an immediate abolitionist meant much more than to simply support the immediate emancipation of the slave. In the 1830s, this new activist identity was tied to a moral politics that altered what the abolitionist Lydia Maria Child described as the individual's "life-web."

"The great majority" of abolitionists, Birney claimed, "are Christians by profession, and are found among the most active, zealous, and well-informed classes of the several churches in which they respectively belong." "In England," Birney observed, they would be called " 'Methodists,' the name by which the *working men* of all the churches there, both established and dissenting, are called, when spoken of by the irreligious part of the community, or by their more indolent and fashionable brethren." Birney was quick to point out that not "*all* the most zealous" members of evangelical churches are abolitionists. "By no means," but it was from these ranks that "the abolitionists have increased their numbers, from the mere handful of two years ago, to it may be 40,000." Abolitionists, according to Birney, believed "in the conversion of the world" and that "human agency is to be the great *instrument* to effect it." They were leading supporters of "foreign and domestic missions" and generous in their donations for the "distribution of the Bible, for Sunday school, for the tract and education causes." "As a class," he thought abolitionists "distinguished for their punctuality in the discharge of pecuniary engagements" and that "such of them as are engaged in profitable pursuits would soon grow rich, were not that they give so much of their money, as well as of their time and personal effort, to the benevolent causes which interest them."

According to Birney, these evangelical and enterprising abolitionists were also particularly abstemious. They refrained from all "that is alcoholic and that produces intoxication." This prohibition extended not only to wine, beer, cider, and all "other disguises of alcohol," but many have also "relinquished the use of tea and coffee, substituting in most cases, water or milk." Birney reported that in his recent journey through Ohio and the East he was "brought in company with a large number of abolitionists" and remembered "but *one* who seemed to be in the habitual use of tabacco." The abolitionists were not just circumspect about bodily diet but were also typically opposed to "theaters, expensive pomps and parade of every kind."[3]

In Birney's vindication, the abolitionist appeared as the model of Christian self-discipline. Birney's reformer also resembled the ultraist depicted in the *Knickerbocker*. Common to both depictions, the glowing and the mocking, was a religious temperament that displayed a compulsive interest with the personal immediacy of extensive but particular social problems. This reform temperament was the product of a new evangelical cosmology that twinned intensive campaigns of personal transformation with extensive struggles against special sins. There had been earlier examples of this pairing, but only in the 1830s did it become widespread in the United States, and only then could it drive national social movements.

From 1790 to 1830, America's eventful religious history—the meteoric rise of populist sects, the disestablishment of New England Congregationalism, the emergence of the national institutions of organized benevolence, and the liberal challenges of Unitarianism and Universalism—reflected the many sides of a cosmological upheaval in the religious experiences of Americans. As Robert Abzug argues, for many evangelicals of the period it seemed as if the "cosmos" was "crumbling." Social reform for the leading abolitionists, teetotalers, and moral reformers reconstructed this shattered cosmology. In this reconstruction, sensibilities, symbols, and practices of the old orders remained but appeared reconfigured to shape a new mode of religious experience. What made antebellum reformers remarkable, and abolitionists particularly so, is that social problems and reform causes that distracted, bemused, or excited ordinary Americans redefined these activists' sense of self. Like many evangelical Christians, reformers were typically twice born: They experienced a rebirth in Christ at some point in their lives. Unlike most evangelical Christians, these activists were also thrice born: They experienced rebirth in a social reform movement.[4]

Any explanation of the reform movements of the 1830s must come to terms with this new religious orientation. The evangelical schemas of this new orientation shaped the way reformers thought and felt about slavery (and alcohol and licentiousness). Attempts by scholars to reduce the religious and emotional dimensions of antebellum reform to material interests, status struggles, or mental pathologies have provided one-sided accounts. The pervasive expressions of guilt and sin cannot be ignored. A historic shift in personal and public patterns of evangelical piety shaped the radical turn in antislavery and other reform movements that swept the nation in the 1830s. A new patterning of personal piety that engaged public matters in an aggressively new way shaped the collective form of immediate abolitionism. Reform of self and society developed into a recursive relationship deeply marking each other. This new religious orientation provides the best account of this wave of movements. Activists possessed no more apt an analogy to capture the significance of their personal commitment to discrete social causes like antislavery than to call them conversions. This remains the most apt term for their experiences.

This chapter explores the intensive dimensions of the reform movements of the 1830s by tracking personal conversions to immediate abolitionism as they appear in the letters, journals, and biographical accounts of six leading antebellum reformers: William Lloyd Garrison, Elizur Wright, Jr., Theodore Weld, James Gillespie Birney, and Sarah and Angelina Grimké. This chapter shows how personal reform bridged with national reform *and* the role of special sins in this realignment of the self and the social. The six reformers analyzed here represent central nodes in a larger interpersonal network of abolitionists. The chronology of conversions extends in time from 1829 to 1836, paralleling the organizational development of immediate abolitionism from isolated voices of dissent to mass movement.

William Lloyd Garrison: "And All Things Became New"

William Lloyd Garrison's break with earlier antislavery sentiment and its gradualist approach to abolition came as he wrestled with the significance of black opposition to colonization plans. He, more than any other white abolitionist, articulated the link between slave emancipation and overcoming racism. His articulation of America's need for a double liberation—black America from slavery and white America from the sin of racism—triggered an awakening, small at first, that spread through distinct and distant networks of white reformers and within a few years gathered together into an extensive movement.[5]

Born in 1805 in Newburyport, Massachusetts, he grew up in a very poor and religious household. Garrison's religious upbringing was evangelical Baptist.[6] He was raised to a religious temperament distinct from the other five abolitionists studied here. Whereas the others were nurtured by the religious traditions of Presbyterians or Congregationalists, Garrison grew up independent from the institutions of orthodoxy but at the center of their influence. As he recounted to an English newspaper in 1847, his mother was raised in an Anglican family but was converted by a Baptist preacher in a barn on Deer Island, New Brunswick. Disowned by her family on account of her public avowal of the Baptist faith, she retained for the rest of her life a combative religious approach to a wicked world, an unwavering willingness to suffer for her faith, and a trust that the love of Christ knew no worldly distinctions.[7] The populist bent to her religious faith wiped away invidious social distinctions that pervaded the wider culture. Late in her life living in Baltimore, sick and without family to care for her, she wrote to her son about the kindness of others:

> Thank God I am well taken care of, for both Black and White are all attention to me, and I have every thing done that is necessary. The ladies are all kind to me and I have a Coloured woman that waits on me, that is so kind no one can tell how kind she is, and although a Slave to Man, yet a free born soul, by the

grace of God. Her name is Henny, and should I never see you again, and you should ever come where she is remember her for your poor mother's sake.[8]

Garrison came by his religious dissent honestly, and he likely felt less compunction and more satisfaction than many of his fellow travelers when he goaded, challenged, and recruited defectors from the ranks of orthodox institutions.[9]

Garrison's fierce public engagement with worldly problems did *not* come from his mother. Her religion exemplified a pietistic withdrawal from a wicked world. As she wrote her son when he was fifteen, "I was taught to see that all my dreams of happiness in this life were chimerical; the efforts we make here all of them imbecility in themselves and illusive, but religion is perennial." A "soteriology of the underprivileged" fired his mother's piety. Religion "fortifies the mind to support trouble, elevates the affections of the heart and its perpetuity has no end." Her religious temperament contrasted with the orthodox disposition characteristic of many New Englanders that engaged the world by seeking proof of personal grace in the steady habits and mastery of material life. Garrison's mother looked for saving grace in responses to suffering and expected all of its rewards in the hereafter. Garrison would take his mother's sense of passion and the redemption of suffering and fuse it to orthodoxy's fierce engagement with the world.[10]

Garrison, unlike most leading white abolitionists, was raised among the working poor of America's eastern towns. His father, a heavy drinker and seaman, abandoned his wife and children before Lloyd (as his mother always referred to Garrison) turned three years of age. Garrison spent his first years under the guidance of his mother, and as he grew older he lived under the stern but caring discipline of nonfamilial caretakers and employers.

Fanny Garrison was forced to put out her children to make a living at an early age. At nine years of age, Lloyd was apprenticed to a shoemaker. From that point on, he bounced around from trade to trade living apart from his mother and under the legal authority of various masters. Finally, at the age of thirteen, he was apprenticed as a printer and found his "calling" in the expanding newspaper trade. His seven-year apprenticeship with the Newburyport *Herald* ended in 1825. During these years, he wrote for the newspaper and developed a scathing style that mixed morality and politics in the defense of Federalist politics and orthodox plans of benevolence. A voracious reader, this autodidact impressed his master with his craftsmanship as both a typesetter and writer.

In 1825, with his independence won, Garrison formed what would become a lifelong partnership with Isaac Knapp and became the editor and publisher of a new paper in Newburyport, the *Free Press*. Garrison, only twenty years of age, held full responsibility for this weekly newspaper. The *Free Press* venture was short-lived, as were his subsequent three forays into the market of newspaper print. Without a job, Garrison made a fateful move to Boston and moved into the boardinghouse of the Reverend William Collier. Collier's Christian boardinghouse, like many others in northern cities, became a hotbed of reformers. In homes like Collier's, young evangelicals found sanctuary from bustling and sinful cities. In these houses of temperance and prayer, contacts were made in the network of intimate relations that structured an evangelical subculture and its emerging radical reform projects.

Garrison soon became the typesetter for Collier's temperance newspaper, the *National Philanthropist*—one of the first reform papers of the period. Collier was a Baptist minister in the Unitarian city of Boston. His alliance with orthodoxy, as evidenced in the causes supported by his newspaper, was not uncommon among the more established eastern clergy of the upstart sects. In the capital of liberal Unitarianism, some Baptists and Congregationalists found common ground and buried the eighteenth-century hatchet. Collier's newspaper was intended as a voice for the temperance societies springing up across Massachusetts in the late 1820s. On July 4th, 1828, Garrison became the editor of this novel special-purpose paper.

As editor, Garrison attacked a "hydra" of sin that assailed northern evangelicals and galvanized support for the institutions of organized benevolence. In addition to intemperance, the paper attacked lotteries, war, and Sabbath violations. But temperance presented the model cause, and its popular appeal in the late 1820s provided the path for other reforms. Garrison envisioned the religious newspaper as playing the role of the vanguard of Christian benevolence. Its duty, as he saw it, was to overcome the trepidation of the "moralists" and "philanthropists" by calling them to meet their duty and impressing them with the moral dangers of inactivity.

That same year, Benjamin Lundy, a Quaker and gradual abolitionist, on one of his many Pauline walks across the United States spreading the gospel of emancipation, visited Boston and lodged at Collier's boardinghouse. There he met Garrison and impressed the young editor with the urgency of the slavery question. In October 1828, Garrison resigned from the *Philanthropist* and moved to Bennington, Vermont, to run the *Journal of the Times.* In an early editorial for the *Journal,* Garrison revealed the impact of his encounter with Lundy.

> His heart is of a gigantic size. Every inch of him is alive with power. He combines the meekness of Howard with the boldness of Luther. No reformer was ever more devoted, zealous, persevering, or sanguine. He has fought single-handed against a host, without missing a blow or faltering a moment; but his forces are rapidly gathering, and he will yet free our land.[11]

Garrison's association with Quakers and that sect's early role in antislavery are worthy of a longer discussion than can be presented here. Radicals within the Society of Friends anticipated the popular combination of personal piety and public activism that exploded in the 1830s. Some Quakers, like Elizabeth Heydrick in Great Britain who promoted immediate abolition in the 1820s, developed a public piety that yoked personal commitments to public activism for discrete causes.[12] In these moral commitments, Friends on both sides of the Atlantic kept the antislavery cause alive during decades of apathy in the United States from the late eighteenth to early nineteenth centuries, but they did not provide the route to popular resistance. This was left, in no small part, to the young Baptist from Newburyport, as he engaged with the causes and goaded the institutions of orthodoxy.

Garrison brought to Bennington, Vermont, similar causes he pursued in Boston but with a tighter focus. In his first notice to the public signaling the direction of the newspaper under his control, Garrison outlined his editorial goals, now grasped as a life calling: "We have three objects in view, which we shall pursue through life, whether in this place or elsewhere—namely the suppression of intemperance and its associate vices, the gradual emancipation of every slave in the republic, and the perpetuity of national peace."[13] Garrison had established himself as one of the many adjuncts of organized benevolence using his paper to contribute to its expanding specialized causes.

The *Journal* also supported John Quincy Adams against Andrew Jackson in the upcoming presidential election. From his early days of working for the *Herald* to this short tenure at the *Journal,* Garrison actively engaged in the electoral politics of the nation. This engagement died in 1828 with the victory of Jackson. The election convinced Garrison of the control slave states held over national politics and undermined his faith in the possibilities of affecting change through electoral politics. For the following three decades, up until the Civil War, Garrison steadfastly resisted mixing reform with electoral politics.

In the spring of 1829, Lundy traveled to Vermont from Baltimore to recruit Garrison to edit his paper the *Genius of Emancipation*. Garrison accepted Lundy's offer. Before he moved to Baltimore, he returned to Boston for the summer. His Fourth of July speech to an assembly of supporters of the colonization society at the Park Street Church provides a window into where he stood on the issues of colonization, racial equality, and emancipation just prior to his experiences in Baltimore. In this speech, he articulated the theme of national guilt and clearly identified northerners as sharing in the sin of slavery.

> [Slavery] should make this a day of fasting and prayer, not of boisterous merriment and idle pageantry—a day of great lamentation, not of congratulatory joy. It should spike every cannon, and haul down every banner. Our garb should be sackcloth—our heads bowed in dust—our supplications, for the pardon and assistance of Heaven.[14]

Recommending they wrap themselves in sackcloth and put their faces in the dust, Garrison invoked the familiar jeremiad that generations of New Englanders had been raised on, but it was yoked not to the general sins of a corporate body of local saints but rather to a special sin of the nation.[15]

At Park Street, he did not directly attack the American Colonization Society, but he was conspicuously quiet about its celebrated colony in Liberia. He also clearly suggested that for all the good work of organized benevolence, it was morally suspect for its passive approach to slavery.

> From one end of the country to the other, [Christianity's] charitable societies form golden links of benevolence, and scatter their contributions like rain drops over parched heath; but they bring no sustenance to the perishing slave. The blood of souls is upon her garments, yet she heeds not the stain. The clankings of the prisoner's chains strike upon her ear, but they cannot penetrate her heart.[16]

This moral outrage had not yet led Garrison to the principles of immediatism. He expressed that removal of African Americans was a necessary component of emancipation (possibly to Haiti as Lundy proposed or to western lands) and that this process need be gradual.

> [The] emancipation of all slaves of this generation is most assuredly out of the question. The fabric which now towers above the Alps, must be taken away

brick by brick, and foot by foot, till is reduced so low that it may be overturned without burying the nation in its ruin. Years may elapse before the completion of the achievement; generations of blacks may go down to the grave, manacled and lacerated, without hope for their children.[17]

What a difference a few months can make.

The direct witness of slavery in Baltimore led Garrison to quickly recant his support of gradual abolition and colonization. In his September 1829 announcement to the readers of Lundy's *Genius,* inaugurating his role as managing editor, immediatism had already started to usurp gradualism: "I am convinced, on mature reflection, that no valid excuse can be given for the continuance of this evil a single hour."[18] In this change of heart, his sense of moral responsibility for sin was also altered. In front of a New England gathering of colonization supporters, Garrison spoke of removing slavery "brick by brick" without "burying the nation in its ruin," but in Baltimore, confronted by manacled slaves and white men getting rich on their traffic, he saw no personal excuse that could justify the persistence of this sin for "a single hour." As he witnessed the immediacy of sin in the actions of slaveholders and merchants, the practicality of emancipation as a corporate issue affecting the nation as a whole became of no concern. No slaveholder could morally justify his or her part in it, and no person with a conscience could stand idly by as the sin continued. As Garrison witnessed "the horrors of the Southern prison house," this dissenting Baptist erased the public versus personal sin distinction affirmed by most orthodox Calvinists.

While still refusing to openly repudiate colonization, he warned in this same announcement that "if we depend on colonization societies, slavery will never be exterminated."[19] Nonetheless, in November 1829, Garrison and Lundy were running ads in the paper seeking slaveholders willing to manumit their slaves in order for them to "remove" to Haiti. By March 1830, Garrison's editorials in the *Genius* turned against colonization schemes and the national society supporting them. Such plans were no longer simply impractical, but Christian commitments to them and the national society promoting them were detrimental to the antislavery cause:

[S]uch is the colonization mania, such the implicit confidence reposed in the operations of the Society, that no demonstration of its inefficiency, however, palpable, can shake the faith of its advocates. . . . My complaint is, that its ability is overrated to a disastrous extent; that this delusion is perpetuated by the conduct and assurances of those who ought to act better—the members of the Society. I complain, moreover, that the lips of these members are sealed upon the subject of slavery, who from their high standing and extensive influence, ought to expose its flagrant enormities, and actively assist in its overthrow.[20]

In Baltimore, Garrison developed an attack on the American Colonization Society that would prove compelling to many of the society's antislavery members. The society, he argued, had a soporific effect on the conscience of whites with regard to the sin of slavery.

At the same time, free African Americans in Baltimore were actively debating the merits of colonization, and public opinion among them sided against the scheme. This activism influenced Garrison's rapidly evolving position on racial equality and immediate emancipation without expatriation. As contact with the domestic slave trade in Baltimore convinced him that personal, racist hatred was the bulwark of the institution of slavery, he began to see this same sin as informing the colonization scheme of removing blacks from the presence of whites. Garrison was acutely sensitive to the deep animus against blacks in the temperament of white Americans and was remarkably free of this racism himself. It was also during this time that he encountered Walker's *Appeal,* which impressed upon him the inevitability of a massive slave insurrection if emancipation did not come quick. He integrated the likelihood of a bloody insurrection into the jeremiad, seeing it as the imminent punishment of an angry God.

Having personalized the sin of slavery, he started to attack sinners in his column in the *Genius.* Like Finneyites in upstate New York, Garrison started to publicly identify sinners by name. He attacked a New England merchant from his hometown, Francis Todd, for his part in the domestic slave trade, and in 1830, Garrison landed himself in jail for libel. The ensuing court case brought him renown. Although he was always quick to point out that his stay in jail was luxurious compared with the conditions of slaves, Garrison's imprisonment confirmed his willingness to suffer for the cause. In the evangelical worldview of an emerging class of radical reformers, this amounted to martyrdom, and it caught the notice of Arthur Tappan. Tappan paid Garrison's fine securing his release from jail after forty-nine days of imprisonment.

At some point between 1829 and 1830, the enormity of the sin of slavery eclipsed if not encompassed all other moral failings for Garrison. In a letter written from the Baltimore jail, Garrison claimed that "there is nothing which the curse of slavery has not tainted. It rests on every herb, and every tree, and every field, and on the people, and on the morals."[21] The young Baptist's hatred for the special sin of slavery proved too fiery for the more genteel Quaker, Lundy, and in less than a year they amicably parted ways. Cut loose and with a small measure of renown, Garrison initiated plans for a new, uncompromising paper, the *Liberator*. Garrison settled on Boston for the home of the paper. To gather support and subscribers for the proposed paper he started a lecture tour. He found great difficulty in securing halls or churches to deliver these speeches, but one venue that was always open to him was black churches.

Shortly after leaving Baltimore, he spoke to a black church in New Haven headed by the white minister Simeon Jocelyn. In New York, he spoke to a small group of gentlemen including Arthur Tappan, but his first success in securing strong commitments among whites came in Boston. In October 1830, he spoke at Julien Hall to an audience that included the Reverend Lyman Beecher and John Tappan (Arthur's brother). The Reverend Samuel J. May, a Unitarian minister, was also present, and described the impression Garrison made that day:

Presently the young man arose, modestly, but with an air of calm determination, and delivered such a lecture as he only, I believe, at that time, could have written; for he had had his eyes so anointed that he could see that outrages perpetrated upon Africans were wrongs done to common humanity; he only, I believe had had his ears so completely unstopped of *prejudice toward color* that the cries of enslaved black men and black women sounded to him as if they came from brothers and sisters.

He began with expressing deep regret and shame for the zeal he had lately manifested in the Colonization cause. It was, he confessed, a zeal without knowledge. He had been deceived by the misrepresentations so diligently given throughout the free States, by Southern agents, of the design and tendency of the Colonization scheme. During his few months residence in Maryland he had been completely undeceived . . . . He exhibited in graphic sketches and glowing colors the suffering of the enslaved, and denounced the plan of Colonization as devised and adapted to perpetuate the system, and intensify the wrongs of American slavery, and therefore utterly undeserving of the patronage of lovers of liberty and friends of humanity.

Never before was I so affected by the speech of man. When he had ceased speaking I said to those around me: "That is a providential man; he is a prophet; he will shake our nation to its centre, but he will shake slavery out of it. We ought to know him, we ought to help him. Come, let us go and give him our hands."[22]

The gospel according to Garrison was "that *immediate, unconditional, emancipation without expatriation, was the right of every slave, and could not be withheld by his master an hour without sin.*" "That night," May testified, "my soul was baptized in his spirit, and ever since I have been a disciple and fellow-laborer of William Lloyd Garrison."[23] Lydia Maria Child described a similar soul-stirring encounter with Garrison. As she recalled, he "got hold of my conscience and pulled me into reforms. It is no use to imagine what might have been, if I had never met him. Old dreams vanished, old associations departed, and all things became new." According to Child, Garrison changed "the whole pattern" of her "life-web."[24]

On January 1, 1831, the first issue of the *Liberator* was released to a mostly black readership. At first his white supporters were few and, like May and Child, mostly liberal Unitarians. When the mayor of Boston was contacted by the governors of Virginia and Georgia, in the wake of Nat Turner's failed insurrection, imploring him to crack down on Garrison's incendiary publication, the mayor assured them that the paper had virtually no support. As he wrote more than a decade after the events,

> [t]he first information received by me of a disposition to agitate this subject [slavery] in our State was from the Governors of Virginia and Georgia, severally remonstrating against an incendiary newspaper published in Boston, and, as they alleged, thrown broadcast among their plantations, inciting to insurrection and its horrid results. It appeared on enquiry that no member of the city government, nor any person of my acquaintance, had ever heard of the publication. Some time afterward it was reported to me by the city officers that they had ferreted out the paper and its editor; that his office was an obscure hole, his only visible auxiliary a negro boy, and his supporters a very few insignificant persons of all colors. This information, with the consent of the alderman, I communicated to the above-named governors with an assurance of my belief that the new fanaticism had not made, nor was likely to make, proselytes among the respectable classes of our people. In this, however, I was mistaken.[25]

Mistaken indeed.

That same year, Garrison joined Simeon Jocelyn and Arthur Tappan as the only white men to attend the first national black convention in Philadelphia. The following year, addressing the second annual convention, Garrison gave witness to the continued importance of temperance in his vision of social reform.

God is my witness that, great as is my detestation of slavery and the foreign slave trade, I had rather be a slaveholder—yea a kidnapper on the African coast—than sell this poison to my fellow-creatures for common consumption. Since the creation of the world there has been no tyrant like INTEMPERANCE, and no slaves so cruelly treated as his.[26]

In this address, Garrison anticipated an argument of equivalence between chattel slavery and intemperance that would resonate with many white evangelicals. As shocking as this claim about intemperance made in front of former slaves may seem now, it came from a man who was more outraged about slavery and racism than any of his white contemporaries, and it serves as a reminder that the fiercest white advocates for racial equality held the sins of the flesh like intemperance and sexual lust as equal to and very much like chattel slavery in their capacity to imprison free moral agents.

White abolitionists saw a moral equivalence because they viewed intemperance as enslaving the free moral agency of the individual. The right to freedom rested on the right to moral autonomy, the right to respond freely to the word of God and the movement of the Holy Spirit. From the perspective of radical reform, chattel slavery and intemperance equally robbed individuals of that freedom. It enslaved them to the desires of man, placing an obstacle between man and God.

The next year, with Arthur Tappan's money, Garrison published *Thoughts on Colonization.* In this pamphlet he pulled together all his arguments against the national society and its scheme of expatriation, concluding that white America's sin of racial hatred was perpetuated rather than ameliorated by the mission of the American Colonization Society. Within months, Garrison's writings were cast as far west as Hudson, Ohio, where at the Congregationalist Western Reserve College, President Charles Storr, professor of sacred literature Beriah Green, and professor of mathematics Elizur Wright, Jr., encountered them as a clarion call.

Elizur Wright, Jr.: "A Revolution of the Soul"

Elizur Wright, Jr., was a leading member of the transplanted New England culture in northern Ohio.[27] In his response to Garrison's attacks on colonization, Wright exemplified the radical temperament of the descendents of Puritans who quested for a second "errand into the wilderness."[28] Wright was born in 1804 in South Canaan, Connecticut. His family arrived in Connecticut in the late seventeenth century. His father was a farmer with a sizeable freehold in Connecticut. The senior Elizur was a man of high standing in South Canaan, and as was typical for the period, his social position mixed religious, civic, and political responsibilities. Like his father before him, the senior Elizur was a deacon of the local Congregationalist church. He was a graduate of Yale, a community schoolteacher, a justice of the peace, a member of the Federalist Party, and a town representative in the state assembly. In all, he was a successful and influential member of New England's pious yeomanry and standing order.

In 1810, he left all this behind. It is likely that he knew the days of the covenanted community in South Canaan and his independence as farmer were numbered. Elizur, Sr., sold his four hundred acres in Connecticut, purchased three thousand acres in Ohio, and moved his family and their possessions along hundreds of miles of rudimentary roads away from a comfortable stone house to a rustic cabin. The Wright family, like so many other New Englanders, sought to preserve their way of life as independent farmers by moving west. With the disappearance of arable land, a depressed economy, and soaring real estate values in the East, Elizur, Sr., could not hope to duplicate for his family what his father had done for him in Connecticut. The Wrights were not alone when they set out to the remote reaches of the U.S. frontier. They moved along with many of their neighbors and settled on a tract of land purchased by a native of South Canaan who sold parcels to residents of their county back in Connecticut. The Wrights were part of a much larger emigration that emptied much of New England's population into western New York and northern Ohio. Typical of this greater pattern of emigration, the Wrights moved as part of a community.[29]

The first community establishment in the new settlement in Ohio was a church. David Bacon, the father of Leonard Bacon, was its minister. Located at the center of the five-square-mile tract, at the crossroads of the major roads, and supported by a tax on each parceled acre, this Congregationalist church replicated the Connecticut tradition of joining community politics and religion. Elizur, Sr., reestablished his Connecticut role of community leader and deacon. The community also established a school that Elizur, Jr., attended along with a handful of other children including Leonard Bacon. Bacon and Wright grew up together under the same social circumstances. As they entered adulthood, their life trajectories looked quite similar. They both seemed destined to be orthodox ministers.[30]

Rich in land, the Wrights were nonetheless strapped for disposable resources, and sacrificed greatly to keep ties with New England. Keeping these ties included preparing Elizur, Jr., for a Yale education and paying for it. In New Haven, Wright encountered a diverse world foreign to his father's New England and to Ohio. Yale's student body in the 1820s became truly national.[31] It included some boys from pious and modest yeomen homes like his, but also the children from wealthy New England, Middle Atlantic, and southern families. At Yale, Wright clashed with the aristocratic attitudes of his southern classmates. His life-defining struggle against slavery was prefigured here. In conflicts over alcohol consumption, hooliganism, and a student tax, Wright banded with fellow children of northern evangelical families to counter what he saw as the moral flabbiness of southern patricians and wealthy merchants. A paradigm of "Yankee saint" and "Southern sinner" took root early in his experiences in the national setting of Yale.[32]

In this his first moral reform campaign, Wright and his pious classmates sided with institutional authority. They banded together to cooperate with school officials in rooting out students guilty of misconduct. Like so many of the activists of his generation, the institutional setting of his education was transformative. It was here that Wright first experienced a wide and intragenerational Christian brotherly love. In moral campaigns and revivals at Yale, he discovered his powers of speech and moral persuasion. He also discovered the thrill of solidarity in moral duty against threats and intimidation. At Yale he began a lifelong career of exposing sinners to public admonishments.

After Yale, Wright planned to enroll at Andover Theological Seminary. In 1826, short on funds, he became a schoolteacher at Groton Academy in Massachusetts and began saving for Andover's tuition. As a teacher for a Congregationalist school, Wright became embroiled in the conflict between Unitarians and Congregationalists that was roiling the state's churches. In 1820, the Massachusetts Supreme Court handed down the Dedham decision establishing that the parish, not the church, had the right to select ministers and held legal title to church property. In the 1820s, Massachusetts's taxpayers continued to support their local Congregationalist churches. The Dedham decision placed church authority in the hands of the parish, which included all taxpayers and wrested control from the more select group of church communicants—that is, those who had passed tests of faith put to them by other church members, the heirs of the Puritan tradition of "visible saints."[33] As a result of the decision, many churches passed from Trinitarian or orthodox Congregationalist control to Unitarian control. When the wider parish population was given the right to choose between liberal Unitarians and abstemious Trinitarians, it often elected the former. By 1830, orthodox congregations were forced to forfeit six hundred thousand dollars worth of ecclesiastical property.

For the first time in Massachusetts, orthodoxy's control over community resources was in doubt. In Groton, Wright was witness and party to this struggle. He lived with a Trinitarian minister, John Todd, who lost his pulpit by the popular vote of the parish to Unitarians. Todd was forced to set up an independent church without state funds. Wright was closely involved in the formation of the new church. In 1827, Todd opened a new meetinghouse and a seceding congregation was formed. On January 3, Lyman Beecher made the trip from Boston to Groton and preached the ordination sermon for the new church. Wright worshiped Beecher at the time: "The Unitarians shrink before him like mice before a lion."[34]

In the late 1820s, although still very committed to orthodoxy, as evidenced by his active part in the struggle against Unitarians in Groton, Wright began to lose his conviction that he had been called to the ministry. Wright had little patience for the metaphysical intricacies of theology and hated the tedium of learning Hebrew. In the summer of 1828, he was faced with a career choice. He disliked teaching and to complicate matters had fallen in love. Enrolling at Andover would mean three years of separation from his new love, Susan Clark. This combination of love and misgivings about his ministerial calling derailed Wright's plan to train for the ministry. Religion remained a central interest, but his enthusiasm for the pulpit waned.

Wright postponed the decision and took a one-year position in the ranks of organized benevolence. He became a colporteur for the American Tract Society in western Pennsylvania. Working for the tract society amounted to a halfway compromise with his previous ministerial aspirations: something of a surrogate ministry. Writing to his fiancée from Pittsburgh, Wright conveyed a heroic figure. "Last Monday early in the morning *your* tract agent set out from his western home—well mounted, equipped with a large pair of saddle bags, stuffed with tracts and wearables, &c.—now he is writing to you in the public room of a crowded hotel in the noisiest of all cities."[35] He was responsible for a depository in Pittsburgh and the distribution of tracts for the surrounding region. Wright's agency was part of the American Tract Society's emerging national strategy of "general supply." Wright zealously committed himself "till the work be done, which is putting at least one tract in every home west of the Alleghanies." Contrasting his role as tract agent with the limited influence of teaching, Elizur wrote Susan, "but here if I succeed, it is to affect the destinies of multitudes to all ages, reclaiming them from degrading [illegible] of sin to that of living in true God."[36]

Wright left the American Tract Society after less than a year of work, but in that short period he distributed over fifty thousand pages of tracts and formed twenty auxiliary societies. He traveled widely among the poorer residents of western Pennsylvania and received an introduction to worlds and lives remote from the orthodox culture that had shaped his youth. The work was arduous and lonely as he expressed to Susan: "If you had been floating about as long as I have in an ocean of strangers you would feel the worth of a letter as you *cannot* now.—You would grasp it like a plank sent to save you from drowning."[37] As a tract agent, Wright pursued an evangelical mission distinct from the ministry: a specialized mission that was focused and practical but expansive not parochial. In the end, like the ministry, Wright did not feel called to devote his life to organized benevolence. Early in 1829, Wright was offered an opportunity to teach math at Western Reserve College, located near to his family's home. He accepted this offer not because he felt called but because he was eager to begin a family. Susan Clark and Elizur Wright, Jr., were married that year, and Susan moved to the Wrights' hometown of Hudson, Ohio.

Western Reserve was an orthodox evangelical college. Elizur Wright, Sr., was a founder and trustee. In this northeastern corner of Ohio, organized benevolence garnered considerable support. This included support for the American Colonization Society. The Wrights were morally opposed to slavery and supporters of colonization. On the Fourth of July, 1829, the same day Garrison addressed a meeting of colonization supporters in Boston, Elizur Wright, Jr., delivered his own talk endorsing African colonization. A few days before the event he wrote Susan, "only think of me shouting on the fourth of July from a stump while the pigs are playing with the children." He described the event as "something like an address;" the local paper pronounced it a success.[38]

Wright was in good company at the college with his antislavery sentiments. The president of Western Reserve, Charles Storr, and fellow faculty member Beriah Green were both outspoken advocates of antislavery and colonization. Among the evangelical Calvinists of this region, antislavery sentiment was solid but uncritical of the idea of colonization. As late as 1831, Elizur, Jr., and his father had worked together on behalf of the American Colonization Society. This support came to an abrupt end that year with the arrival of William Lloyd Garrison's newspaper and its call to immediatism.

The writings of Garrison appeared in Ohio almost immediately after they did in the East. Wright was reading the *Liberator* in 1831 and received a copy of *Thoughts on Colonization* a month after it had appeared in

Boston and New York. There is no record that Wright had a religious conversion experience, but his conversion to immediatism was clearly religious. Preparing for the ministry and working as an agent for organized benevolence, Wright was looking for but had failed to find a soul-stirring vocation. He found it in immediate abolitionism. He described his adoption of immediatism as "an entire change of thought and feeling, a revolution of the soul." What first stirred his heart was guilt. "When I look a little backward and remember my own apathy while my eyes rested on scenes that were enough to move stones to pity, I am covered with shame."[39]

The conversion was not instantaneous but it evolved rapidly. It involved a short period of wrestling with the truth as it was presented by Garrison's writings: "[T]he more I was troubled with his great principles—the more sick was I of that flexible expediency on which I say my own cause was based. In short, I burned up my colonizationism." With his heart changed, Garrison's immediatism seemed to Wright to compare with colonization as "religious sincerity" did to "hypocrisy."[40]

Exactly why Wright was disposed to embrace Garrison's message as a sacred calling is difficult to answer, but immediate abolitionism tapped visceral feelings of guilt. His work as a tract agent suggests that he was looking for a religiously inspired cause to assist the disadvantaged. In a letter to Susan, he confessed that he was deeply moved by the popular messages of the tracts he distributed. Included in his saddlebags were popular and implicitly antislavery tracts like number 92, *The Praying African: An Authentic Narrative,* distributed in the American Tract Society's national campaign of general supply. It tells of an encounter by a man journeying on business through the western part of New York with a devout slave. The story begins when the narrator stops at an inn to "put up for the Sabbath." Venturing out to find a place of solitude to pray, he happens upon a black woman praying to God for herself and her master:

> I listened, and was struck with astonishment, to hear one of the sable daughters of Ethiopia, in the most importunate manner, raising her prayer to God. Never before did I witness such simplicity, such fervour, such engagedness.

She prayed for her cruel master.

> *O Lord, bless my master. When he calls upon thee to damn his soul, do not hear him, do not hear him, but hear me—save him—make him know he his wicked, and he will pray to thee.* For herself, she said, *I am afraid, O Lord, I have wished*

him bad wishes in my heart—keep me from wishing him bad—though he whips me and beats me sore, tell me of my sins, and make me pray more to thee—make me more glad for what thou hast done for me, a poor Negro.[41]

These patronizing and often bigoted tracts nonetheless eroded the justification of slavery on very personal and moral grounds. Although the tracts did not say it, the readers could scarcely fail to conclude that it was indefensible to hold God's children in bondage.

Almost immediately after encountering Garrison's message, Wright along with Beriah Green and Charles Storr led the first college rebellion against the mainstream of organized benevolence on the issue of slavery. In the following few years, the students from orthodox schools like Lane Seminary and Andover Academy followed suit. Western Reserve College was unique in that faculty and the president initiated the organizing for immediatism and took a stand against the board of trustees by refusing to desist. The trustees of Western Reserve College moved to silence the call for immediate abolition. Charles Storr died soon after the immediate abolitionists organized the students, Wright moved to New York to become the corresponding secretary for the newly formed American Anti-Slavery Society, and Beriah Green was eventually run out of the school and moved to lead the Oneida Institute. But the damage was done. News had spread, and the controversy started to envelop one orthodox institution after another in the North. For example, on August 21, 1833, David Kimball, Jr., wrote Wright the following:

> All that is wanting is that some influential individual or individuals would come in here and . . . Old Andover may be converted. The heresy is spreading rapidly thro' this county. There is no danger that the Colonizationists will subjugate this rebellious population.[42]

The most important outcome of the conversions to immediatism at Western Reserve College may have been its influence on Finney's prized protégé, leader of the Lane Rebellion.

Theodore Weld: "Trouble the Dead Water of My Stagnant Soul"

In the fall of 1832, Theodore Weld came to Hudson as a stop along a tour of the West, north and south, to raise funds and awareness for two evangelical causes: temperance and manual labor. Western Reserve College was implementing the principles of manual labor, as were other evangelical schools at the time. Weld, a young man of considerable renown for his part in Finney's Rochester revival, met Wright and encountered the growing impulse for immediate abolition, an impulse he would augment with his own revivalistic fervor. Antislavery was not new to Weld. His patron and adoring friend, the Englishman Charles Stuart, had already impressed on him the evils of slavery; but when he arrived in Hudson, he had not *felt* it an immediate duty to renounce slavery as always and everywhere a sin.

Weld was one year younger than Wright, and like him he was also born in Connecticut.[43] His father, a graduate from Harvard in the years before it was captured by Unitarians, was a minister of the Congregationalist church in the village of Hampton. His father's lineage in America went back just about as far as a white man's can. It went back to Thomas Welde who arrived in the Bay Colony in 1632. On his mother's side, the lineage included none other than Jonathan Edwards. Both of Weld's grandfathers were ministers. His upbringing was typical for his social position of high status but modest means. Although his mother tempered the moral discipline of their Puritan forebears with a measure of loving affection, the anxious Calvinist call of the "saint" haunted Theodore.

He was raised to be independent and to find his own calling, but from his earliest days, the expectation was that he too would become a minister. Weld's father embodied that calling. Ludovicus was a typical eighteenth-century orthodox minister, unfortunately placed in the nineteenth century. He presided over a settled pulpit that he expected to hold until his death. Ludovicus was a community leader, and he and his family lived under the pressure of this status. Like most of his congregants, he was also a farmer. At an early age, he saddled his son with considerable responsibility for the family farm.

Theodore was the product of the steady habits of Connecticut Yankees. Like Elizur Wright, he was educated in preparation for the ministry. He attended Andover where he discovered and developed his prodigious skills as an orator. To earn money, he toured the neighboring towns lecturing on the "science" of mnemonics. Success at the local level led to greater ambition. It also sowed seeds of doubt about being called to the ministry. In Hartford, Weld impressed Thomas Gallaudet, principal of the American Asylum; in Litchfield, he impressed the Reverend Lyman Beecher. Weld secured letters of recommendation from both and used them as credentials as he moved his lecture tour from town to town. From 1822 to 1825, Weld traveled America's growing network of turnpikes and new canals bringing the "science" of mnemonics to the instant cities, farm towns, and new schools of the expanding nation. During these years he found the freedom of the road and the pleasing yet disturbing pride evoked by adoring crowds. All the while, he made little headway in his studies at Andover.

In 1825, his father resigned his pulpit in Hampton. Ludovicus's ministry had come to an unhappy end. As he grew old, his congregation proved neglectful and desirous of a youthful replacement. The covenanted community of the eighteenth century that married clergy and congregation for life had come to a close. A mobile, market society disrupted even the steady habits of Hampton, Connecticut. His pulpit ceased to be an office for life and became a competitive professional post. Ludovicus moved to Fabius, New York, to be close to his wife's family and live out the remainder of his life in retirement. Theodore decided to quit Andover and enroll in nearby Hamilton College. The move placed Weld in the middle of a fast current of cultural and economic activity channeled through that region by the newly completed Erie Canal. His father was disappointed and wished he had stayed at Andover, the educational bulwark of orthodoxy.

The following year, Finney's revival work in Utica caught the attention of the young Weld at nearby Hamilton. His initial reaction was disdain. "My father," he told fellow students at Hamilton, "was a real minister of the Gospel, grave and courteous, and an honor to the profession. This man is not a minister, and I will never acknowledge him as such."[44] But as the end to his father's tenure in Hampton suggested, there were few places left for "real" ministers, and, insofar as his father represented the ministerial calling to Weld, that calling was growing faint in the hustle and bustle of the Erie Canal. Weld's aunt, Sophia Clark, a founding member of the benevolent society that first commissioned Finney as an itinerant preacher and a leading resident of Utica, had already been touched by the revival spirit, and she conspired with Finney to bring Weld into the enthusiasm. They tricked Weld into attending an unscheduled sermon delivered by Finney. The sermon, "One Sinner Destroyeth Much Good," was directed right at Weld, and he felt publicly humiliated. The next day the two encountered each other in a store in Utica, and Weld berated the minister in public. That night, Weld was tormented by guilt. The following evening, on his own accord, he attended Finney's revival meeting. According to Finney, Weld "got up" and asked "if he might make confession."

> I told him Yes, and he made public confession before the whole congregation. He said it became him to remove the stumbling-block which he had cast before the whole people; and he wanted opportunity to make the most

public confession he could. He did make a very humble, earnest, broken-hearted confession.[45]

For the next year, Weld worked as Finney's lieutenant promoting revivals in booming upstate New York.

In this revival work, Weld worked not only to capture souls but also evangelical institutions. Weld's charisma as a public speaker made him a powerful adjunct in this battle. During this period, Weld developed an interest in a number of benevolent causes including most notably temperance and manual labor. He saw these causes as part of the revival campaign. Temperance was a challenge to an orthodox clergy set in its tippling ways. Manual labor was a challenge to the cold, bookish traditions of orthodox seminaries. By integrating vigorous physical activity into the educational course of religious training, "new measure" evangelicals sought to curb the supposed debilitating affects of a life devoted to mental labor and provide a cheap means for establishing new schools. Implicit in this challenge was the opposition between learned orthodox ministers and the practical and plain approach of new measure revivals—yet another echo of the eighteenth-century Great Awakening.[46]

Shortly after his conversion under Finney, Weld left Hamilton College for the Oneida Institute in Whitesboro just outside of Utica, a pioneer school in the manual labor program. Hamilton's faculty and board of trustees had come out against Finney, and Oneida established itself as an alternative for those friendly to the new measures. Weld's conversion at the hands of Finney meant much more than a spiritual rebirth. It put him at the center of a cultural battle between evangelicals. By the late 1820s, he had chosen sides, repudiated much of his father's orthodox ways, and become an active partisan.

It is also in Utica that Weld met Charles Stuart, an Englishman and abolitionist. Stuart witnessed Weld's public confession, and the two of them from 1826 to the spring of 1827 worked directly with Finney. In Stuart, Weld found a companion who unashamedly entrusted him with his soul. Their letters to each other contain a loving affection relatively new to the emotional culture of Yankee evangelicals. The brotherly love between Stuart and Weld, expressed in the following letter, was something Weld would bring with him and spread among the students of Lane Seminary in the early 1830s.

If agre[e]able to you, let *Sun-rise* be our time of heart meeting. This will probably approximate us as much in *time* as may be practicable amidst the diversity

of hours, of light, and darkness, which overspreads society; and it is not to the
formal act of retiring or bending the knee that we wish to resort to; but the
spontanious Swell mutually, of sacred and kindred feeling, seeking to bear each
other and those we love to the footstool of the Glorious Majesty![47]

This loving kindness was of a temperament alien to the orthodox religion
of his father, which retained too much of the Calvinist anxiety to let itself
go in such sweet sentiment. As Ludovicus once admitted to his son hurt-
ing from feelings of paternal neglect, "I have ever found it easier to write
sermons than letters."[48]

In these days of revival excitement, the loving kingdom of Christ was displacing the harsher judgments of the Old Testament God, and this opened
a rift between the emerging reform cosmology of evangelicals like Weld
and the orthodox worldview of his father's generation. In the late 1820s,
this inchoate cosmology still seemed to be pointing Weld in the direction
of the ministry. Or, at least, that is what Stuart was encouraging in 1828:

> Often my beloved Theodore, does my soul turn to you and contemplate you with
> solemn affection; sometimes it trembles for you. Dearest Theodore, it says, do
> not, on any account or for any considerations overlook the main object of your
> residence at Whitesboro', your studious preparation for the Gospel ministry,
> and the great object of all human existence, an humble, wise and faithful walk
> with God to His glory; and whenever you find that local calls or duties interfere
> with these, cast them off without hesitation, pursuing steadily and in love your
> own more immediate calling.[49]

But Weld was having doubts that he was walking in God's glory.

Only two years after his conversion, Weld complained of his own spiritual declension. In a letter written in April of 1828 as Finney was preaching
in Philadelphia and building his national reputation, Weld voiced fear.

> My wretched cold heart hardly rejoices at all at the glorious conquests of the
> Lord Jesus in Phila. 'Tis true—I know it—and with shame and confusion of face,
> confess it. I do feel a something that the Devil would have me *call joy,* but it de-
> serves not even the nickname; it just moves over the soul's surface but so gently
> as scarsely to ruffle it. Oh for that joy *unspeakable,* that full-of-glory-joy, that
> would stir the sluggish spirit and trouble the dead water of my stagnant soul.[50]

He would not find that joy in the ministry or in revivals. Instead, particular causes like temperance and manual labor seized more and more of

his religious attention. By the early 1830s, Finney expressed concern that Weld's particular commitments were distracting him from the main object of religious revivals. Stuart's letters, on the other hand, began to acknowledge that social reforms like antislavery and temperance might be a more immediate calling than religious revival. In a letter written in the spring of 1831, Stuart asked Weld, "How is your soul?" He wrote that he longed "to hear" that Weld was "engaged in the Sacred cause of Negro emancipation." Stuart no longer seemed concerned with obstacles to the ministry but excited in the specific reform causes that vied for Weld's attention and commitment.

> Let me hear from you—about you—about Finney—Revivals—Temperance "Joe"—The Negroes—The missionaries and Indians in Georgia—The Colonization Society—The free coloured people—your family—Oneida Academy etc., and write *plainly,* and ever believe me your ardently and tenderly attached.[51]

After Finney's Rochester revival, Weld's name was widely associated with the temperance cause, and he was in high demand as a public speaker. In Whitestown, New York, he was mobbed for the first of many times to come when trying to organize a temperance society. He was earning his stripes as a radical reformer. Weld had also made a number of powerful contacts through his work with Finney and at the Oneida Institute. At Oneida he came in contact with the Tappan family. Lewis Tappan had enrolled his two sons at Oneida on the suggestion of Finney. There they fell under the care of Weld, their "Monitor General," and were converted under his influence. Impressed with Oneida and with Weld, Lewis agreed to form a society to promote Oneida's manual labor program and paid for Weld to travel as its agent.

In 1832, with the munificence of the Tappan family to support him, Weld launched a lecturing tour across the Northwest and Southwest. Preaching manual labor and temperance, this tour brought him into contact with emerging leaders of immediate abolitionism. In October of that year, he visited Wright, Beriah Green, and Charles Storr in Hudson, Ohio, to discuss their college's manual labor program. Weld's biographer, Robert Abzug, convincingly argues that Weld was converted to immediatism during this stay. Letters between Wright and Weld shortly after this visit support the claim. On December 7, 1832, Wright wrote Weld, "I will plead no apology for calling your attention to a subject which I trust is daily, of itself, gaining a larger place in your thoughts." Wright related that Beriah

Green had "come out nobly," lately preaching on abolition from Isaiah 58 in the neighboring town of Tallmadge—the same biblical text on atonement that Garrison had drawn from when he started to make his abolitionist break a few years earlier. Wright then pressed Weld to make a deeper moral commitment to the antislavery cause:

> Often I have thought that if Providence had fu[rnished] me as it has Brother Weld, I would devote myself as a [word mutilated—*EDS*] advocate in the cause of our persecuted colored brethren—[the] great trial cause of human rights; but in my circumstances I feel clear to stick to our beloved college, and act through it as long as possible. Should the storm that now seems to be gathering, or any other cause, drive me off, I should rejoice to be deemed worthy to exert a more direct influence in favor of *immediate, universal emancipation.* This is the doctrine of the Savior, and *must be* preached, from one end of the land to the other, tho' the very "Stars of Heaven" should be shaken by it.
>
> What would benevolent men in N. York think of a convention on this subject, about the time of the anniversaries next spring? My wife wishes a place in your remembrances—would like of all things, she says, to hear you plead the cause of the slave. May the God who commands *temperance,* righteousness, and godliness bless you.[52]

Weld's response made clear that Wright had gotten a hold of his conscience, and he too was "coming out" for immediate abolition.

> I have just returned to this City [New York] after an absence of five weeks and have this moment read your letter of the 7th Dec. I long to write you a whole sheet-letter but when I tell you that I have now on my table more than sixty letters (according to Mr. Tappans counting) and have as yet read but half a dozen of them, you will forgive me for making my words few. And Firstly and mostly: Abolition *immediate universal* is my desire and prayer to God; and as long as I am a moral agent I am fully prepared to *act out* my belief in that thus saith the Lord—*"Faith without WORKS is dead."*
>
> Since I saw you my soul has been in travail upon that subject. I hardly know how to contain myself. If I was not positively pledged for two or three years to come, and if I had finished my education, I would devote myself to the holy work, come life or death.[53]

As the coming months would confirm, Weld had discovered a moral campaign to stir his "stagnant soul."

Weld's pledged commitments included participating in the founding of Lane Seminary just outside of Cincinnati, Ohio, on the manual labor principle. Weld secured Arthur Tappan's financial support for the new seminary and sought to enlist Finney as its president. Finney declined but Lyman Beecher, now reconciled with the new measure revivals, accepted. Leaving his pulpit in Boston, he told his congregants, "If we gain the West all is safe; if we lose it, all is lost."[54] Beecher, like Weld and so many other Americans, saw the future of the nation to be decided in the Ohio River Valley. With Tappan's money, Beecher's name, and its location just outside the Queen City, Lane Seminary immediately assumed national prominence among prorevivalist Presbyterians and Congregationalists. Beecher wanted to hire Weld as a professor, but in his characteristic aversion to anything that might smack of vainglory, Weld chose to enroll as a student. He brought with him twenty-four classmates from Oneida, more than half of the inaugural class. As student or faculty member, it mattered not, Weld was destined to lead the school and its students. Beecher considered Weld a genius, but feared his fellow students thought him a "God."[55]

From the start, the seminary suffered grave trials. Evangelicals of the 1830s still saw the hand of God in every disaster and every delivery from harm. In 1832 on his travels as an itinerant agent, Weld had "miraculously" survived a deadly stagecoach accident. He, his friends, and family saw in this deliverance a confirmation that God intended Weld to be his instrument. In the summer of 1833, an epidemic of cholera visited the seminary. For ten days, almost without sleep, Weld tended to the sick. A few died, one damned, the others saved. If the student body was not completely devoted to Weld before this point, they were after. The next trial would be for the cause of the slave.

In New York, Wright had joined forces with Arthur Tappan, and a national antislavery society was formed around Garrison's call for immediate abolition. Battle lines were being drawn between this new abolition society and the American Colonization Society. In this context, Weld suggested a debate on the merits of the Colonization Society among the Lane students. For eighteen evenings, the matter was discussed. The event took less the form of a debate than a protracted revival meeting with a series of testimonials. Eight of the eighteen speakers were born and raised in slave states. In the end, they all made public confessions renouncing slavery and colonization. At the end of the "debate," the entire student body, save a handful that refused to attend, renounced their support of colonization and confessed themselves to immediate abolition.[56]

A letter from Weld to Lewis Tappan written in the early spring of 1834 provides a capsule of the events.

> The Lord has done great things for us here. Eight months ago there was not a single immediate abolitionist in this seminary. Many students were from slave states, and some of them the most influential and intelligent in the institution. A large colonization society existed, and abolitionism was regarded as the climax of absurdity, fanaticism and blood.
>
> The first change was brought about in some of the first minds in the seminary, and especially in an individual of great sway among the students, who was from Alabama; born, bred, and educated in the midst of slavery; his father an owner of slaves, and himself heir to a slave inheritance. After some weeks of inquiry, and struggling with conscience, *his noble soul broke loose from its shackles*. He is now President of our Anti-Slavery Society.[57]

Born again as immediate abolitionists, most everything in the lives of these Lane rebels crystallized around the battle against the sin of slavery. Few, if any, of the students at Lane had ever doubted that slavery was evil, but they had never felt it a personally punishable sin—they had never felt it as *immediate*. As the historian Gilbert Barnes described the impact of the Lane debate, it meant "more than a change of opinion; for scores of the students it meant *a change in their lives*."[58] Wary of the hostile response from the residents of Cincinnati, local members of the board of trustees moved to silence the students' antislavery pronouncements and ban their activities. Refusing to renounce their new confession, virtually the entire student body withdrew from the school. Many of them, following Weld, became agents for the new American Anti-Slavery Society.

James Birney: "Your Trials Are Touchstones of God's Promises"

News of the Lane Rebellion attracted great attention in evangelical circles. Most prominent among those affected was James Gillespie Birney, a leading agent of the American Colonization Society. At the time of the rebellion, Birney was suffering misgivings about the practicality and principles of colonization. A few years earlier, in 1832, he was visited by Weld at his then home in Huntsville, Alabama, on the same tour that took Weld to Hudson, Ohio. At that point, Birney was in the middle of deciding to abandon his successful law practice to assume a full-time position as agent to the American Colonization Society for the Southwest. Weld had then encouraged him to follow his heart on the importance of working against slavery. Now in 1834, Weld pressed Birney again on his convictions. Weld's loving pressure convinced Birney of what he had suspected: Colonization had to be repudiated. There could be no quarter with the sin of slavery; it demanded immediate abolition; anything less was sinful.

James Gillespie Birney's father arrived in Philadelphia from Ireland in 1784.[59] The family of James Birney, Sr., can be traced back to the De Birneys who immigrated to England from France in the fifteenth century. Three brothers of the clan accompanied Cromwell to Ireland and established a family homestead at Cotehill, County Cavan. It was from there that James, Sr., ran away to America. Four years later, with modest savings, he ventured west to Danville, Kentucky, setting up a bagging and rope manufactory. He proved a very successful shopkeeper. He married Martha Reed against the wishes of her father, a man also from Ireland and of considerable prominence in Danville. The senior Birney and his wife's father, John Reed, were soon reconciled. Before Martha died five years into the marriage, she gave birth to two children, James and Nancy. Left alone to parent two children, the father sent for his widowed sister back in Ireland for help. Accompanying Mrs. Doyle from Ireland were two more sisters with their husbands and children. Together the clan lived in a Georgian-style mansion just outside of Danville built by James Birney, Sr. Here James, Jr., spent his childhood among his many cousins and Michael, a child slave gifted to him by his maternal grandfather.

At age eleven, James Gillespie was packed off to boarding school, Transylvania University in Lexington. It is in Lexington that Birney encountered the antislavery teachings of Robert Hamilton Bishop, a member of the school's faculty. Back home, during school recesses and for a longer period of preparation to enroll at the College of New Jersey in Princeton, Birney encountered other expressions of antislavery sentiment. Both his father and grandfather had supported the admission of Kentucky to the Union as a free state. The delegates they backed to the state constitutional convention all pledged to vote for an emancipation clause. The Birneys were also attracted to antislavery elements within the religious community of Danville. Most prominent were Rev. David Rice, a Presbyterian, and Rev. David Barrow, a Baptist. The Birneys had close contact with both ministers and undoubtedly considered slavery an evil.

Birney's father and grandfather nonetheless held slaves. They counseled benevolent treatment of blacks until the state legislature devised a plan to rid Kentucky of the burden of slavery. Aunt Doyle, Birney's surrogate mother, was more resolute in her antislavery and refused to own a fellow human being. In 1808, the sixteen-year-old Birney arrived at Princeton, New Jersey. That year Congress banned the importation of slaves and slavery was a hot issue, North and South. At Princeton, Birney encountered liberal arguments of the unity of the human race and of the environmental conditioning of the differences between the races. Here he mingled with the children of distinguished families from the South, New England, and the Middle Atlantic. Birney excelled academically at Princeton but was suspended twice for disciplinary purposes. He had a taste for "spirituous liquors." In spite of running afoul of school rules, he graduated with honors.

After Princeton, Birney's father arranged for him to read law with Alexander J. Dallas, a prominent lawyer in Philadelphia. Dallas was counsel to the great. His clients included Jefferson, Madison, and Monroe. His house had been the refuge of Aaron Burr after he fatally wounded Alexander Hamilton in a duel. Birney was being groomed for a distinguished public life. Accordingly, his family afforded him the life of a gentleman in the cultural capital of the new republic. These were also the years of the second war against Great Britain, and, in a climate of charges of sedition, Birney's apprenticeship dealt with more than the mundane cases of property law. In Philadelphia, he met James Forten, a free African American who had made a fortune as a sail maker. Forten was active in antislavery and had received schooling at the Quaker school of the abolitionist Anthony Benezet. Birney made other Quaker contacts in Philadelphia suggesting that the slavery issue remained prominent in his life. In 1814, with Dallas headed to Washington to fulfill his appointment as secretary of the treasury, Birney went back to Kentucky as a lawyer with the best possible credentials.

In his hometown of Danville, Birney's family connections and grooming translated into immediate success. He became the lawyer for a bank established by his father and two partners. In 1815, he stumped for an old family friend, Henry Clay, and began to make a name for himself in the politics of Kentucky. That same year he met and courted Agatha McDowell. Their marriage in February 1816 was well received by both sides of the family. The Episcopalian Birneys and the Presbyterian McDowells did not differ over the union, but Agatha and James Birney worshiped together as Presbyterians. Both sides of the family gave the couple slaves as wedding gifts.

In the same year as his wedding, James Gillespie Birney was elected to the state legislature in Kentucky. Through contacts in Lexington, he planned the purchase of over three hundred acres in the Alabama Territory north of Huntsville. In 1818, Agatha and their son, James, Jr., joined Birney and his growing number of slaves in Alabama. Soon to be a state, Alabama afforded Birney the opportunity to establish himself as a distinguished planter and a politician, but he fared poorly in both ventures. In the process, cotton farming involved him more deeply in slavery. He added nineteen slaves to the twenty-four he brought from Kentucky. He and Agatha participated liberally in the cultural life of planters. They entertained lavishly and Birney took to reckless gambling and heavy drinking.

In politics, Birney proved too principled to be successful for statewide election. He refused to align himself with Andrew Jackson and remained out of step with the party politics of the southwestern frontier. Failed crops, the death of a new daughter, deep gambling debts, and failed election bids caused a broken Birney to sell his plantation and entrust all his slaves to an overseer—except for his lifelong slave Michael and his family, which he retained as servants. Together, the two families moved into the town of Huntsville, and Birney established a law practice.

His fall from planter and would-be politician to town lawyer was accompanied by a religious crisis and conversion. As Birney worked to establish a successful law practice, he deepened his commitment to religion and became active in the benevolent enterprises of the period. He became deeply involved in the Presbyterian Church, established a local and regional temperance society, supported the distribution of tracts, and worked as a lawyer against the removal of Cherokees from Georgia and Alabama. Birney also became involved in education: first working for the American Sunday School Union and later as recruitment agent for the University of Alabama. Under this capacity, in the summer of 1830, Birney traveled through the East to recruit faculty. His trip took him to Philadelphia, Princeton, New York, New Haven, and Boston. At each stop he met with leading academics and religious figures.

The following summer events caused Birney to despair of the future of the slave states. Nat Turner's revolt in Virginia and the beginnings of abolitionist agitation in the North prompted a harsh backlash against slaves and free blacks. In Alabama in the early 1830s, the number of African Americans equaled that of whites. Deeper south, the balance tilted toward the slaves. Birney feared that the situation would end in a bloodbath, and he grew uncomfortable with the influence the "slaveholding spirit" was having on his growing family. In 1832, Birney made plans to move to Illinois. He arranged to sell his property and wind down his law practice. A letter from Ralph R. Gurley arrested these plans. Gurley, president of the American Colonization Society, extended to Birney an offer of complete responsibility for the society's Southwest circuit. While Birney was weighing his options, Theodore Weld arrived in Huntsville on his tour to generate support for manual labor and temperance. Weld and Birney met and spoke of slavery. A letter from Weld following their meeting indicates that Birney was struggling with his conscience on the great matter of slavery and his Christian duty:

> I can hardly tell you my dear brother how much I am interested in your decision upon the *great question* which you have under consideration. May the Lord direct you to such a result as shall magnify his name and greatly lighten the burden of human woe.[60]

Weld, writing before he visited Wright, encouraged Birney to accept Gurley's offer.

> Your present circumstances my dear brother, and the great question of personal disposal which occupies your mind, rests upon *my own individual concernment.* When I look at the great slave question, trace its innumerable and illimitable bearings upon the weal of the world, every year augmenting the difficulties, its dangers, its woe and its guilt, my heart aches with hope deferred, mocks all prescriptions and refuses to be comforted. I am ripe in the conviction that if the Colonization Society does not dissipate the horror of darkness which overhangs the southern country, we are undone. Light breaks *in from no other quarter.* I have very little doubt—in fact none at all—about your ultimate determination. May the Lord guide you into all truth and duty.[61]

This letter confirms that before Weld's visit with Wright he shared in the colonizationist view that the amelioration of slavery entailed removal of African Americans.

Birney decided to remain in the South and work for the American Colonization Society. His agency began with cautious optimism. He worked delicately with southern interests. He sought to dissuade slaveholders that colonization would incite unrest among the slaves. As immediatism gained strength in the North in 1833, he presented colonization as the South's only safe means to address the problem of slavery. He thought colonization could give slaveholders an acceptable route out of their painful predicament. His work proceeded in two directions: First, he planned for a well-publicized voyage of "return" for a large number of manumitted slaves. He thought the sight of Christian blacks "returning" to Africa as missionaries would make a favorable impression on slaveholders and the antislavery evangelicals of the North. Second, he also sought state support for colonization, lobbying legislators to commit funds to the American Colonization Society. Both ends met with frustration. He found free blacks generally reluctant to participate in colonization. His own slaves refused to participate in the mission to Liberia. Although he did successfully plan one shipload of "freed" blacks from New Orleans to Liberia, the mission did not have the intended effect. If anything it convinced him of the impracticality of colonization. He found legislators generally unwilling to commit support for colonization. He was politely received everywhere in the Southwest, but he generated little interest.

In 1834, Birney resigned his commission and moved back to Kentucky. In April, he visited Weld at Lane Seminary, and his conversion to immediatism began. Throughout the spring he struggled with his conscience over his duty. In June, Weld wrote him the following:

> My dear brother the Lord WILL help you—*we bear you on our hearts* in *constant* prayer—such trials as now afflict you are precious touchstones with which to test the heavenly gold of God's promises. Be of good courage and HE shall *strengthen thy heart. Wait* I say on the Lord. The God of the poor and needy will surely not forsake those who plead their cause. Cleave fast to Him my brother. Verily "More are they that be with *us* than those that be with *them.*" See Elisha's words to his servant. Adieu—*dear brother of my soul—May God speed thee.*[62]

Elisha's servant despaired when the soldiers of Syria surrounded him and his master in the city of Dothan. He asked his master, "What shall we do?" Elisha told him, "Fear not" because, as Weld wrote Birney, "there were more with them than with the Syrians." Elisha then prayed to God that he open his servant's eyes. *Awakened,* the servant saw the mountains alive with chariots of fire. The Syrians came no more to subjugate the land of Israel.[63]

In August, another letter from Weld indicated that Birney had awakened to immediatism and his period of trial had come to an end.

> My heart greatly rejoices at the news you give me of the relief from *peculiar trial.* "*Wait* on the Lord—be of good courage and He shall strengthen thine heart." How gloriously God is opening the door for you in Kentucky! Let us be ashamed of our unbelief. Trust in the Lord and DO GOOD.[64]

That same year Birney freed his slaves, formed the Kentucky Anti-Slavery Society, and wrote his influential and widely distributed "Letter on Colonization" renouncing that society and endorsing immediatism.

In the spring of 1835, Birney wrote Gerrit Smith—a prominent leader of organized benevolence, temperance, and the American Colonization Society about to come out for immediatism—of the transformation he experienced after publicly confessing himself an abolitionist:

> Altho' I am in the midst of enemies (tho' I must say, not *personal,* unless they
> have transferred their malignant feelings from the cause of freedom to its hum-
> ble advocate) and am often much perplexed, yet altogether I have never had
> so much peace—never before have I felt God to be a Help so present, or the
> character of the Savior, in his invariable holiness and constancy so altogether
> precious. Let my soul magnify the Lord![65]

The same year he established an antislavery newspaper in Cincinnati, the *Philanthropist.* He soon discovered—via threats like the ones made by the Alabama vigilante committee and riots that destroyed his press and menaced his home—that the anger of the enemies in his midst *was* personal. And so was Birney's commitment to the cause. In spite of the violence, he found peace in magnifying the Lord through the special lens of immediate abolition. As Wright described the commitment in a letter of the same year to Birney celebrating the conversion of Smith, in the immediatist move to "magnify the Lord," God had "thrust" abolitionists like Birney "into the very midst of *his* battlefield, filled with moral perils to be sure, yet to be yielded, living or dying, only with immortal honors."[66]

Sarah and Angelina Grimké: "The First Long Breath of Liberty Which My Imprisoned Spirit Dared to Respire"

Next to Birney, the most prominent southern converts to immediate abolitionism were two sisters from South Carolina, Sarah and Angelina Grimké.[67] Sarah was born in 1792, the sixth child and second daughter of Mary Smith Grimké. More than twelve years later, Angelina was born, the last of fourteen children Mary brought into the world in a space of twenty years. Two of the fourteen died in infancy and a third at a young age. Mary Smith came from a most distinguished South Carolina family.

Her ancestors included Thomas Smith, one of the earliest plantation holders in the Carolinas. Her line of American ancestors included two colonial governors. Her father was one of the richest men in South Carolina.
Mary's husband, Sarah and Angelina's father, John Faucheraud Grimké,
was similarly distinguished. He was a planter, slaveholder, legislator, and
judge. His ancestors were Huguenots and had settled in the Carolinas early in the eighteenth century. He was a decorated officer of the
American Revolution and rewarded richly for his service. The Grimkés
split their time between a Beaufort plantation and a Charleston mansion.
During the long summer season of fevers, the family fled the swampy
rice plantation for the high society of Charleston's planters and shippers.

   Sarah was particularly close to her brother Thomas, the secondborn.
Thomas was six years older than Sarah, but they played and learned together as children. Thomas graduated at the top of his class at the College of Charleston. When Sarah was twelve, just before Angelina's birth,
Thomas went off to Yale. Unlike her brother, Sarah received limited formal education, but she was well read. Thomas returned from New Haven
a convert from the religious revival led by that school's president, Timothy
Dwight. He wanted to be a minister, but his father's will prevailed and he
trained for the law. He became a prominent lawyer in Charleston. He was
also a generous philanthropist and very involved in benevolent causes. He
helped launch the American Peace Society and the American Colonization Society of South Carolina and supported temperance. He developed
a national reputation and was well respected by northern orthodox leaders
of benevolence. In his early years of public life, he was assisted by Sarah
in writing speeches and correspondences. As he grew older and independent, he left Sarah behind, trapped in a society that consigned women to a
culture of gaiety, vanity, and frivolity. Although her father recognized that
Sarah possessed a unique intellect, at least the equal of Thomas's, he saw
no future in it.

   As Thomas moved out of her life, Sarah found in her baby sister Angelina new purpose. Sarah became a surrogate parent for her beloved "Nina,"
and the latter returned her affection, referring to her as "Mother." At an
early age, both sisters were acutely sensitive to the suffering of the many
slaves that lived in their midst. Slaves attended to every detail of the daily
life of the members of the Grimké family. At a very early age, the Grimké
children took personal charge of their own slaves. In their diaries and
recollections, Sarah and Angelina report many experiences of sorrow and
horror over the harsh treatment of slaves. As evidenced by the response
of adults to Sarah and Angelina's upset, sensitive children recoiling from

the violence of slavery was not unusual. That these feelings of tenderness about the mistreatment of slaves persisted into adulthood and crystallized into a well-articulated moral outrage *was* unusual.

As Sarah became an adult, she refused to apply herself to the central ambition of the female circles she was confined to, attracting a husband. She turned against the elite culture of Charleston with its balls, races, and courtship games. As a young adult, she turned against the high church ways of her Episcopalian family and was converted in a Presbyterian revival. Religion was central to the Grimké family, and Sarah's commitment to Presbyterianism was not scandalous. It did indicate a level of religious devotion that was critical of the more relaxed mores of both her family and its social circle. Sarah's stepped-up religious devotion marked a growing alienation from elite Charleston and southern planter culture. Hers was an orthodox conversion taking place over many days of private conferences with the Reverend Kollock. Born again, she gave up novels, dancing, and the parties of genteel Carolinians substituting them for prayer meetings and the work of Christian benevolence.

When Sarah was twenty-six years old, her father became very sick. This illness provided a physical rupture in Sarah's life that allowed her to act on an emotional and moral distance that had been growing between her and the cultural milieu of her upbringing. In April 1819, Sarah traveled with her sick father to Philadelphia where he went under the care of a renowned surgeon.

Dr. Phillip Synge Physick, a Quaker, arranged for Sarah to stay at a Friends boardinghouse during her father's hospitalization. There was no known treatment for his illness. From Philadelphia, Sarah took her dying father to spend the summer at the Jersey shore and there, the two of them alone, waited for death. Of this time Sarah said, "our attachment became strengthened day by day. I regard this as the greatest blessing next to my conversion that I have ever received from God."[68] Gerda Lerner convincingly argues that on his deathbed Judge Grimké gave his daughter what he had denied her all her life—freedom and equality. He had long recognized her as brilliant. He is supposed to have said that if she had been born a boy she would have made the best lawyer in South Carolina. On the Jersey shore, maybe the dying father did give his daughter her due. Sarah, alone, with the help of a few strangers, buried her father, a distinguished southern planter, in a Methodist plot.

In mourning and traveling home to Charleston by boat, Sarah met a group of Quakers. Among them was Israel Morris, who gave her a copy of the journal of John Woolman—an eighteenth-century Quaker abolitionist.

Sarah had long hated slavery, but upon her return from Philadelphia she found living in a slave society "insupportable, it burst on my mind with renewed horror."[69] She spoke with her brother Thomas about the evils of slavery. He was no defender of the system, but to his mind emancipation could be achieved only though the gradual removal of the black population. The two races could not live side by side in a free society, the inferior next to the superior. Still in mourning and increasingly alone in South Carolina, Sarah turned Quaker. She read Woolman's journal and attended a Friends meeting in Charleston. She changed her dress to conform to the Friends standard of modesty and disdain for luxury. She made herself a stranger in her family's world. In a short time, she made the fateful and difficult decision to move to Philadelphia and join a community of Friends. It was a bold choice to leave her extended family and to live as a single woman with a despised sect.

Prior to Sarah's move north, Angelina refused confirmation in the Episcopalian Church. After reading the content of the pledge, she said she could not make it with a good conscience. Angelina soon became very active in the Presbyterian Church. She threw herself into the church. She taught at the Sunday school and led prayer meetings among her family's slaves. She even dared to teach her personal slave how to read.

Angelina developed a close relationship with her Presbyterian minister who shared her hatred of slavery, but he dared not voice his antislavery from the pulpit. He knew what the consequences would be if he challenged his slaveholding congregation. Angelina, young and naïve, did raise the issue of the evils of slavery to a meeting of the elders of her church. They handled her gently, letting her know that they understood her sympathies for the slave but also that she would understand with time why things were the way they were. Angelina was not appeased. She pressed her antislavery sentiments incessantly on her siblings and mother. She scolded family members for mistreatment of slaves and criticized her family's comfort with the slaveholding society of Charleston.

Alienated from church and family, Angelina felt on spiritual trial. On January 10, 1828, she made the following entry in her diary:

> This text rests much on my mind: "I have many things to say unto you, but you cannot hear them now." It does appear to me, & it has appeared so ever since I had a hope that there was a work before me to which all my other duties & trials were only preparatory. I have no idea what it is, & I may be mistaken, but it does seem that *if* I am obedient to the still small voice of Jesus in my heart

that he will lead into more difficult paths & cause me to glorify Him in a more honorable & trying work than any in which I have yet been engaged.[70]

Searching for divine purpose, Angelina followed her sister's lead and joined a small Quaker meeting in Charleston.

The following year, Sarah returned to Charleston to "save" Angelina. She brought her sister back with her to Philadelphia. Sarah and Angelina became very involved in a conservative Quaker meeting. Neither sister was very happy in the Philadelphia meeting. They both expressed uncertainty about their religious calling and frustration that they had not found a more satisfying path to glorify God. Sarah, painfully shy, aspired to the ministry, but she struggled to assert herself in this circle of Friends. Angelina, who never found difficulty in asserting herself in public, chafed at the group discipline the Friends expected.

Antislavery had led Sarah and Angelina to join the Society of Friends, but the meeting they joined in Philadelphia was not particularly aggressive on the issue. At their meeting, blacks had to sit on a bench in the back. These Friends likely supported colonization, but they did not support independent protest by members against slavery. In 1829, Sarah contributed money to the American Colonization Society. In the early 1830s, Sarah, Angelina, and their fellow Friends rejected the radical notions of immediate abolition Garrison was beginning to espouse. In 1834, Angelina's position changed.

A diary entry in May of that year reveals that she had discovered in abolition the "honorable & trying work" to glorify God that she had been in search of for years.

> Five months have elapsed since I wrote in this diary, since which time I have become deeply interested in the subject of abolition. I had long regarded this cause as utterly hopeless, but since I have examined Antislavery principles, I find them so full of the power of Truth, that I am confident not many years will roll over before the horrible traffic in human beings will be destroyed in this land of Gospel privileges.

In the summer of 1835, as mobs attacked abolitionist meetings across the North and southerners flogged the agents and burned the publications of abolitionists, Angelina wrote a letter to Garrison expressing her commitment to the cause of immediate abolition. The letter was prompted by Garrison's "Appeal to our Fellow Citizens" appearing in the *Liberator* on

August 22, 1835, in which he vowed in the face of mob violence not to "yield an inch." Describing the impact of Garrison's "Appeal," Angelina confessed that she

> could not read it without tears, so much did its spirit harmonize with my own feelings. This introduced my mind into deep sympathy with Wm. Lloyd Garrison. I found in that piece the spirit of my Master; my heart was drawn out in prayer for him, and I felt as if I would like to write him.[71]

In the letter to Garrison, she professed herself willing to sacrifice her life for the "cause of bleeding humanity."

> It is my deep, solemn, deliberate conviction, that this is a cause worth dying for. I say so, from what I have seen, and heard and known in a land of slavery, where rests the darkness of Egypt, and where is found the sin of Sodom.[72]

Garrison published the letter in the *Liberator*. In introducing the letter to his readers, he said he was "thrilled—subdued—strengthened—soul-animated, on reading it."

The letter was an abolitionist coming out for Angelina. It dismayed her sister, outraged her community of Friends, and must have mortified her family in Charleston. After the publication of her sister's letter, Sarah wrote in her diary that

> [t]he suffering which my precious sister has brought upon herself, by her connection with the anti slavery society, which has been a sorrow of heart to me, is another proof how dangerous it is to slight the clear convictions of Truth. But, like myself, she listened to the tempter, & oh that she may learn obedience by the things that she suffers. Of myself, I can say the Lord brought me out of the horrible pit, & my prayer for her is that she may be willing to bear the first chastisement *patiently*.[73]

From Sarah's perspective and the members of her Quaker meeting, pride had led Angelina to a sinful assertion of self against the moral guidance of her loved ones. In her diary of the same time, Angelina wrote about the pain she experienced when she first heard that her letter had been published.

> O! the extreme strain of extravagant praise—to be held up as saint in a public newspaper before thousands of people, when I felt I was the chief of sinners.

Blushing & confusion of face were mine, & I tho't the walls of a prison would hav been preferable to such an exposure. Then again, to hav my name, not so much *my* name, as the name of Grimké associated with that of the despised Garrison, seemd like disgrace upon my *family,* not myself alone. I felt as tho' the name had been tarnished in the eye of thousands who had before lovd and & reverd it. Nevertheless, I was helpd with a little strength, and tho' I suffered so deeply, I could not blame the publication of my letter, nor would I have recalled it if I could. I believed I had done right, that tho' condemnd by human judges, I was acquitted by him whom I believ qualifyd me to write it, & I feel willing to bear all, if it was only made instrumental of good. I felt my great unworthiness of being used in such a work but remembered that "God hath chosen the *weak things* of this world to confound the wise" & so was comforted. Since this time, my greatest trial is the continued opposition of my precious sister S.[74]

Soon thereafter in October 1835, as she confided in her diary, she felt redeemed in her decision:

O, the goodness & mercy of God. He has been graciously pleased to deliver me from the trial & apprehension of trial with regard to the writing of that letter. The storm seems to hav gone over for the present . . . O, I sometimes feel as if I am willing to become any thing if the Lord will only purify & refine & make me useful in his Church militant. . . .[75]

A few years later, in a letter to Weld, she described the writing of the let- ter this way:

You speak of my letter to W.L.G. Ah! You felt then that it was written under tre- mendous pressure of feelings bursting up with volcanic violence from the bot- tom of my soul—you felt that it was the first long breath of liberty which my im- prisoned spirit dared to respire whilst it pined in hopeless bondage, panting after freedom to *think aloud.* O! how I suffered for that letter, but IT WAS GOOD![76]

Having joined the militant antislavery church and freed her own im- prisoned soul, Angelina, the child of a powerful and prominent slavehold- ing family, started to receive letters from fellow abolitionists. Among the many letters was one from Wright, corresponding secretary of the Ameri- can Anti-Slavery Society, inviting her on behalf of the Executive Commit- tee to come to New York to talk with sewing circles of women on the sin of slavery. Angelina did not at first accept the society's invitation to act as an antislavery agent. Instead, she wrote *Appeal to the Christian Women of the South* to "open their eyes" to the principle that it is "sinful to hold a human being in bondage." Angelina's *Appeal* was widely circulated by the antislavery press, securing her fame in the ranks of abolitionists and infamy in the South. By the end of the summer of 1836, Sarah had reconciled with Angelina and pledged her support to the abolitionist campaign. That fall, the two sisters joined a workshop for abolitionist agents in New York sponsored by the American Anti-Slavery Society and led by Weld. In the coming year, the sisters launched a lecture tour throughout New England that brought great public attention to the cause of antislavery and challenged the unity of the movement.

*   *   *

These six leading reformers all took different paths to their abolitionist commitments. Garrison came from urban poverty, was nurtured by the populist faith of his Baptist mother, made a name for himself as a newspaper man, and from the outside challenged the orthodox institutions of organized benevolence to live up to their moral calling. Wright grew up in a Yankee emigrant community in the Northwest and was schooled within orthodox institutions. At an early age he committed himself to the mission of organized benevolence, and within these institutions he agitated for a radicalization of evangelical commitments to antislavery. Weld's trajectory was most similar to Wright's; they were both expected to be ministers. Weld became caught up in and helped lead the religious fervor of the new measure revivals that roiled orthodox institutions. He was a religious virtuoso that stirred the spiritual passions of an emerging middle class against the conservatism of organized benevolence. Birney early on seemed destined to be a leader of the planter societies of the South, but profligacy and then religious conversion altered that path. His religious quest within orthodoxy led him to colonization and through contact with radical reformers like Weld ultimately to abolitionism and ostracism from his native land. The Grimké sisters also suffered ostracism from their birthplace on account of following their consciences. Raised Episcopalian, converted by Presbyterians, supporters of benevolent societies, and drawn to the Quakers, these daughters of the South searched restlessly for divine purpose until they found their calling in abolitionism.

What could these activists and their very different spiritual paths possibly share in common? They all in one way or another came into contact with the agencies and causes of organized benevolence. Although most were deeply touched by the religion of orthodoxy—either through personal conversion or through work in benevolence, or both—they all remained restless. Weld, for example, complained of his "wretched cold heart" even after conversion at the hands of Finney. He described Birney as "afflicted" by "peculiar trials" even after his conversion to Presbyterianism and his commitment to the American Colonization Society. Sarah and Angelina's religious travels from Episcopalians to Presbyterians to Quakers reflected spiritual unease and internal moral struggle. And finally and most importantly, when the enormity of the special sin of slavery pressed on their consciences, they at first felt like Garrison "deep regret and shame" for their complicity with slavery. Wright, for example, felt "sick" for his "flexible expediency." Struggling through these "travails," "trials," and "apprehensions" on the subject of slavery, they all experienced a breaking loose of their souls as they committed themselves to the cause of immediate abolitionism. These trials came to be seen as "tests" of the "promise of God" and preparations to let the "soul magnify the Lord." Confessions of sin and faith directly tied to the issue of slavery projected these activists out of internal moral battles and into a national campaign, and they found in these confessional projections personal redemption and social purpose. From very different backgrounds and through different paths of preparation, they testified to this similar religious and psychological dynamic.

"For the Movement and for Myself"

In December 1835, Theodore Weld wrote a letter to Lewis Tappan just as he finished an antislavery lecture tour through Ohio and was about to begin six months of agitation throughout western New York. The letter reveals Weld's frame of mind and emotional state at the pinnacle of his influence as an itinerant agent for immediate abolitionism. In it he reacted to news about what came to be known as the Great Fire of 1835, a fire in New York City that destroyed close to seven hundred buildings. He interpreted the disaster as a divine act: "a single herald sent in advance to announce the coming of a host." Weld launched into a jeremiad similar in form to the temperance and abolitionist lectures that had made him a sensation among reformers: "The poor have cried, and ears have been stopped"; "avarice has clutched the last pittance, and lust has gorged itself with spoil"; "prejudice has spurned God's image with loathing, and passion has trodden down the needy in the gates"; and "when iniquity has been visited by terrible rebuke, it has swelled with pride and gnashed with rage." Weld brought the letter to a close with a hint of embarrassment for the harangue:

> I have run on and on almost incoherently perchance, but this awful calamity . . . seems to me so like Jehovah's voice, its last warning spoken in articulate thunder over the sealed ear of a besotted people drugged by its sins into the sleep of death, that my forebodings have all rushed out *en masse.*

Despite the divine rebuke, Weld had not given up all hope: "What can save us as a nation but repentance—immediate, profound, *public,* proclaimed abroad, wide as our infamy and damning guilt have gone!"[1]

Antebellum reformers like Weld had a peculiar view of the modern world—a prophetic one. They did not see in the rapidly developing events around them the gradual necessity of progress and advancement. Quite the opposite, they saw the necessity of personal interventions to save "progress" from itself. From their perspective, extensive problems would not simply go away as advances weeded out the imperfections of the world. To the contrary, social problems like slavery and intemperance appeared to grow more serious, risking collective cataclysm.[2] They believed this mounting risk called for Americans to take moral responsibility for these problems in their own lives and in society at large. Reformers called for immediate and profound confession proclaimed as wide as the guilt of slavery or intemperance extended. They demanded that Americans acknowledge that these sins touched their very souls *as they* imperiled their great nation. They called for intensive and personal but also extensive and public witnessing. Depending on the response of the people, the nation could be redeemed or it would suffer judgment. They seesawed between hope and despair.

Like many social movements to follow, antebellum reform called for both intensive and extensive commitments to change society. Getting this type of engagement is more difficult than making the call. It depends on articulating coherent campaigns that speak to far-flung people *and* shape the deep understandings, motives, and actions of this extensive constituency. This is not a simple task. Figuring out how such commitments are won is the goal of both activists seeking to launch movements for change and social scientists trying to understand them. Antebellum reformers proved surprisingly successful at it. Explaining how not only reveals mechanisms central to the unprecedented wave of moral protests that broke out across the United States in the 1830s but also to modern protest more generally. Today's activists struggle to arouse similar commitments; more than ever, launching and sustaining social movements involves telescoping the intimate and the far-flung.

In the early nineteenth century, population growth, geographic conquest, extending capitalist markets, and new transportation and communication technologies expanded the social world of white Americans. Mobilizing collective action to agitate for changes across this immense and mobile society posed serious challenges. Temperance activists, abolitionists, and other antebellum reformers confronted these challenges with an innovative form of moral protest. This form shared essential features with other social movements emerging at the same time in Great Britain and elsewhere in Western Europe. The widespread reach of this form of protest depended on the organization of modular associations, the articulation of special purposes, and the emergence of detached protest identities. Evangelical Christianity, more than any other social force, shaped the form, purposes, and collective identities behind this national wave of American protest.

During this restless period, few institutions could stand in the gap between individual and nation. Drawing on evangelical schemas, reformers created a new cosmology to confront this reality. This reform cosmology envisioned the individual as morally implicated in national expansion and taught that she could not ignore large-scale problems *because* they held the keys to her spiritual fate. This reform perspective countered feelings that the individual was untouched, dwarfed, or disoriented by this expanded national reality; and it demanded moral engagement with this reality for reasons that fused the personal and the public. It informed an innovative type of collective engagement that called on individuals to use confession to simultaneously project themselves "arm and soul" into "great struggles" and introject these national battles in order to release a "shackled spirit."

This witnessing depended on a delicate balance of personal and public engagement, one that Weld described in his letter to Tappan in the winter of 1835. Profound and public repentance meant not just

> [t]he *breaking off* by righteousness and turning to the Lord, not merely the ashes and sackcloth and sitting in dust, with disheveled hair and streaming tears and lamentation and wailing, *but* confession—yea on the house tops—and *restoration* to the uttermost tho' it bring to beggary, and loosing the bonds, undoing the burdens, breaking every yoke, dealing bread to the hungry, hiring the poor that are cast out, and satisfying the afflicted *soul*. This may save us.[3]

This confessional form of protest drew on traditional evangelical schemas, but it mixed them in a surprising and contentious fashion. From populist traditions came the mass appeal of public confessions. These confessions provided a popular vehicle to convey messages of reform, but as practiced in the populist revivals of the time they—to use Weld's words—called on individuals to "break off" from sin "lamenting and wailing" *without* demanding "restoration to the uttermost" or "the breaking of every yoke." Public and extensive in their appeal, the work of these public confessions focused primarily on the reform of the self.

From orthodox traditions came organized campaigns to reform public institutions and attack the specific moral failings of groups of Americans like the Sabbath-breaking and hard-drinking ways of the unchurched. These public campaigns against special sins externalized the problem and looked to saints to pressure sinners to reform. The new form of collective action that emerged in the 1830s mixed elements from both traditions demanding commitment to confront an extensive national problem that deeply implicated the self in the campaign for change. This twinning of the intimate and the far-flung is evident in the personal writings of leading activists. In their own words, reformers found "peace" or the awakening of a "slumbering soul" through engagement in a cause that "magnified the Lord" because it was the "great trial cause" of the nation and humanity. Restless men and women, who had struggled with spiritual quests for much of their lives, who had been plagued by guilt and had sought but not found redemption in different churches and evangelical campaigns, discovered new purpose and identity as they thrust themselves into confessional protests against special sins. The popular influence of this twinning is also evidenced in the formal resolutions of the thousands of reform societies that pressed for individual and collective repentance. By fusing intensive and extensive moral projects, this form of protest presented detached and dispersed evangelicals a coherent purpose and identity in national movements.

These movements did not just awaken moral commitments where orthodox institutions had long sought to reform public sins. These movements were interregional because their mix of public confession and special sins resonated in evangelical communities across the North and even in the South. Particularly in the fluid communities of the Northwest, where orthodox and populist evangelicals mixed, bearing witness against special sins provided new moral purposes and collective identities to a mobile population. It was support from these communities that led this wave of protest and made it national in scope and influence.

Reformers working to mobilize widespread support successfully spoke to split registers of early nineteenth-century American life. In a social context of demographic upheaval, expanding markets, and public institutions outpaced by these social forces, they tapped meanings and forms of actions that seized the conscience of individuals detached from traditional arrangements. Bearing witness against special sins provided a moral project that was at once introspective and nationally extensive. This moral project thrived on widespread feelings of an evangelical guilt that was inclined to project the self into a cosmic battle of good and evil and introject that battle into the self. These feelings were mediated through the schemas of public confession and special sins providing the cultural and social-psychological mechanism to propel the first sustained and interregional U.S. movements. Religious virtuosos like Garrison, Weld, and Sarah and Angelina Grimké tapped these feelings by interlacing intimate moral responsibility and far-flung social problems. And when institutions in between these registers of the repentant self and the guilty nation resisted the call to bear witness—when churches refused to repent, when the politicians refused to listen, and when mobs moved to silence reformers—these movements carried on because many evangelicals had effectively telescoped the self and nation.

How was this accomplished? The answer, in part, has to do with the central emotion of these movements. Guilt is not a simple affective response to personal or social conditions. Many scholars of emotion view it as a socialized variant of fear and anxiety.[4] Its distinctiveness comes from its being a moral and reflexive emotion.[5] Guilt is a culturally mediated emotion with a distinctive inward dynamic. It is an emotion experienced by believers in hierarchies of values and by persons capable of and prone to self-judgment. Moral guilt arises "from the choice of a lower order value at the expense of a higher order one." Only persons living in a universe of ordered values or desires experience guilt. Individuals can and do distinguish first-order desires or simple wishes—like a taste for sugar, the touch of soft fabrics, an urge to have sex or get drunk—from second- or higher-order desires—like to be a person that is good to others, a defender of community, or faithful to God. These orders easily come into conflict. If a person is true to the higher order, he often must renounce the lower order. When a conscientious person fails to do this, he feels guilty.[6]

Guilt testifies to a self at war with itself: "I say I want to promote the happiness of others, and yet I indulge in consuming sugar produced on slave plantations; I say I want to promote the happiness of others, and yet I enjoy wine produced by an industry that turns thousands into drunks." An individual's conscience calls or appeals to her to live up to higher values. It calls the individual to reorder the values and desires of her life, but it reaches a divided self. The appeal comes against a will. The guilty self is split, as if there is someone else in this world with her, calling her, appealing to her. To feel guilty implies something unresolved. There are many images and explanations for this internal dissent, including Freud's garrison in the middle of an occupied city, Mead's internalization of the other, or Heidegger's appeal of possible selves.[7] Antebellum reformers most often referred to this internal struggle as a "trial." Common to these different images is the sense that the emotion testifies to an internally divided and judged self.

Evangelicals are conditioned to feel guilty about their engagement with the world. For evangelicals, the presence of sin in the heart, the urge to indulge in lower-order desires, is representative of the moral depravity of all humanity—evidence of their fallen nature. The conscience, on the other hand, the appeal to live up to a higher order, is God's representative in the person—evidence of the presence of the divine. The moral intro-spection triggered by Christian guilt, the looking inside for evil and good that moral disquiet prompts, leads the believer to disclose forces that "in one moment seem to be alternative forces within the self and in the next are recognized as forces which transcend the self."[8] For the purposes of this argument, it does not matter what we think of these religious evalua-tions of the internal division of the guilty self encountered on moral intro-spection. What matters is that this emotional process leads the evangelical to form an immediate link or identification of the self with an external force. Evangelical guilt establishes links between polarized registers—it telescopes the personal and the cosmic. The dynamic of evangelical guilt quite naturally projects the self into a cosmic battle of good and evil and introjects that battle into the self. In the words of Weld to Birney as he struggled with his concerns over immediate abolitionism, "such trials as now afflict you are precious touchstones which to test heaven's gold of God's promise."[9]

This emotional dynamic did not in itself lead to deep, personal commit-ments to far-flung causes and movements, but a particular combination of intensive and extensive schemas that channeled the *reflexive* dimensions of Christian guilt did. This cultural and social-psychological mechanism propelled national U.S. movements through a form of life politics. In ear-ly nineteenth-century American Christianity, as evangelicals reacted to disorienting events, they adjusted and extended the schemas of sin and confession to make sense of what they were feeling. These adjustments came from different religious sources, and in the reform movements they combined in a particular and powerful way.

Through the rationalized organizations and broadcast media of ortho-dox benevolence, the general schema of sin was specialized. Particular campaigns and particular agencies with directives to combat special sins worked to disassociate the problem of sin from concrete social settings and extended it to an "imagined community" of members and readers. In the process, sin became focused and attention-grabbing.[10] This new specialized schema of sin amplified problems relevant to scattered individuals displaced from local traditions and to society as a whole. Making sin particular extended the reach of campaigns against it. It also made pervasive feelings of guilt actionable.

Traditionally, the Christian schema of sin not only informs actions and conditions the individual is free to choose; it also reveals the imperfection of the actions he is forced to take and the conditions he cannot escape. In the latter instance, "the moral guilt of conscious evil is transmuted into a sense of religious guilt which feels a general responsibility for that which the individual agent cannot be immediately responsible."[11] This difference between general responsibility tied to inability and immediate responsibility tied to a duty to act nicely distinguishes the operation of sin on the hearts and minds of more conservative evangelicals from its operation on the radical evangelicals driving and supporting the reform movements of the 1830s. The traditional Calvinist belief in human inability allowed many to excuse inaction for "inherited" sins like owning slaves or holding property tied to the production or selling of alcohol. The specialization of sin shifted the sense of responsibility from the general to the immediate form—from conditions in which the individual is not free to choose higher possibilities to conditions that are open to direct change. As special sins like intemperance and slavery were sorted out from the general state of sin, the struggle against them became more actionable and the victory over them more attainable.

The specialized purpose of battling particular sins enabled reformers to project personal struggles against sin onto particular social issues. Specialization extended the intensive schema of personal struggle against sin into a focused, national drama framed for broadcast. Far-flung social problems like drinking and slavery were grasped as immediate, personal sins. Immediate personal battles with sin were projected as national struggles for reform. This resonated with the reflexive dynamic of evangelical guilt. The battle against special sins resonated with the affective disposition of evangelical Americans to form an immediate link between the self and external forces of a vastly different scale.

The practical vehicle for this projection of the self onto far-flung problems and the introjection of abstract national problems into personal struggles was confession—specifically, public confession. In the evangelical Protestant tradition, confession is a reaction to a personal conviction of guilt and a renunciation of sin. For individuals raised in an evangelical tradition, the experience of confession and conversion is not so much the acceptance of a radically new belief system as the resolution of the inner battle of guilt, a healing of the divided self. As William James observed in his lectures on religious experiences, "There are dead feelings, dead ideas, and cold beliefs, and there are hot and live ones; and when one grows hot and alive within us, everything has to re-crystallize about it." A person "converts" when religious ideas, previously dead, cold, or peripheral, become alive, hot, and central to her being. Emotional states precipitate these personal "rearrangements." Emotions like guilt can "seize" the person, and when they do, they "seldom leave things as they found them." [12] They transform identities.

Confession is the trigger of conversion and redemption. It reaches inward to remake the self as it renounces sinful states of being and lays claim to "a new heart." Confession breaks the bonds of sin and binds the convert anew by pledging allegiance to a new moral order. [13] It is an act of profound adjustment that responds to emotional situations of personal crisis. The populist evangelical movement of the early nineteenth century transformed the practice and experience of confession by making it public. As an intensive schema of transformation, confession made public provided a practice for the rapid and collective formation of new moral associations and identities. In bearing witness against special sins, however, these associations and identities were marked by the nature of the sins that were being confessed.

The combination of cultural schemas—public confession and special sins—generated a highly transposable or modular form of collective action. In towns scattered over hundreds of miles, Americans gathered together in the same fashion to bear witness against sin. The combination of schemas generated special purposes that united and focused this form of collective action across the length of the nation against specific social problems. In this bearing witness against special sins, Americans were converted and new collective identities were shaped: detached protest identities like the teetotaler, the immediate abolitionist, or as their critics preferred to refer to them, the "Ultra Moral-Reformer." This form, purpose, and identity to protest were essential to the interregional success of these movements. Not only did this combination of schemas extend the movements, it fixed the commitment of activists to deeply personal motives. Public confession represented an extension of an intensive schema—a broadcast of the personal experience of transformation. For some, this undermined the saliency of confession. It was too showy; it was inauthentic. Specialization of sin also marked an extension of an intensive schema.

For some, it spelled the publicity and overexposure of very personal struggles. There was the risk of the attenuation of meaning in these transformations of the two evangelical schemas. Although critics cried hypocrisy, these innovative cultural schemas, playing off the reflexive dimensions of Christian guilt, offered many evangelicals moral projects of reform that resonated at bipolar registers: moral projects that were, in Abzug's terms, at once "self-scrutinizing" and "national."[14] Special sins and public confession extended intensive schemas but kept the two registers in creative play. Moreover, the fusion of the schemas, bearing witness against special sins, brought two schemas, extended from different evangelical sources, converging on intensive counterparts. Where an extending schema of public confession risked attenuation it met and revivified with an intensive schema of sin. Where an extending schema of special sins risked attenuation it met and revivified with an intensive schema of confession. This zone of combination was not stable, but it lasted long enough to launch national movements.

Given the material and human resources structuring the extending schemas and the social spaces where they combined, certain evangelicals were more centrally situated and therefore more likely to move and to be moved by these reforms. Middle-class evangelicals located geographically between the core and periphery where populist and orthodox evangelicals freely interacted, were so situated. Within this mixing space of evangelical currents and class, the intensive and extensive dynamics of bearing witness against special sins resonated especially with women. The combination of self-scrutiny and public pressure appealed to women as it empowered them to draw on their moral authority derived from the cult of domesticity to act against the male-dominated institutions of the marketplace and politics. Within these broad social categories of religion, class, geography, and gender, it was religious virtuosos that came up with the creative fusion of schemas that launched the movements.

Antebellum reformers grasped for a time a way to mobilize engagement with the world that remains quite current. It was hard to hold onto. By the end of the 1830s, significant elements of temperance and abolitionist support veered off into either more private campaigns for personal reform or more public struggles to control political institutions. But for a period, they inspired a popular form of what contemporary social theorists term life politics.

There is a long legacy to these antebellum reform movements. The reform impulse of the 1830s diffused into an array of movements that extend to the present. The men and women who experienced activist awakenings in the 1830s continued on for decades to shape the women's rights movement, the battle for temperance, and the fight for African American rights during Reconstruction. They influenced the next generation that continued these lines of activism into the twentieth century with the movement for women's suffrage, prohibition, and the founding of the NAACP. These movements and organizations, in turn, shaped the protests of the 1960s and beyond.[15]

But the influence of this antebellum reform goes well beyond these direct historical lineaments. In the revival spirit of the early bus boycott meetings in Montgomery, in the "prefigurative" protests of Students for a Democratic Society, in making the "personal political" in the Women's Liberation Movement, and in countless other instances of social protest that telescoped the intimate feelings of the individual and extensive projects for social change, a variant of the form of bearing witness against special sin remained present.[16] Why? Because activists continue to seek ways to inspire intensive and extensive commitments to their causes, and bearing witness remains a key form of protest to tap these different registers of engagement.

For some movements with close ties to Christianity, like the prolife movement or the recent U.S. Central America peace movement, religious traditions of bearing witness directly shape how they think about protest and how they inspire personal commitments to large-scale social change. But even for actors who do not consider themselves especially religious or who have angrily rejected Christianity, witnessing continues to shape dissent. Take, for example, two quite different accounts of protest published in contemporary activist newspapers. The first is from an interview with Bob Lawrence that appeared in the October 31, 1998, edition of *Earth First!* Bob was asked why he had turned down a court deal to do community service instead of prison time for disrupting logging in the Mount Hood National Forest. This is how he responded:

> I've been following really closely over the past couple of years the activities of the Plowshares activists and the Catholic peace movement. The Plowshares activists always refused to pay fines or accept probation, to become involved in that system at all in anyway, because that system is corrupt and wrong. So, they always end up going to prison for what they do. They feel it is another way of bearing witness. You can't ask anybody to do something you haven't done yourself. So, I felt it was in the best interest *for the movement, and for myself,* to take my time and come to prison.[17]

The second is from an article in the September 3, 2002, edition of the *Advocate*. The article responded to the impact of the child molestation scandal in the Roman Catholic Church on the gay community and called for gay priests to come out.

> The problem is that by saying nothing, by refusing to take the risk of coming out and bearing witness to the reality of their lives, they are adding to the impression that they are all somehow shameful and guilty, denying us the witness we need and powerfully undermining both their own cause and the cause of gay liberation. For decades gay men and lesbians have taken enormous personal cost in order to right the ancient wrongs of homophobia. From the teenager who comes out and risks homelessness to the marine who comes out and risks court-martial, gay people have bravely borne witness, have suffered great losses, and in so doing have changed the world. For priests, whose calling is one of sacrifice, self-negation, and bearing witness, to refuse to do the same is a blot on their mission.[18]

Radical ecology and gay and lesbian liberation do not have particularly close ties with the institutions of Christianity. And yet, activists in these and many other secular movements recognize the power of bearing witness and hope to enlist this power to change, to better, to redeem the individual and society. It may surprise them and some social scientists that teetotalers and evangelical abolitionists from the early nineteenth century help explain why.

Notes

Introduction

1. *Knickerbocker,* October 1842, pp. 337–344.

2. See Anthony Giddens, *Modernity and Self-Identity: Self and Society in the Late Modern Age* (Stanford: Stanford University Press, 1991) for a theoretical discussion of life politics. For an excellent empirical use of the concept see Verta Taylor, *Rock-A-By Baby: Feminism, Self-Help, and Postpartum Depression* (New York and London: Routledge, 1996).

3. For data on auxiliary societies, see *Journal of Humanity* 2, nos. 36–49 (Jan. 27–April 28, 1831); American Temperance Union, *Permanent Temperance Documents,* vol. 1 (New York: American Temperance Union, 1852), p. 474; American Anti-Slavery Society, *Annual Reports* (New York: William S. Dorr, 1836–38); and Paul Goodman, *Of One Blood: Abolitionism and the Origins of Racial Equality* (Berkeley: University of California Press, 1998).

4. Following Mark A. Noll, *America's God: From Jonathan Edwards to Abraham Lincoln* (New York: Oxford, 2006), p. 5, by evangelicals, this books refers to "a welter of Protestants" united by four basic characteristics: "biblicism (or reliance on the Bible as ultimate religious authority), conversionism (or an emphasis on the new birth), activism (or energetic, individualistic engagement in personal and social duties, and crucicentrism (or focus on Christ's redeeming work as the heart of religion)." In terms of Protestant denominations or sects, this designation includes Presbyterians, Congregationalists, Baptists, Dutch and German Reformed, Methodists, "Christians," Restorationists, African American churches, and even Lutherans and low-church Episcopalians. It excludes Unitarians, Roman Catholics, and high-church Episcopalians. Also see Nathan O. Hatch, *Democratization of American Christianity,* (New Haven and London: Yale University Press, 1989) for a similar categorization.

5. *New York Evangelist,* April 29, 1837, p. 69.

Chapter One

1. Important examples of increased research in the historical sociology of American movements after the Civil War include Edwin Amenta, *When Movements Matter: The Townsend Plan and U.S. Social Spending Challengers* (Princeton, NJ: Princeton University Press, forthcoming); Edwin Amenta, Kathleen Dunleavy, and Mary Bernstein, "Stolen Thunder? Huey Long's Share Our Wealth, Political Mediation and the Second New Deal," *American Sociological Review* 59 (1994): 678–702; Edwin Amenta and Yvonne Zylan, "It Happened Here: Political Opportunity, the New Institutionalism, and the Townsend Movement," *American Sociological Review* 56 (1991): 250–65; Sarah Babb, "'A True American System of Finance': Frame Resonance in the U.S. Labor Movement, 1866 to 1886," *American Sociological Review* 61 (1996): 1033–1052; Elizabeth Clemens, *The People's Lobby: Organizational Innovation and the Rise of Interest Group Politics in the United States, 1890–1925* (Chicago: University of Chicago Press, 1997); Kent Redding, "Failed Populism: Movement-Party Disjuncture in North Carolina, 1890 to 1900," *American Sociological Review* 57 (1992): 340–352; and Kim Voss, *The Making of American Exceptionalism: The Knights of Labor and Class Formation in the Nineteenth Century* (Ithaca, NY: Cornell University Press, 1993). Important exceptions to this pattern include Stephen Ellingson, "Understanding the Dialectic of Discourse and Collective Action: Public Debate and Rioting in Antebellum Cincinnati," *American Journal of Sociology* 101 (1995): 100–44; Craig Calhoun, "'New Social Movements' of the Early Nineteenth Century," *Social Science History* 17 (1993): 385–427; Joseph R. Gusfield, *Symbolic Crusade: Status Politics and the American Temperance Movement* (Urbana: University of Illinois Press, 1963); and George M. Thomas, *Revivalism and Cultural Change: Christianity, Nation Building, and the Market in the Nineteenth-Century United States* (Chicago: University of Chicago Press, 1989).

2. Although the core of his research is on Western Europe, Charles Tilly has written on changing patterns of protest in North America in "Collective Action in England and America, 1765–1775," in *Tradition, Conflict, and Modernization: Perspectives on the American Revolution,* ed. Richard Maxwell Brown and Don Fehrenbacher (New York: Academic Press, 1977) and in "Repertoires of Contention in America and Britain," in *Dynamics of Social Movements,* ed. Mayer N. Zald and John D. McCarthy (Cambridge, MA: Winthrop, 1979); Sidney Tarrow discusses the historical significance of American protest in *Power in Movement: Social Movements, Collective Action and Politics* (New York: Cambridge University Press, 1994) and in "'The Very Excess of Democracy': State Building and Contentious Politics in America," in *Social Movements and American Political Institutions,* ed. Anne N. Costain and Andrew S. McFarland (Lanham, MD: Rowman and Littlefield, 1998).

3. In this use of the concept of a national social movement, I extend Tilly's definition to include sustained protests that not only challenge national state authorities but also the dominant cultural patterns of a nation. To be genuinely national,

these movements cannot be parochial or narrowly limited in geographic support. Therefore, central to explaining the emergence of national social movements is explaining how sustained and interregional protests emerge. For a discussion of definitions of national social movements, see Tilly, "Buried Gold," *American Sociological Review* 67 (2002): 689–92.

4. Charles Tilly, *From Mobilization to Revolution* (Reading, MA: Addison-Wesley, 1978); *The Contentious French* (Cambridge, MA: Belknap Press of Harvard University Press, 1986); and *Popular Contention in Great Britain, 1758–1834* (Cambridge, MA: Harvard University Press, 1995), p. 44.

5. For a discussion of the concept of modularity see Tarrow, *Power in Movement,* and idem, "Modular Collective Action and the Rise of the Social Movement: Why the French Revolution Was Not Enough," *Politics and Society* 21 (1993): 69–90; and also Benedict Anderson, *Imagined Communities: Reflections on the Origin and Spread of Nationalism* (London: Verso, 1983).

6. Charles Tilly, "The Parliamentarization of Popular Contention in Great Britain, 1758–1834," in *Roads from Past to Future, Legacies of Social Thought,* ed. C. Lemert, 217–44 (Lanham, MD: Rowman & Littlefield Publishers, Inc., 1997).

7. Charles Tilly, "From Interactions to Outcomes in Social Movements," in *How Social Movements Matter,* ed. Marco Giugni, Doug McAdam, and Charles Tilly (Minneapolis: University of Minnesota Press, 1999), and *Popular Contention in Great Britain, 1758–1834,* p. 13.

8. Tarrow, *Power in Movement.*

9. For a detailed discussion of rough music, see E. P. Thompson, *Customs in Common: Studies in Traditional Popular Culture* (New York: New Press, 1993); for an example of it in early nineteenth-century America, see Sherlock Bristol, *The Pioneer Preacher: Incidents of Interest, and Experience in the Author's Life* (Urbana: University of Illinois Press, 1989), pp. 15–17.

10. Tilly, "Parliamentarization of Popular Contention in Great Britain, 1758–1834," p. 236; and *Popular Contention in Great Britain, 1758–1834,* p. 13.

11. Pauline Maier, *From Resistance to Revolution: Colonial Radicals and the Development of American Opposition to Britain, 1765–1776* (New York: Knopf, 1972); Tarrow, *Power in Movement.*

12. Theda Skocpol, *Protecting Soldiers and Mothers* (Cambridge, MA: Belknap Press, 1992), p. 67.

13. Stephen Skowronek, *Building a New American State: The Expansion of National Administrative Capacities 1877–1920* (New York: Cambridge University Press, 1982); Skocpol, *Protecting Soldiers and Mothers;* and Michael Mann, *The Rise of Classes and Nation-States, 1760–1914,* vol. 2 of *The Sources of Social Power* (New York: Cambridge University Press, 1993).

14. Hatch, *The Democratization of American Christianity*; Stephen R. Warner, "Work in Progress toward a New Paradigm for the Sociology of Religion in the United States," *American Journal of Sociology* 98 (1993): 1044–93; Roger Finke and Rodney Stark, *The Churching of America, 1776–1990: Winners and Losers in*

Our Religious Economy (New Brunswick, NJ: Rutgers University Press, 1992); and Noll, *America's God*.

15. C. Wright Mills, "Situated Actions and Vocabularies of Motive," *American Sociological Review* 5 (1940): 904–13.

16. For examples of this research, see Charles A. Beard and Mary Beard, *The Rise of American Civilization* (New York: Macmillan Co., 1927); and Arthur C. Cole, *The Irrepressible Conflict, 1850–1865* (New York: Macmillan Co., 1934); for a review of the "progressive historians," see Merton L. Dillon, "Gilbert H. Barnes and Dwight L. Dumond: An Appraisal," *Reviews in American History* 21 (1993): 539–52; and Eric Foner, *Free Soil, Free Labor, Free Men: The Ideology of the Republican Party Before the Civil War* (New York: Oxford University Press, 1995), pp. 2–4.

17. Charles W. Ramsdell, "The Changing Interpretation of the Civil War," *Journal of Southern History* 3 (1937): 2–27; Avery Craven, *The Coming of the Civil War* (New York: Scribner's Sons, 1942); J. G. Randall, "The Blundering Generation," *Mississippi Valley Historical Review* 27 (1940): 3–28, quotation on p. 15; see also Betty L. Fladeland, "Revisionists vs. Abolitionists: The Historiographical Cold War of the 1940s and 1950s," *Journal of the Early Republic* 6 (1986): 1–21.

18. See Craven, *Coming of the Civil War,* pp. 11–12; and Alice Felt Tyler, *Freedom's Ferment* (Minneapolis: University of Minnesota Press, 1944) for good examples of clustering the many antebellum reforms into a coherent whole.

19. Craven, *Coming of the Civil War,* pp. 136, 139.

20. Craven, *Coming of the Civil War,* p. 150.

21. Stanley M. Elkins, *Slavery: A Problem in American Institutional and Intellectual Life* (Chicago: University of Chicago Press, 1959); David H. Donald, *Lincoln Reconsidered: Essays on the Civil War Era* (New York: Knopf, 1956).

22. Elkins, *Slavery.*

23. Herbert Blumer, "Collective Behavior," in *An Outline of the Principles of Sociology,* ed. R. E. Park, pp. 221–80 (New York: Barnes and Noble, 1939), pp. 228, 237, 255, 260, 263.

24. Neil J. Smelser, *Theory of Collective Behavior* (New York: Free Press, 1962).

25. Aileen S. Kraditor, *Means and Ends in American Abolitionism: Garrison and His Critics on Strategy and Tactics, 1834–1850* (New York: Pantheon Books, 1969); Bertram Wyatt-Brown, *Lewis Tappan and the Evangelical War against Slavery* (Cleveland: Press of Case Western Reserve University, 1969). Critical accounts of reformers continued in studies of temperance, Sabbath observance, and asylum and school reform. David J. Rothman, *The Discovery of the Asylum: Social Order and Disorder in the New Republic* (Boston: Little, Brown and Co., 1971); Michael B. Katz, *The Irony of Early School Reform: Educational Innovation in Mid-Nineteenth Century Massachusetts* (Cambridge, MA: Harvard University Press, 1968); Paul

Boyer, *Urban Masses and Moral Order in America, 1820–1920* (Cambridge, MA: Harvard University Press, 1978).

26. Robert Allen Skotheim, "A Note on Historical Method: David Donald's 'Toward a Reconsideration of Abolitionists,'" *Journal of Southern History* 25 (1959): 356–65; Martin B. Duberman, "The Abolitionists and Psychology," *Journal of Negro History* 47 (1962): 183–91; Martin Duberman, ed., *The Antislavery Vanguard: New Essays on the Abolitionists* (Princeton, NJ: Princeton University Press, 1965); Betty Fladeland, "Who Were the Abolitionists?" *Journal of Negro History* 49 (1964): 99–115.

27. Merton L. Dillon, *Elijah P. Lovejoy, Abolitionist Editor* (Urbana, IL: University of Illinois Press, 1961); Wyatt-Brown, *Lewis Tappan*.

28. Kraditor, *Means and Ends in American Abolitionism*, p. 21; also see Dwight L. Dumond, *Antislavery: The Crusade for Freedom in America* (Ann Arbor: University of Michigan Press, 1961) and Donald G. Matthews, "Abolitionists on Slavery: The Critique behind the Social Movement," *Journal of Southern History* 33 (1967): 163–82, for similar accounts. This new perspective fit better with a series of historical studies written a few years earlier on the forces shaping American Victorianism. Centered mainly on the benevolence societies of Presbyterians and Congregationalists—societies like the American Sunday School Union and the American Tract Society—these studies documented the close association between these mainstream national institutions of the 1820s and the reform associations of the 1830s. An important implication of this work on the so-called evangelical united front—one that did not get much attention at the time Elkins and Donald were describing abolitionists as anti-institutionalists—was that antebellum reformers were actually more securely embedded in social institutions than most of their fellow Americans. John R. Bodo, *The Protestant Clergy and Public Issues, 1812–1848* (Princeton, NJ: Princeton University Press, 1954); Charles C. Cole, *The Social Ideas of the Northern Evangelists, 1826–1860* (New York: Columbia University Press, 1954); Charles I. Foster, *An Errand of Mercy: The Evangelical United Front, 1790–1837* (Chapel Hill: University of North Carolina Press, 1960); Clifford Griffin, *Their Brothers' Keepers: Moral Stewardship in the Unites States, 1800–1865* (New Brunswick, NJ: Rutgers University Press, 1960).

29. Lois W. Banner, "Religion and Reform in the Early Republic: The Role of Youth," *American Quarterly* 23 (1971): 677–95; idem "Religious Benevolence as Social Control: A Critique of an Interpretation," *Journal of American History* 60 (1973): 23–41; Anne M. Boylan, "Women in Groups: An Analysis of Women's Benevolent Organizations in New York and Boston, 1797–1840," *Journal of American History* 71 (1984): 497–523; David Brion Davis, *The Problem of Slavery in the Age of Revolution, 1770–1823* (Ithaca, NY: Cornell University Press, 1975); John J. Rumbarger, "The Social Origins and Function of the Political Temperance Movement in the Reconstruction of American Society, 1825–1927" (Ph.D. diss., University of Pennsylvania, 1969), idem, *Profits, Power, and Prohibition: Alcohol Reform*

and the Industrializing of America, 1800–1930 (Albany: State University of New York Press, 1989); Carroll Smith-Rosenberg, *Religion and Rise of the American City: The New York City Mission Movement, 1812–1870* (Ithaca, NY: Cornell University Press, 1971); Nancy F. Cott, *The Bonds of Womanhood: "Woman's Sphere" in New England, 1780–1835* (New Haven, CN: Yale University Press, 1977). On the rise of a new humanitarian spirit, see Thomas L. Haskell, "Capitalism and the Origins of Humanitarian Sensibility, Part 1 and 2," in *The Antislavery Debate*, ed. Thomas Bender, pp. 107–60 (Berkeley: University of California Press, 1992). The quotation is from Donald, *Lincoln Reconsidered*, p. 33.

30. Paul E. Johnson, *A Shopkeeper's Millennium: Society and Revivals in Rochester, New York, 1815–1837* (New York: Hill and Wang, 1978); Mary P. Ryan, *Cradle of the Middle Class: The Family in Oneida County, New York, 1790–1865* (New York: Cambridge University, 1981).

31. Gilbert H. Barnes, *The Antislavery Impulse, 1830–1844* (New York and London: D. Appleton-Century Company, 1933); Gilbert H. Barnes and Dwight L. Dumond, eds., *Letters of Theodore Dwight Weld, Angelina Grimké Weld and Sarah Grimké*, 2 vols. (Gloucester, MA: Peter Smith, 1934); Dwight L. Dumond, *Letters of James Gillespie Birney, 1831–1857*, 2 vols. (New York: D. Appleton-Century Co., 1938), and Dumond, *Antislavery*; see Dillon, "Gilbert H. Barnes and Dwight L. Dumond: An Appraisal."

32. Whitney R. Cross established a strong correlation between religious revivals and reforms like temperance and antislavery in a detailed analysis of the counties of western New York. Cross, *The Burned-over District: The Social and Intellectual History of Enthusiastic Religion in Western New York* (Ithaca: Cornell University Press, 1950). The research of sociologists Hammond and Thomas confirm this strong association. John L. Hammond, "Revival Religion and Antislavery Politics," *American Sociological Review* 38 (1974): 175–86. Thomas, *Revivalism and Cultural Change*. And a series of broad surveys over the past quarter century of antebellum reform movements remain tied to Barnes's and Dumonds's basic thesis. See Lawrence J. Friedman, *Gregarious Saints: Self and Community in American Abolitionism, 1830–1870* (New York: Cambridge University Press, 1982); Louis S. Gerteis, *Morality and Utility in American Antislavery Reform* (Chapel Hill: University of North Carolina Press, 1987); James B. Stewart, *Holy Warriors: The Abolitionists and American Slavery* (New York: Hill and Wang, 1996); Donald M. Scott, "Abolition as a Sacred Vocation," in *Antislavery Reconsidered: New Perspectives on the Abolitionists*, ed. Lewis Perry and Michael Fellman, pp. 51–74 (Baton Rouge: Louisiana State University Press, 1979); Bertram Wyatt-Brown, *Yankee Saints and Southern Sinners* (Baton Rouge: Louisiana State University Press, 1985); Robert H. Abzug, *Passionate Liberator: Theodore Dwight Weld and the Dilemma of Reform* (New York: Oxford University Press, 1980); Paul Goodman, *Of One Blood*.

33. David Brion Davis, "The Emergence of Immediatism in British and American Antislavery Thought," *Mississippi Valley Historical Review* 49 (1962): 209–30,

quotation on p. 228; Anne C. Loveland, "Evangelicalism and 'Immediate Emancipation' in American Antislavery Thought," *Journal of Southern History* 32 (1966): 172–88, quotation on p. 178.

34. Smith-Rosenberg, *Religion and Rise of the American City;* Ian R. Tyrell, *Sobering Up: From Temperance to Prohibition in Antebellum America, 1800–1860* (Westport, CN: Greenwood Press, 1979). For example, Smith-Rosenberg's study of female Magdalen and Moral Reform societies in the city of New York concluded that revivals freed women to assume more public and aggressive roles in the battle against the sexual sin of men, leading to a widespread movement against prostitution and adultery. Ian Tyrell's exhaustive study of temperance in Massachusetts credited the first popular expansion of teetotalism (or the immediate renunciation of all forms of alcohol) in the late 1820s and early 1830s to the youthful evangelism of groups set ablaze by religious revivals. Robert H. Abzug, *Cosmos Crumbling: American Reform and the Religious Imagination* (New York: Oxford University Press, 1994), partakes of a similar spirit.

35. Ronald G. Walters, *American Reformers, 1815–1860,* ed. Eric Foner (New York: Hill and Wang, 1997), quotation on p. xvi.

36. For example, on the role of collective identity construction, see Jean L. Cohen, "Strategy or Identity: New Theoretical Paradigms and Contemporary Social Movements," *Social Research* 52 (1985): 663–716; and Nancy Fraser, "From Redistribution to Recognition? Dilemmas of Justice in a 'Post Socialist' Age," *New Left Review* 212 (1995): 68–93; and on the role of narrative, see Francesca Polletta, "Contending Stories: Narrative in Social Movements," *Qualitative Sociology* 21 (1998): 419–46.

37. David A. Snow et al., "Frame Alignment Processes, Micromobilization, and Movement Participation," *American Sociological Review* 51 (1986): 464–81, quotation on p. 464; and David A. Snow and Robert D. Benford, "Master Frames and Cycles of Protest," in *Frontiers in Social Movement Theory,* ed. Aldon D. Morris and Carol McClurg Mueller, pp. 133–155 (New Haven: Yale University Press, 1992), quotation on p. 137.

38. The literature on framing processes in social movements is extensive. For defining works, see Snow et al., "Frame Alignment Processes"; Snow and Benford, "Master Frames and Cycles of Protest"; and William A. Gamson, *Talking Politics* (New York: Cambridge University Press, 1992).

39. Pamela Oliver, Jorge Cadena-Roa, and Kelley D. Strawin, "Emerging Trends in the Study of Protest and Social Movements," *Research in Political Sociology* 12 (2003); Snow and Benford, "Master Frames and Cycles of Protest"; Robert Benford, "An Insider's Critique of the Social Movement Framing Perspective," *Sociological Inquiry* 67 (1997): 409–30. For an overview of the role of emotions and social movements, see Jeff Goodwin, James M. Jasper, and Francesca Polletta, "The Return of the Repressed: The Fall and Rise of Emotions in Social Movement Theory," *Mobilization* (2000): 565–84.

40. Barnes, *Antislavery Impulse,* p. 68; Davis, "Emergence of Immediatism," p. 228; Loveland, "Evangelicalism and 'Immediate Emancipation,'" p. 174.

41. Abzug, *Cosmos Crumbling,* p. 7; Max Weber, "Science as a Vocation," in *From Max Weber: Essays in Sociology,* ed. H. H. Gerth and C. Wright Mills, pp. 129–56 (New York: Oxford University Press, 1946), p. 143, idem, "Science as a Vocation," p. 153; Wyatt-Brown, *Yankee Saints and Southern Sinners* (Baton Rouge: Louisiana State University Press, 1985), p. 28.

42. Erving Goffman, *Frame Analysis* (New York: Harper & Row, 1974), pp. 11–12, 236; William H. Sewell, Jr., "A Theory of Structure: Duality, Agency, and Transformation," *American Journal of Sociology* 98 (1992): 1–29. See also Darren E. Sherkat and Christopher G. Ellison, "The Cognitive Structure of a Moral Crusade: Conservative Protestant Opposition to Pornography," *Social Forces* 75 (1997): 957–80.

43. Anne E. Kane, "Theorizing Meaning Construction in Social Movements: Symbolic Structures and Interpretation during the Irish Land War, 1879–1882," *Sociological Theory* 15 (1997): 249–76; Pierre Bourdieu, *The Logic of Practice* (Stanford: Stanford University Press, 1980); Tarrow raised this point about framing and agency in response to a talk I gave at the Sociology Department at Cornell University in 2002.

44. Sewell, "A Theory of Structure," idem, "Political Events as Structural Transformations: Inventing Revolution at the Bastille," *Theory and Society* 25 (1996): 841–81; Bourdieu, *Logic of Practice,* pp. 66–70; Giddens, *Modernity and Self-Identity.*

45. In drawing this distinction between types of schemas, I have applied Michael Mann's distinction between intensive and extensive forms of power to theories of cultural schemas. Intensive schemas are not to be confused with the deep symbolic structures of cultural structuralism. Indeed, deep structures may correspond more clearly to what I refer to as extensive schemas. Michael Mann, *A History of Power from the Beginning to A.D. 1760,* vol. 1 of *The Sources of Social Power* (New York: Cambridge University Press, 1986).

46. Roger Gould, in "Collective Violence and Group Solidarity: Evidence from a Feuding Society," *American Sociological Review* 64 (1999): 356–80, has demonstrated how limited the extension of the Corsican vendetta actually was in nineteenth-century Italy. Kinship acts of vengeance depended on prior experiences of group contention; Tilly touches on a related point in his discussion of how augmenting the number of supporters and the intensity of support for a movement often work against each other; and also in his discussion of how the distinction between embedded and detached collective identities matters when explaining the strength of commitment and the scope of emulation of different experiences exhibited in movements. Tilly, "From Interactions to Outcomes in Social Movements," pp. 262–66.

47. Clifford Geertz's ethnographic research and Gould's research on vendettas in nineteenth-century Corsica both suggest that the intensive schema of vengeance needs the reinforcement of past actions that enhance clan solidarity and its

reputation for taking deadly risks. This nicely illustrates the recursive relationship between action and structure in cultural schemas. The schema needs repeated instantiation in violent clan action to remain salient. Clifford Geertz, *The Interpretation of Cultures* (New York: Basic Books, 1973), p. 93; Gould, "Collective Violence and Group Solidarity."

48. Clemens, *People's Lobby;* Jeffrey Haydu, "Business Citizenship at Work: Cultural Transposition and Class Formation in Cincinnati, 1870–1910," *American Journal of Sociolgy* 107 (2002): 1424–67.

49. John Dewey, *A Common Faith* (New Haven: Yale University Press, 1934), p. 14.

50. Hans Joas, *The Creativity of Action* (Chicago: University of Chicago Press, 1996).

51. Martin Heidegger, *Being and Time* (New York: Harper & Row, 1962); Paul Ricoeur, *Hermeneutics and Human Sciences: Essays on Language, Action, and Interpretation* (New York: Cambridge University Press, 1981).

52. For a good example of the role of binary oppositions in cultural theory, see Alexander, "The Binary Discourse of Civil Society," ed. Michele Lamont and Marcel Fournier, pp. 289–308 (Chicago: University of Chicago Press, 1992).

53. Clemens, *People's Lobby.*

54. Abzug, *Cosmos Crumbling.*

55. Giddens, *Modernity and Self-Identity;* Taylor, *Rock-A-By Baby.*

56. The phrase "cosmos crumbling" comes from Abzug's book with the same title. On rates of alcohol consumption, see W. J. Rorabaugh, *Alcoholic Republic: An American Tradition* (New York: Oxford University Press, 1979); on a new sensibility, see Haskell, "Capitalism and the Origins of Humanitarian Sensibility"; and most importantly on the novel linking of the individual and national redemption through religious revival see Thomas, *Revivalism and Cultural Change.* I will draw again on Thomas's work at the conclusion of chapter 4 which charts the changing forms of American revivals.

Chapter Two

1. For the local dimensions and role of patronage in the Whiskey Rebellion, see Gould, "Patron-Client Ties, State Centralization, and the Whiskey Rebellion," *American Journal of Sociology* 102 (1996): 400–29. For the regional nature of Shays's Rebellion, see David P. Szatmary, *Shays' Rebellion: The Making of an Agrarian Insurrection* (Amherst: University of Massachusetts Press, 1980). And for the mostly parochial nature of labor organizing up to and through the 1830s, see Sean Wilentz, *Chants Democratic: New York City and the Rise of the American Working Class, 1788–1850* (New York: Oxford University Press, 1984).

2. Alexis de Tocqueville, *Democracy in America* (Chicago: University of Chicago Press, 2000), pp. 232, 528–29, 529.

3. The apt phrase "meandering rivulets" characterizing Tocqueville's under-standing of American political and civic engagement comes from Tarrow, "The Very Excess of Democracy", p. 32.

4. Tocqueville, *Democracy in America,* pp. 282, 517, 280.

5. Tocqueville, *Democracy in America,* p. 512; Peter D. McClelland and Richard J. Zeckhauser, *Demographic Dimensions of the New Republic: American Interregional Migration, Vital Statistics, and Manumissions, 1800–1860* (Cambridge: Cambridge University Press, 1982); George R. Taylor, *Transportation Revolution, 1815–1860* (White Plains, NY: M. E. Sharpe, 1951).

6. Hatch, *Democratization of American Christianity,* p. 30.

7. Historical Statistics of the United States from Colonial Times to 1970. Washington, D. C.: U.S. GPO, 1975.

8. Allan Kulikoff, *The Agrarian Origins of American Capitalism* (Charlottesville: University Press of Virginia, 1992); Cross, *Burned-over District;* Ryan, *Cradle of the Middle Class.*

9. Taylor, *Transportation Revolution,* p. 143.

10. Charles Sellers, *The Market Revolution* (New York and Oxford: Oxford University Press, 1991); *Niles Register,* Nov. 3. 1827, p. 154.

11. D. B. Davis, "Perils of Doing History by Ahistorial Abstraction," in *The Antislavery Debate: Capitalism and Abolitionism as a Problem of Historical Interpretation,* ed. Thomas Bender, pp. 290–309 (Berkeley: University of California Press, 1992).

12. The phrase "midget institution in a giant land" comes from John Murrin, "The Great Inversion, or Court Verses Country: A Comparison of the Revolution Settlements in England (1688–1721) and America (1776–1816)," in *Three British Revolutions: 1641, 1688, 1776,* ed. J. G. A. Pocock (Princeton: Princeton University Press, 1980), p. 425; George Wilson Pierson, *Tocqueville in America* (Baltimore: John Hopkins Press, 1996), p. 185; Edwin Amenta, *Bold Relief: Institutional Politics and the Origins of American Social Policy* (Princeton: Princeton University Press, 1998).

13. Sellers, *Market Revolution.*

14. United States Bureau of Census 1976; Skocpol, "The Tocqueville Problem: Civic Engagement in American Democracy," *Social Science History* 21 (1997): 455–79; Richard R. John, *Spreading the News: The American Postal System from Franklin to Morse* (Cambridge, MA: Harvard University Press, 1995); Richard D. Brown, "The Emergence of Urban Society in Rural Massachusetts, 1760–1820," *Journal of American History* 61 (1974): 29–51.

15. See Michael P. Young, "Tocqueville's America: A Critical Reappraisal of Voluntary Associations before the Civil War," paper presented at the 2001 ASA meeting in Anaheim, 2001, for an analysis of the lack of cross-sectional association between state expenditures and moral reform societies.

16. Richard L. McCormick, *The Party Period and Public Policy: American Politics from the Age of Jackson to the Progressive Era* (New York: Oxford University, 1986).

17. Glenn C. Altschuler and Stuart M. Blumin, "Limits of Political Engagement in Antebellum America: A New Look at the Golden Age of Participatory Democracy," *Journal of American History* 84 (1997): 855–85; Clemens, *People's Lobby;* Ronald P. Formisano, *The Birth of Mass Political Parties: Michigan, 1827–1861* (Princeton: Princeton University Press, 1971).

18. Formisano, *Transformation of Political Culture;* McCormick, *Party Period and Public Policy;* Sellers, *Market Revolution.*

19. Amenta, *Bold Relief,* and Clemens, *People's Lobby,* both argue that patronage parties are averse to programmatic and national purposes.

20. See Young, "Tocqueville's America," for a detailed statistical analysis of the cross-sectional association between party politics and moral reform societies; Leonard L. Richards, *'Gentlemen of Property and Standing': Anti-Abolition Mobs in Jacksonian America* (New York: Oxford University Press, 1970); Tyrell, *Sobering Up;* Research of members of temperance and antislavery society show that they were not Jacksonians and more often than not simply uninvolved in party politics.

21. Noll, *America's God;* Hatch, *Democratization of American Christianity.*

22. Jon Butler, *Awash in a Sea of Faith: Christianizing the American People* (Cambridge, MA: Harvard University Press, 1990); Noll, *America's God.*

23. Finke and Stark, *Churching of America.*

24. Butler, *Awash in a Sea of Faith;* Noll, *America's God.*

25. Donald G. Matthews, "The Second Great Awakening as an Organizing Process, 1790–1830," *American Quarterly* 21 (1969): 23–43, p. 37; Edwin Gaustad, *Historical Atlas of American Religion;* Finke and Stark, *Churching of America.*

26. Paul Johnson, *A History of Christianity* (London: Weidenfeld and Nicolson, 1976). See also Perry Miller, *The Life of the Mind in America: From the Revolution to the Civil War* (New York: Harcourt, Brace and World, 1965), p. 7.

27. Butler, *Awash in a Sea of Faith.*

28. Hatch discusses the essentially centrifugal nature of the religious movements that Christianized America. Noll, on the other hand, sees a little more theological coherence to these movements, but does not contradict the general point that American evangelical churches in the 1820s were at best weakly united around a loose theological consensus and organizationally independent and even factious. For these discussions see Hatch, *Democratization of American Christianity;* and Noll, *America's God.*

29. David Paul Nord, "The Evangelical Origins of Mass Media in America, 1815–1835," *Journalism Monographs* 88 (1984): 1–30; Butler, *Awash in a Sea of Faith;* R. Laurence Moore, *Selling God: American Religion in the Marketplace of Culture* (New York and Oxford: Oxford University Press, 1994).

30. Curtis D. Johnson, *Redeeming America: Evangelicals and the Road to the Civil War* (Chicago: Ivan R. Dee, 1993); and Hatch, *Democratization of American Christianity.* Noll in *America's God* also uses formalist and antiformalist designations to draw distinctions among evangelicals. Both Congregationalist and Pres-

byterians subscribed to the Dort Confession (1618–19) and remained avowedly anti-Arminian at the turn of the nineteenth century. The seventeenth-century Reformed Confessions of Dort and Westminster (1643–48) established the contentious distinction between Calvinist and Arminian, a distinction that would endure long after the seventeenth-century principles of the split had been hopelessly confused. Formally, New England Congregationalists did not subscribe to the Westminster Confession. American Puritans had fled Great Britain before its articulation. Nonetheless, the Confession's even stronger rejection of Arminian heresies was widely accepted by them. In simple terms, Jacob Harmensen (Arminius) opposed the doctrine of double predestination—that God chooses the elect and the damned. It is significant to note that this doctrine played nowhere near as central a role in Calvin's work as it would in the doctrines of those Reformed sects that took his name into the seventeenth and eighteenth centuries. Arminius smuggled human choice into God's schema of saving grace. Individuals were free to respond to or restrain from the covenant of grace. For the orthodox Calvinists in England and Holland, this seemed a heretical affront to the sovereignty of God. In 1618, a conference at Dort was called to convince Arminius to reconsider. He did not, but the Dort conference resulted in a new confession captured in the now famous five points of Calvinism: total depravity, unconditional election, limited atonement, irresistible grace, and the perseverance of saints. While Arminius and his early followers considered themselves Calvinists, the Dort Confession monopolized the label for the anti-Arminian camp, and the Westminster Confession only escalated hostility between Calvinists and Arminians. This understanding of orthodox doctrine and its differences from other evangelical sects comes from Paul K. Conkin, *The Uneasy Center: Reformed Christianity in Antebellum America* (Chapel Hill: University of North Carolina Press, 1995), pp. 36–37, 48.

Chapter Three

1. American Education Society, *The Quarterly Register and Journal of the American Education Society* (Boston: Perkins and Marvin, 1825–1829). The phrase "evangelical united front" comes from Foster, *Errand of Mercy*.

2. American Education Society, *The Quarterly Register and Journal of the American Education Society* vol. 2, no. 1, August 1829, pp. 3–6; For Bacon's comments, see Introduction, p. 6 of this book.

3. See Conkin, *Uneasy Center;* also Finke and Stark, *Churching of America,* p. 55; Allan Heimert and Perry Miller, introduction to *The Great Awakening: Documents Illustrating the Crisis and Its Consequences,* ed. Alan Heimert and Perry Miller (Indianapolis and New York: Bobbs-Merrill Company, 1967); and Miller, *Errand into the Wilderness* (Cambridge, MA: Belknap Press, 1984).

4. For discussions of the motives and uniqueness of organized benevolence, see Banner, "Religious Benevolence as Social Control"; Sellers, *Market Revolution;*

Peter Dobkin Hall, *The Organization of American Culture, 1700–1900: Private Institutions, Elites, and the Origins of American Nationality* (New York: New York University Press, 1984); and Donald M. Scott, *From Office to Profession: The New England Ministry* (Philadelphia: University of Pennsylvania, 1978).

5. On the populist opposition to organized benevolence, see Paul E. Johnson and Sean Wilentz, *The Kingdom of Matthias: A Story of Sex and Salvation in 19th Century America* (New York: Oxford University Press, 1994); Conkin, *Uneasy Center;* and Hatch, *Democratization of American Christianity.*

6. Quoted in Hatch, *Democratization of American Christianity,* p. 18.

7. On the operation of organized benevolence, see Banner, "Religious Benevolence as Social Control"; Bodo, *Protestant Clergy and Public Issues;* Cole, *Social Ideas of the Northern Evangelists;* Foster, *Errand of Mercy;* Griffin, *Their Brothers' Keepers;* and Wyatt-Brown, *Lewis Tappan,* pp. 45–46.

8. On these political changes, see Formisano, *Transformation of Political Culture;* and Griffin, *Their Brothers' Keepers.*

9. Quoted in Hatch, *Democratization of American Christianity,* p. 98. Hatch provides an excellent discussion of how populist Christianity and Jeffersonian politics mixed. Noll, in *America's God,* argues that during this period evangelical Christianity was fusing with a republican and common sense ideology in a way that threatened orthodox theocratic thinking. See Sellers, *Market Revolution,* for a broad overview of these competing political and religious dynamics. Butler, *Awash in a Sea of Faith* is also illuminating on this topic.

10. For discussions of disestablishment see Bodo, *Protestant Clergy and Public Issues,* pp. 31–37; Finke and Stark, *Churching of America,* p. 60; and Butler, *Awash in a Sea of Faith.*

11. Quoted in Lyman Beecher, *Autobiography,* ed. Barbara M. Cross (1864; Cambridge, MA: Belknap Press of Harvard University Press, 1961), vol. 1, p. 344; and also in Bodo, *Protestant Clergy and Public Issues,* p. 33.

12. Quoted in Beecher, *Autobiography,* 1: 344–45.

13. Finke and Stark, *Churching of America.*

14. For evidence of orthodoxy's concern with losing ground to upstart sects, particularly in the West, see the two following missionary reports: John F. Schermerhorn and Samuel J. Mills, *A Correct View of that Part of the United States which lies West of the Allegany Mountains, with Regard to Religion and Morals* (Hartford: Peter B. Gleason, 1814); and Samuel J. Mills and Daniel Smith, *Report of a Missionary Tour Through That Part of the United States which Lies West of the Allegany Mountains; Performed Under the Direction of the Massachusetts Missionary Society* (Andover, MA: Flagg and Gould, 1815); also see Banner, "Religious Benevolence as Social Control."

15. For arguments that organized benevolence was above all else an elite enterprise in social control see Cole, *Social Ideas of the Northern Evangelists;* Foster, *Errand of Mercy;* and Griffin, *Their Brothers' Keepers.*

16. Quoted in Hatch, *Democratization of American Christianity,* p. 100.

17. Wyatt–Brown, *Lewis Tappan.*

18. For notions of benevolence that extend beyond orthodoxy, see Banner, "Religious Benevolence as Social Control." For the ties of benevolence to the New Divinity theology developed by the disciples of Edwards, see Griffin, *Their Brothers' Keepers;* Conkin, *Uneasy Center;* and Leo P. Hirrel, *Children of Wrath: New School Calvinism and Antebellum Reform* (Lexington: University of Kentucky Press, 1998). Noll in *America's God* argues that Edward's theology was not genuinely American (it was still European in its roots), but the next generation's response to it was.

19. On this point, see Hirrel, *Children of Wrath.*

20. Quoted in Noll, *America's God,* p. 273.

21. This account of disinterested benevolence synthesizes arguments from Cole, *Social Ideas of the Northern Evangelists;* Sidney E. Ahlstrom, *A Religious History of the American People* (New Haven and New London: Yale University Press, 1972); Conkin, *Uneasy Center;* and Griffin, *Their Brothers' Keepers.*

22. Romans 11: 6; and see John Calvin, *Institutes of the Christian Religion* (Philadelphia: Westminster Press, 1960), chap. 21.

23. Quoted in Noll, *America's God,* p. 45. This conservative wing of orthodoxy still held strong theocratic views and worked within a covenant theology famously described by the historian Perry Miller. This theology and the corporate structure of covenanted communities extended into the nineteenth century for many heirs of Calvinism, particularly for Presbyterians in southern Middle Atlantic States and a minority of Congregationalists in New England. Archibald Alexander was a good representative of this mind set. These staunch Calvinists remained emotionally embedded in the corporate structure of eighteenth-century America. They felt the new republic's relationship with God to be one of a collective contract like that of the Israelites with the Old Testament God. For this reason, the theocrats associated with organized benevolence expected popular deference to be shown to the pious in matters of civil governance. The saints had a right to protect themselves from violations of the public covenant even against the interests of the irreligious. This sentiment extended in a modified form to the New Divinity advocates, but this sense of covenant and saints was refracted through the lens of benevolence and a republican sense of the mass regeneration of individuals. For support of this argument see Bodo, *Protestant Clergy and Public Issues;* Miller, *Errand into the Wilderness;* Alan Heimert, *Religion and the American Mind: From Awakening to the Revolution* (Cambridge, MA: Harvard University Press, 1966); Scott, *From Office to Profession;* and Noll, *America's God.*

24. James 2:26.

25. See Hirrel, *Children of Wrath.*

26. Quoted in Bodo, *Protestant Clergy and Public Issues,* pp. 19–20.

27. For the group migration of New Englanders, see Cross, *Burned-Over District,* p. 5; Lawrence Goodheart, *Abolitionist, Actuary, Atheist: Elizur Wright and*

the Reform Impulse (Kent, Ohio: Kent State University Press, 1990), p. 7; and D. W. Meinig, *The Shaping of America: A Geographical Perspective on 500 Years of History,* vol. 2, *Continental America, 1800–1967* (New Haven: Yale University Press, 1993), pp. 264–73.

28. Griffin, *Their Brothers' Keepers,* pp. 24–25, discusses the separate efforts of the home missionary societies because of different migration patterns. The reports of Schermerhorn and Mills, *Correct View of that Part of the United States* and Mills and Smith, *Report of a Missionary Tour* provide strong evidence of interdenominational cooperation.

29. *Evangelist,* Sept. 1825, p. 357. Griffin, in *Their Brothers' Keepers* also makes this point about the missionary pressures to cooperate among emigrant communities in the West.

30. United Domestic Missionary Society, *Fourth Annual Report* (New York, 1826).

31. Banner, in "Religious Benevolence as Social Control," discusses the different initiatives Presbyterians and Congregationalists took in building the united front. Schermerhorn and Mills, *A Correct View of that Part of the United States,* and its influence on the leaders of organized benevolence, demonstrate how concerned orthodoxy was with religion in the West and the success of the populist sects in this region. Griffin, in *Their Brothers' Keepers,* pp. 26–28, provides an overview of the events leading up to the formation of the American Bible Society.

32. *New York Evangelist,* May 15, 1830.

33. See the constitutions published in the annual reports of the American Bible Society, the American Board of Commissioners for Foreign Missions, the American Home Missionary Society, American Sunday School Union, and the American Tract Society for the voluntary associative nature of these societies. Peter J. Wosh in "Bibles, Benevolence and Emerging Bureaucracy: The Persistence of the American Bible Society, 1816–1890" (Ph.D. dissertation in History from NYU) provides evidence of the rationalized and bureaucratic nature of the Bible Society—a model followed by other parachurch institutions.

34. On the influence of orthodox Sunday schools and the Union's curriculum, see Conkin, *Uneasy Center.*

35. See Griffin, *Their Brothers' Keepers.*

36. *Missionary Herald,* June 25, 1824, vol. 21, p. 184.

37. *Missionary Herald,* June 25, 1824, vol. 21, p. 188.

38. For an account of the American Tract Society's plan of "general supply," see Nord, "Evangelical Origins of Mass Media in America."

39. For a discussion of the general influence of print capitalism, see Anderson, *Imagined Communities,* and for the emergence of the penny presses in America, see Johnson and Wilentz, *Kingdom of Matthias.* Moore, *Selling God,* argues convincingly that print evangelism reached a national audience before these commercial interests did.

40. American Education Society, *Quarterly Register*, 1830, p. 107.

41. American Education Society, *Quarterly Register*, 1831, p. 303.

42. On the national character of these schools see Hall, *The Organization of American Culture*. On these schools as stepping stones to involvement in organized benevolence see Hugh Davis, *Joshua Leavitt: Evangelical Abolitionist* (Baton Rouge: Louisiana State University Press, 1990); and Goodheart, *Abolitionist, Actuary, Atheist*.

43. These figures are cited in Sellers, *Market Revolution*. The survey of income to benevolent societies published by the American Education Society in 1830 in its *Quarterly Register* supports them.

44. See Young, "Tocqueville's America."

45. See Abzug, *Cosmos Crumbling*, for the role of accounting in the evangelism and reform movements of the early nineteenth century.

46. Quoted in Sellers, *Market Revolution*, p. 217.

47. Quoted in Foster, *Errand of Mercy*, p. 58.

48. On the specialization of organized benevolence, see American Education Society, *Quarterly Register*, 1830, p. 63; Abzug, *Cosmos Crumbling*, p. 70; Davis, *Joshua Leavitt*, pp. 51–52; Griffin, *Their Brothers' Keepers*, chap. 4; and Wyatt-Brown, *Lewis Tappan*.

49. See Davis, *Joshua Leavitt*.

50. *Missionary Herald*, May 1824, vol. 20, p. 167.

51. *African Repository and Colonial Journal*, Aug. 1825, 1, 6: 174–75.

52. The organization's original name was the American Society for the Promotion of Temperance, but the name was soon simplified.

53. See Tyrrell, *Sobering Up;* and Walters, *American Reformers* for a discussion of the origins of the American Temperance Society. Lyman Beecher, *Six Sermons on the Nature, Occasions, Signs, Evils, and Remedy of Intemperance* (Boston: T. R. Marvin, 1828).

54. John Allen Krout, *Origins of Prohibition* (New York: Alfred A. Knopf, 1925), is still the best study of the early years of the American Temperance Society.

55. Again, see Miller, *Errand into the Wilderness*, for an account of the covenant theology.

56. Randolph A. Roth, *Democratic Dilemma: Religion, Reform, and the Social Order of the Connecticut River Valley of Vermont, 1791–1850* (New York: Cambridge University Press, 1987), p. 46 and Ryan, *Cradle of the Middle Class*, pp. 115–16, provide evidence for the decline of church trials. Glenn C. Altschuler and Jan M. Saltzgaber, *Revivalism, Social Conscience, and Community in the Burned-over District: The Trial of Rhoda Bement* (Ithaca, NY: Cornell University Press, 1983) shows in wonderful detail how communicants in the new era of disestablishment could rebel against church authority.

57. For evidence of this, see Conkin, *Uneasy Center*, p. 52; Johnson, *Shopkeeper's Millennium*, chap. 1; and Ryan, *Cradle of the Middle Class*, chap. 1.

58. *Weekly Recorder,* February 9, 1815, vol. 1, no. 32, p. 253.

59. *Utica Christian Magazine,* Dec. 1814, vol. 2, no. 6, p. 196.

60. Quoted in *Panoplist and Missionary Magazine,* June 1817, p. 262. For similar reports see *Connecticut Evangelical Magazine,* July 1814.

61. Quoted in *Miscellaneous Magazine,* Jan. 1824, vol. 1, no. 1, p. 9.

62. Quoted in Krout, *Origins of Prohibition,* p. 95.

63. Davis, *Joshua Leavitt;* John McDowall, *McDowall's Journal* (New York, 1833); Wyatt-Brown, *Lewis Tappan.*

64. Friedman, in *Gregarious Saints,* p. 19, makes the argument that reform and benevolence served as something of a surrogate ministry. See Scott, *From Office to Profession,* for the changing nature of the ministry in the early nineteenth century.

65. A sample of the studies demonstrating the active role of women in benevolence include Cott, *Bonds of Womanhood;* Ann Douglas, *The Feminization of American Culture* (New York: Alfred A. Knopf, 1979); Barbara Epstein, *The Politics of Domesticity: Women, Evangelism, and Temperance in Nineteenth-Century America* (Middletown, CN: Wesleyan University Press, 1981); Nancy Hewitt, *Women's Activism and Social Change* (Ithaca, NY: Cornell University Press, 1984); Smith-Rosenberg, *Religion and Rise of the American City;* Ryan, *Cradle of the Middle Class;* Ryan, *Women in Public: Between Banners and Ballots, 1825–1880* (Baltimore: The Johns Hopkins University Press, 1990), chap. 3.

66. *Western Recorder,* Dec. 28, 1830.

67. *Philanthropist,* April 25, 1828, quoted in Wendell Phillips Garrison and Francis Jackson Garrison, *William Lloyd Garrison, 1805–1879: The Story of His Life Told By His Children* (1885; New York: Negro Universities Press, 1969), vol. 1, pp. 82–83.

68. See Henry Mayer, *All on Fire: William Lloyd Garrison and the Abolition of Slavery* (New York: St. Martin's Press, 1998), for William Lloyd Garrison's views of temperance in the late 1820s. See Davis, *Joshua Leavitt,* chap. 6, and John McDowall, *Memoir and Select Remains of the Late Rev. John R. McDowall* (New York, 1838) for the radicalization of these two agents of organized benevolence. Also see Smith-Rosenberg, *Religion and Rise of the American City,* chap. 5, for the contentious issues surrounding the moral reform or Magdalen societies within organized benevolence.

Chapter Four

1. On the different forms of revivalism, see Randall Herbert Balmer and John R. Fitzmier, *The Presbyterians* (Westport, CN: Green Wood Press, 1993); Richard Carwardine, *Transatlantic Revivalism: Popular Evangelicalism in Britain and America, 1790–1865* (Westport, CN and London: Greenwood Press, 1978);

and William Warren Sweet, *Revivalism in America: Its Origin, Growth and Decline* (New York: Charles Scribner's Sons, 1945).

2. Bernard A. Weisberger, *They Gathered at the River: The Story of the Great Revivalists and Their Impact upon Religion in America* (Boston: Little, Brown and Company, 1958), p. 27; Noll, *America's God*, p. 5.

3. On this point of regional, class, and sectarian differences over revivals, see Hatch, *Democratization of American Christianity.*

4. This is how the paper described itself in its earliest editions, see, e.g., *New York Evangelist,* April 17, 1830, p. 5.

5. *New York Evangelist,* April 10, 1830, p. 9.

6. Finke and Stark, *Churching of America.*

7. For accounts of this revival, see Sweet, *Revivalism in America;* and John B. Boles, *The Great Revival: Beginnings of the Bible Belt* (Lexington, KY: University Press of Kentucky, 1996).

8. Balmer and Fitzmier, *Presbyterians.*

9. Accounts of the Kentucky revival come from Boles, *Great Revival,* chap. 5; and Sweet, *Revivalism in America,* pp. 122–23. McGee's account is quoted in Boles, p. 54.

10. For the number of people attending the revival, see Balmer and Fitzmier, *Presbyterians,* p. 63; and *New-York Missionary Magazine and Repository of Religious Intelligence,* 1802, vol. 3, no. 2, p. 83.

11. *New-York Missionary Magazine and Repository of Religious Intelligence,* 1802, vol. 3, no. 2, p. 83.

12. For accounts of the Cane Ridge revival, see Balmer and Fitzmier, *Presbyterians,* p. 63; Boles, *Great Revival,* pp. 66–67; and Weisberger, *They Gathered at the River,* pp. 34–35.

13. Synod of Kentucky, "Minutes of the Synod of Kentucky," in *Religion on the American Frontier: The Presbyterians, 1783–1840: A Collection of Source Materials,* ed. William Warren Sweet (New York and London: Harper & Brothers Publishers, 1936), vol. 2, pp. 318–19.

14. Cumberland Presbytery, "Minutes," in *Religion on the American Frontier,* vol. 2, p. 305.

15. See Weisberger, *They Gathered at the River,* p. 38; and Hatch, *Democratization of American Christianity,* pp. 60–61, 70 on the Cumberland Presbyterian split.

16. The quotation is from Hatch, *Democratization of American Christianity,* p. 7. For a general discussion of the ramified effects of the western revivals, see Carwardine, *Transatlantic Revivals.*

17. The Jezebel quotation comes from Ryan, *Cradle of the Middle Class;* Cross reports on the two female preachers in western New York in *Burned-Over District,* p. 38.

18. *Western Missionary Magazine,* March 1803, vol. 1, p. 51.

19. See Hatch, *Democratization of American Christianity,* for an extended discussion of African American religion, especially pp. 102–13.

20. Quoted in Balmer and Fitzmier, *Presbyterians,* pp. 229–30.

21. Quoted in Heimert, *Religion and the American Mind,* pp. 164–5.

22. Cedric B. Cowing, *The Great Awakening and the American Revolution: Colonial Thought in the 18th Century* (Chicago: Rand McNally, 1971), pp. 45–53.

23. On Whitefield's tour, see Sweet, *Revivalism in America,* p. 33; and Henry S. Stout, "Religion, Communication, and the Ideological Origins of the American Revolution," *William and Mary Quarterly* 34 (1977): 519–41.

24. The term is Jonathan Edwards's, who contended that the "heart of true religion is holy affection . . . Our people do not so much need to have their heads stored, as to have their hearts touched." Quoted in Sweet, *Revivalism in America,* p. 30. As illustrated in the passage quoted above from the *Evangelist,* the term became a favorite of the defenders of the "new measure" revivals in the 1820s.

25. On the Old-Side (Light) / New-Side (Light) split and the popular role of the laity, see Marilyn J. Westerkamp, *Triumph of the Laity: Scots-Irish Piety and the Great Awakening, 1625–1760* (New York and Oxford: Oxford University Press, 1988).

26. Quoted in Heimert and Miller, introduction, pp. xxvi.

27. Quoted in Miller, *New England Mind: From Colony to Province* (Cambridge, MA: Belknap Press, 1953), p. 70.

28. The term "short-cut to heaven" comes from Carwardine, *Transatlantic Revivals,* chap. 1. For a more general discussion of the changing shape of revivals in the early nineteenth century, see Miller, "From the Covenant to the Revival," in *The Shaping of American Religion,* ed. James Ward Smith and A. Leland Jamison (Princeton: Princeton University Press, 1961); and Noll, *America's God.*

29. Heimert, *Religion and the American Mind,* gives the account of Davenport burning his vestment. The quote from the *Boston Evening Report* can be found in Sweet, *Revivalism in America,* p. 59. A general account of the compromise between the opposing sides can be found in Balmer and Fitzmier, *Presbyterians.*

30. Boles, *Great Revival,* p. 87.

31. See Conkin, *Uneasy Center;* and John Kent, *Holding the Fort: Studies in Victorian Revivalism* (London: Epworth Press, 1978), on the sharp distinctions between populist and orthodox revivals.

32. *Connecticut Evangelical Magazine,* March 1802, p. 354.

33. Ibid., p. 356.

34. See Balmer and Fitzmier, *Presbyterians,* p. 66; Conkin, *Uneasy Center,* p. 221; and Sweet, *Revivalism in America,* p. 125, on Baxter and Alexander's change of heart.

35. Quoted in Westerkamp, *Triumph of the Laity,* p. 191.

36. Quoted in Hatch, *Democratization of American Christianity,* p. 19.

37. Ibid., p. 13.

38. See Rev. Alexander's letter in Sprague, *Lectures on Revivals of Religion* (Albany: Webster and Skinners, 1832), p. 4.

39. *Connecticut Evangelical Magazine,* November 1803, pp. 180–81.

40. Ibid., pp. 182–83.

41. Ibid., p. 183.

42. Ibid., p. 188.

43. Ibid., pp. 188–89.

44. Lyman Beecher, *The Government of God Desirable* (New London: Samuel Green, 1811).

45. *Vermont Evangelical Magazine,* April 1811, vol. 3, no. 4, p. 127.

46. Davis, *Joshua Leavitt;* Goodheart, *Abolitionist, Actuary, Atheist;* Hall, *Organization of American Culture.*

47. Weisberger, *They Gathered at the River,* pp. 64–69, describes Nettleton's style of revivalism.

48. These numbers come from Scott, *From Office to Profession.*

49. Cross, *Burned-Over District,* pp. 6–7, describes how New England migration outpaced the reach of orthodox institutions.

50. Quoted in Cross, *Burned-Over District,* p. 41.

51. See Charles Grandison Finney, *The Memoirs of Charles G. Finney: The Complete Restored Text* (Grand Rapids, Michigan: Zondervan Publishing House, 1989), chap. 10.

52. Quoted in Ryan, *Cradle of the Middle Class,* p. 67.

53. See the American Home Missionary Society, "First Annual Report," in American Home Missionary Society, *Reports of the American Home Missionary Society* (New York: Claton and Van Norden, 1827–1830); and Cross, *Burned-Over District,* p. 22.

54. For discussions of the demographic and economic changes of New York, see Cross, *Burned-Over District,* pp. 56–73; Keith Hardman, *Charles Grandison Finney, 1792–1875: Revivalist and Reformer* (Syracuse: Syracuse University Press, 1987); and Johnson, *Shopkeeper's Millennium,* p. 92. The phrase "instant city" comes from Ryan, *Cradle of the Middle Class,* p. 67.

55. Finney, *Memoirs,* p. 18.

56. Ibid., p. 18.

57. See Finney, *Memoirs,* chap. 10–11, quotation on p. 86. See also Edwin Gaustad, *Historical Atlas of American Religion* (New York: Harper & Row, 1962), for the religious composition of this region.

58. Quoted in Hardman, *Charles Grandison Finney,* p. 66.

59. On this point, see Barnes and Dumond, *Letters,* p. 23; and Finney, *Memoirs,* p. 84.

60. Hardman, *Charles Grandison Finney,* p. 84.

61. Abzug, *Passionate Liberator,* makes this point that the new measure revivals were a struggle over the control of pulpits and churches.

62. Quoted in Abzug, *Passionate Liberator,* p. 48.

63. Quoted in Finney, *Memoirs,* p. 186n.

64. See Carwardine, *Transatlantic Revivalism,* p. 6; and Weisberger, *They Gathered at the River,* pp. 111–12.

65. These figures come from John L. Hammond's ICPSR (7754) data set. In a survey of ten religious newspapers, Hammond recorded all revivals reported in New York and Ohio from 1825 to 1835.

66. Quoted in Abzug, *Passionate Liberator,* p. 41.

67. See Johnson, *Shopkeeper's Millennium.*

68. Quoted in Hardman, *Charles Grandison Finney,* p. 204.

69. *New York Evangelist,* January 22, 1831.

70. See Finney, *Lectures on Revivals of Religion,* p. 50.

71. For support of this claim, see Barnes, *Antislavery Impulse;* and Scott, "Abolition as a Sacred Vocation."

72. Thomas, *Revivalism and Cultural Change,* p. 78. On the fusion of individualism and nation in revivalism, Thomas's argument, though much broader than the one made here, is very much in accord with the central theme of this book. The phrase "irresistible power" of the revival comes from Miller, *Life of the Mind in America,* p. 7.

Chapter Five

1. "Secret Circular of 1831" in *Religion on the American Frontier: The Presbyterians, 1783–1840: A Collection of Source Materials,* ed. William Warren Sweet (New York and London: Harper & Brothers Publishers, 1936), p. 829.

2. See Balmer and Fitzmier, *Presbyterians,* p. 68.

3. On this point, see Robert L. Hampel, *Temperance and Prohibition in Massachusetts, 1813–1852* (Ann Arbor: UMI Research Press, 1982), p. 28.

4. Beecher, *Six Sermons,* p. 7.

5. *American Quarterly Temperance Magazine,* February 1833, p. 7.

6. Krout, *Origins of Prohibition.*

7. Quoted in *American Quarterly Temperance Magazine,* November 1833, pp. 315, 317.

8. See Calvin Colton, *Protestant Jesuitism* (New York: Harper and Brothers, 1836).

9. *Western Recorder,* July 16, 1833, p. 116.

10. See Griffin, *Their Brothers' Keepers,* pp. 69–70; and Rorabaugh, *Alcoholic Republic,* p. 196.

11. *New York Evangelist,* May 31, 1834, p. 87.

12. See Hampel, *Temperance and Prohibition,* p. 50; and Tyrrell, *Sobering Up,* chap. 6.

13. See Krout, *Origins of Prohibition*, p. 108.

14. See Tyrrell, *Sobering Up*, pp. 237–39.

15. See Jed Dannenbaum, *Drink and Disorder: Temperance Reform in Cincinnati from the Washington Revival to the WCTU* (Chicago: University of Illinois Press, 1984), chap. 2; Hampel, *Temperance and Prohibition;* and Tyrrell, *Sobering Up*.

16. *Baltimore Clipper,* Jan. 15, 1841.

17. *Baltimore Sun,* Jan. 1, 1841.

18. *Baltimore Clipper,* March 27, 1841.

19. *American and Commercial Daily Advertiser,* March 26, 1841, p. 2.

20. See Tyrrell, *Sobering Up*, p. 172.

21. Ibid., chap. 8.

22. For the repressive measures of the antivice campaigns of the late nineteenth century, see Nicola Beisel's excellent study, *Imperiled Innocents: Anthony Comstock and Family Reproduction in Victorian America* (Princeton: Princeton University Press, 1997).

23. Quoted in Garrison and Garrison, *William Lloyd Garrison*, p. 136.

24. Goodman, *Of One Blood*.

25. *Liberator,* Jan. 1, 1831, p. 1.

26. *Liberator,* Sept. 3, 1831, p. 143.

27. *Liberator,* Jan. 7, 1832, p. 1.

28. *Abolitionist,* Jan. 1833, vol. 1, no. 1, p. 29.

29. Goodheart, *Abolitionist, Actuary, Atheist*, p. 43.

30. American Anti-Slavery Society, *Declaration of Sentiments* (New York: W. S. Dorr, 1833), p. 1.

31. On events at Lane Seminary, see Barnes, *Antislavery Impulse;* and Thomas Lawrence Lesick, *The Lane Rebels: Evangelicalism and Antislavery in Antebellum America* (Metuchen, NJ: The Scarecrow Press, Inc., 1980).

32. *New York Evangelist,* May 10, 1834, p. 74.

33. *New York Evangelist,* Oct. 29, 1836, p. 174.

34. See, for example, *New York Evangelist,* Oct. 11, 1834, Nov. 22, 1834; *Liberator,* Jan. 2, 1837; *Zion's Herald,* Nov. 22, 1837.

35. Lewis Perry, in *Radical Abolitionism: Anarchy and the Government of God in Antislavery Thought* (Ithaca: Cornell University Press, 1973), argues that the Garrisonians withdrew into a type of Christian anarchism that eschewed all institutional authority—a conclusion not unlike the one Elkins arrived at (see chap. 1).

36. On the political wing of abolitionism, see Richard H. Sewell, *Ballots for Freedom: Antislavery Politics in the United States, 1837–1860* (New York: Oxford University Press, 1976). For a discussion of the impact of the abolitionists on the coming of the Civil War, see Doug McAdam, Sidney Tarrow, and Charles Tilly, *Dynamics of Contention* (New York: Cambridge University Press, 2001).

37. *McDowall's Journal,* Jan. 1833, vol. 1, no. 1, p. 5.

38. *McDowall's Journal,* Nov. 1834, vol. 2, no. 11, p. 87.

39. McDowall, *Memoir and Select Remains*.

40. *Advocate of Moral Reform,* Jan. and Feb. 1835, vol. 1, no. 1, p. 1.

41. *Advocate of Moral Reform,* Oct. 1835, p. 73.

42. *New York Evangelist,* May 13, 1837, p. 79.

43. Barbara Berg, *Remembered Gate: The Woman and the City, 1800–1860* (New York: Oxford University Press, 1978); and Smith-Rosenberg, *Religion and the Rise of the American City: The New York City,* chap. 5.

44. Ryan, *Cradle of the Middle Class;* and Beisel, *Imperiled Innocents.*

45. *New York Evangelist,* Dec. 7, 1833, p. 192.

46. *New York Evangelist,* Oct. 11, 1834, p. 163.

47. *Advocate of Moral Reform,* Jan. 1836, p. 7.

48. *Liberator,* Dec.10, 1836, p. 198.

49. *Liberator,* Nov. 5, 1836, p. 177.

50. *McDowall's Journal,* Nov. 1834, vol. 2, no. 11, p. 87.

51. *Western Recorder,* July 16, 1833, p. 116; and *New York Evangelist,* Oct. 29, 1836, p.174.

52. *New York Evangelist,* May 23, 1835, p. 82.

53. *Advocate of Moral Reform,* January 1836, p. 7.

54. Ralph Waldo Emerson, "New England Reformers," in *The Selected Writings of Ralph Waldo Emerson,* ed. Brooks Atkinson (New York: Modern Library, 1992), p. 403.

55. *Liberator,* Dec. 24, 1836, p. 205.

56. *New York Evangelist,* March 4, 1837, p. 37.

57. *Liberator,* Dec. 3, 1836, p. 195.

58. *Liberator,* March 22, 1834, p. 46.

59. *McDowall's Journal,* June 1834, vol. 2, no. 6, p. 45.

60. *New York Evangelist,* June 7, 1834, p. 92.

61. See, for examples, *New York Evangelist,* April 1, 1837; *Zion's Herald,* Sept. 20, 1837; Ryan, *Cradle of the Middle Class;* and Deborah Van Broekhoven, "'Better than a Clay Club': The Organization of Anti-Slavery Fairs, 1835–1860," *Slavery and Abolition* 19 (1998): 24–45.

62. Stuart M. Blumin, *The Emergence of the Middle Class: Social Experience in the American City, 1760–1900* (New York: Cambridge University Press, 1989); Hampel, *Temperance and Prohibition;* Edward Magdol, *The Antislavery Rank and File: A Social Profile of the Abolitionists' Constituency* (New York: Greenwood Press, 1986); Ryan, *Cradle of the Middle Class;* Tyrrell, *Sobering Up.*

63. *McDowall's Journal,* Nov. 1834, vol. 2, no. 11, p. 87.

64. *Liberator,* Oct. 29, 1836, p. 175.

65. Ibid.

66. *New York Evangelist,* May 31, 1834, p. 86.

67. *Liberator,* Jan. 2, 1837, p. 2.

68. *New York Evangelist,* May 24, 1834, p. 83.

69. *Liberator,* April 19, 1834, p. 62.

70. Craven, *Coming of the Civil War;* Elkins, *Slavery.*

71. *New York Evangelist,* Feb. 25, 1837, p. 35.

72. *New York Evangelist,* Dec. 13, 1834, p. 198.

73. *Advocate of Moral Reform,* Dec. 1835, pp. 89–90.

74. Quoted in *Western Recorder,* April 5, 1831, p. 54.

75. *Western Recorder,* Feb. 1, 1831, p. 18.

76. Barnes and Dumond, *Letters,* p. 303.

77. *New York Evangelist,* April 15, 1837, p. 61.

78. *New York Evangelist,* May 17, 1834, p. 78.

Chapter Six

1. Ryan, *Cradle of the Middle Class;* and Johnson, *Shopkeeper's Millennium.*

2. See introduction and chapter 3 for more on Bacon's and Alexander's observations.

3. *Liberator,* Jan. 16, 1836, p. 9.

4. Abzug, *Cosmos Crumbling.*

5. Goodman, *Of One Blood.*

6. In the following biographical account I have relied heavily on the hagiography assembled by his children, Wendell Phillips Garrison and Francis Jackson Garrison, *William Lloyd Garrison.* Although rarely even handed in its treatment of their father, this biography pulls together many invaluable letters, newspaper accounts, and firsthand recollections (often presented in their entirety and without much comment). The book is in many ways Garrison's memoir. I have also drawn from two of the six published volumes of Garrison's letters, covering the years from 1822 to 1840, Walter M. Merrill and Louis Ruchames, *The Letters of William Lloyd Garrison, 1822–1840* (Cambridge, MA: Belknap Press, 1971). More important than any other source is the *Liberator.* Published from 1831 to 1865, the newspaper presents Garrison's life of activism told in his own words. My account also follows Goodman's interpretation of Garrison's influence on the movement as set down in his unfinished book *Of One Blood* and Mayer's biography of Garrison, *All on Fire.*

7. Garrison and Garrison, *William Lloyd Garrison,* p. 15.

8. May 12, 1820, in Garrison and Garrison, *William Lloyd Garrison,* p. 38.

9. See Friedman, *Gregarious Saints,* for the source of this claim.

10. Quotes from letter are from May 24, 1820 in Garrison and Garrison, *William Lloyd Garrison,* p. 39. The concept of a soteriology of the underprivileged is from Weber, "Soteriology of the Underprivileged," in *Max Weber: Selections in Translation,* ed. W. G. Runciman (New York: Cambridge University Press, 1978).

11. *Journal of the Times,* Dec. 12, 1828, in Garrison and Garrison, *William Lloyd Garrison,* p. 92.

12. See Davis, "Emergence of Immediatism," on this point.

13. *Journal of the Times,* Oct. 3 1828, in Garrison and Garrison, *William Lloyd Garrison,* p. 103.

14. Garrison and Garrison, *William Lloyd Garrison,* p. 128.

15. Garrison invoked the words of the Hebrew prophets as seventeenth and eighteenth-century Puritans had before him. For a discussion of the American jeremiad, see Miller, *New England Mind.* For the biblical source of this imagery, see Isaiah 58—a favorite of immediate abolitionists to come.

16. Garrison and Garrison, *William Lloyd Garrison,* p. 131.

17. Garrison and Garrison, *William Lloyd Garrison,* p. 135.

18. Garrison and Garrison, *William Lloyd Garrison,* p. 143.

19. Garrison and Garrison, *William Lloyd Garrison,* p. 143.

20. Garrison and Garrison, *William Lloyd Garrison,* p. 149.

21. Letter to Harriet Farnham Horton dated May 12, 1830 in Merril and Ruchames, *Letters,* p. 92.

22. Garrison and Garrison, *William Lloyd Garrison,* pp. 213–14, emphasis in original.

23. Garrison and Garrison, *William Lloyd Garrison,* p. 214, emphasis in original.

24. Quoted in Deborah Pickman Clifford, *Crusader for Freedom: A Life of Lydia Maria Child* (Boston: Beacon Press, 1992), p. 97.

25. Garrison and Garrison, *William Lloyd Garrison,* pp. 244–45.

26. Garrison and Garrison, *William Lloyd Garrison,* p. 268.

27. The following biographical account of Elizur Wright Jr., draws on Goodheart's biography, *Abolitionist, Actuary, Atheist.* I have also used the Library of Congress's collection of Wright's papers and letters as well as those letters written to James Gillespie Birney, Theodore Weld, and Sarah and Angelina Grimké appearing in two published collections: Barnes and Dumond, *Letters;* and Dumond, *Letters.*

28. Miller, *Errand into the Wilderness.*

29. See Cross, *Burned-over District,* chap. 2; and Meinig, *Shaping of America,* part 2, chap. 1.

30. See Hugh Davis's biography: *Leonard Bacon: New England Reformer and Antislavery Moderate* (Baton Rouge: Louisiana State University Press, 1998).

31. See Hall, *Organization of American Culture* on the unique national character of early nineteenth-century elite educational institutions like Yale.

32. Wyatt-Brown, *Yankee Saints and Southern Sinners* sketches the moral polarization that emerged in antebellum America. This polarization was in early evidence in student conflicts at Yale in the 1820s.

33. See Edmund S. Morgan, *Visible Saints: The History of the Puritan Idea* (Ithaca: Cornell University Press, 1965).

34. Goodheart, *Abolitionist, Actuary, Atheist,* p. 27.

35. Wright to Susan Clark Nov. 6, 1828, Wright Papers, Library of Congress.

36. See chapter 4 for a discussion of the American Tract Society's national strategy of "general supply." Quotes are from Wright to Susan Clark, Oct. 12, 1828, Wright Papers.

37. Wright to Susan Clark, Nov. 24, 1828, Wright Papers.

38. Wright to Susan Clark, June 15, 1829, Wright Papers.

39. Goodheart, *Abolitionist, Actuary, Atheist,* p. 43.

40. Goodheart, *Abolitionist, Actuary, Atheist,* p. 41.

41. American Tract Society, *Tract no. 92. The Praying African: An Authentic Narrative* (New York: 1827–1831) (italics in the original).

42. David Kimball, Jr., to Wright, August 21, 1833, Wright Papers.

43. This biographical account draws from Robert Abzug's excellent biography of Weld, *Passionate Liberator;* Barnes and Dumond, *Letters;* and Finney, *Memoirs.*

44. Abzug, *Passionate Liberator,* p. 47.

45. Finney, *Memoirs,* pp. 187–88.

46. Abzug, *Passionate Liberator,* p. 59.

47. Weld to Stuart, Jan. 10, 1826, in Barnes and Dumond, *Letters,* p. 7.

48. Abzug, *Passionate Liberator,* p. 72.

49. Barnes and Dumond, *Letters,* p. 22.

50. Barnes and Dumond, *Letters,* p. 14.

51. Barnes and Dumond, *Letters,* p. 49.

52. Barnes and Dumond, *Letters,* p. 97.

53. Barnes and Dumond, *Letters,* p. 99.

54. Abzug, *Passionate Liberator,* p. 76.

55. Abzug, *Passionate Liberator,* p. 80.

56. Lesick, *Lane Rebels.*

57. Barnes and Dumond, *Letters,* p. 132, emphasis added.

58. Barnes, *Antislavery Impulse,* p. 68.

59. This biographical account draws from Betty Fladeland's biography, *James Gillespie Birney: Slaveholder to Abolitionist* (New York: Greewood Press, 1969), and the published volumes of Birney's letters edited by Dumond.

60. Weld to Birney, July 24, 1832, in Dumond, *Letters,* p. 13.

61. Weld to Birney, Sept. 27, 1832, in Dumond, *Letters,* p. 27.

62. Weld to Birney, June 1834, in Dumond, *Letters,* p. 118.

63. 2 Kings 6: 15–23.

64. Weld to Birney, August 1834, in Dumond, *Letters,* p. 131.

65. Birney wrote Gerrit Smith, spring 1835, in Dumond, *Letters,* p. 190.

66. Wright to Birney, 1835, in Dumond, *Letters,* p. 261.

67. This account of Sarah and Angelina Grimké draws on Gerda Lerner's biography of the sisters, *The Grimké Sisters from South Carolina: Pioneers for Women's Rights and Abolition* (New York: Schocken Books, 1971); Larry Ceplair's biographical work and the letters and diary fragments collected in that same work, *The Public Years of Sarah and Angelina Grimké: Selected Writings, 1835–1839* (New York: Columbia University Press, 1989); and on the letters published in Barnes and Dumond, *Letters.*

68. Lerner, *Grimké Sisters from South Carolina,* p. 45.

69. Lerner, *Grimké Sisters from South Carolina,* p. 52. See John 16:12 for biblical quotation.

70. Ceplair, *Public Years of Sarah and Angelina Grimké,* p. 16.

71. Ceplair, *Public Years of Sarah and Angelina Grimké,* p. 28.

72. Ceplair *Public Years of Sarah and Angelina Grimké,* p. 26.

73. Ceplair, *Public Years of Sarah and Angelina Grimké,* p. 27.

74. Ceplair, *Public Years of Sarah and Angelina Grimké,* p. 30.

75. Ceplair, *Public Years of Sarah and Angelina Grimké,* p. 31.

76. Angelina Grimké to Weld, in Barnes and Dumond, *Letters,* p. 537.

Conclusion

1. Quoted in Barnes and Dumond, *Letters,* pp. 247–48.

2. Weld's activism expressed a sensibility about the world that was far from the Enlightenment and closer to what Walter Benjamin captured in his writings about the angel of history or Ulrich Beck in his concept of a risk society.

3. Quoted in Barnes and Dumond, *Letters,* pp. 247–48.

4. See for example, Sigmund Freud, *Civilization and Its Discontents* (London: Hogarth Press, 1949).

5. See Thomas Fuchs, "Shame, Guilt, and the Body: A Phenomenological View," unpublished manuscript, 2003.

6. The quote is from Cornelius Golightly, "Race, Values, and Guilt," *Social Forces* 26 (1947): 125–139. Harry Frankfurt, "Freedom of the Will and the Concept of a Person," *Journal of Philosophy* 68 (1971): 5–20, presents the argument for different orders of desire. The theory of guilt presented here draws on the development of Frankfurt's insights by Charles Taylor, *Sources of the Self: The Making of the Modern Identity* (Cambridge, MA: Harvard University Press, 1989); and Christian Smith, *Moral, Believing Animals: Human Personhood and Culture* (New York: Oxford University Press, 2003).

7. See Freud, *Civilization and Its Discontents;* George Herbert Mead, *Mind, Self, and Society from the Standpoint of a Social Behaviorist* (Chicago: University of Chicago Press, 1962); and Martin Heidegger, *Being and Time.* Calvin, in the *Institutes of Christian Religion,* p. 1182, described guilt in a similar fashion, "the feeling, which draws men to God's judgement," as "a keeper assigned to man, that watches and observes all his secrets so that nothing may remain buried in the darkness. Hence that ancient proverb: conscience is a thousand witnesses."

8. See Rheinhold Niebuhr, *An Interpretation of Christian Ethics* (San Francisco: Harper & Row, 1963), p. 49. Niebuhr points out that this phenomenon is captured "in the two contrasting words of Saint Paul, 'I, yet not I, but Christ who liveth in me,' and, 'It is no more I that do it, but sin that dwelleth in me.'" In both phrases, good and evil point to the believer but also beyond her.

9. Weld to Birney, August 1834, in Dumond, *Letters,* p. 190. See chapter 6 for a discussion of the context of this letter.

10. See Anderson, *Imagined Communities;* Calhoun, "Indirect Relationships and Imagined Communities," in *Social Theory for a Changing Society,* ed. Pierre Bourdieu and James S. Coleman (Boulder, CO: Westview Press, 1991); and Habermas, *Between Facts and Norms: Contributions toward a Discourse Theory of Law and Democracy* (Cambridge, MA: MIT Press, 1996) on the social processes behind extending senses of community.

11. See Niebuhr, *Interpretation of Christian Ethics,* p. 47.

12. See William James, *The Varieties of Religious Experience: A Study in Human Nature* (New York: Penguin Books, 1982), p. 198.

13. See Mike Hepworth and Bryan S., Turner, *Confession: Studies in Deviance and Religion* (London: Routledge and Kegan Paul, 1982).

14. Abzug, *Cosmos Crumbling,* p. 7.

15. See James M. McPherson, *The Abolitionist Legacy: From Reconstruction to the NAACP* (Princeton: Princeton University Press, 1975); and Steven M. Beuchler, *Women's Movements in the United States: Woman Suffrage, Equal Rights, and Beyond* (New Brunswick: Rutgers University Press, 1990).

16. For these parallels, see Aldon Morris, *The Origins of the Civil Rights Movement: Black Communities Organizing for Change* (New York: Free Press, 1984), pp. 47–48; Wini Breinis, *Community and Organizing in the New Left, 1962–1968* (New Brunswick: Rutgers University Press, 1989); John D'Emilio, *Sexual Politics, Sexual Communities: The Making of a Homosexual Minority in the United States, 1940–1970* (Chicago: University of Chicago Press, 1983); and Bonnie Zimmerman, "The Politics of Transliteration," in *The Lesbian Issue,* ed. Estelle Freedman et al. (Chicago: University of Chicago Press, 1985).

17. *Earth First!* Oct. 1998, p. 16. Emphasis added.

18. *Advocate,* Sept. 3, 2002, p. 72.

Reference List

Newspapers, Magazines, and Periodicals

Abolitionist
Advocate
Advocate for Moral Reform [New York]
African Repository and Colonial Journal
American and Commercial Daily Advertiser [Baltimore]
American Quarterly Temperance Magazine [Albany]
Baltimore Clipper
Baltimore Sun
Connecticut Evangelical Magazine
Earth First!
Evangelist
Journal of Humanity
Knickerbocker [New York]
Liberator [Boston]
McDowall's Journal
Miscellaneous Magazine
Missionary Herald
New York Evangelist
New York Missionary Magazine and Repository of Religious Intelligence
New York Weekly Messenger
Nile's Register [Baltimore]
Panoplist and Missionary Magazine
Utica Christian Magazine
Vermont Evangelical Magazine
Weekly Recorder
Western Missionary Magazine
Western Recorder [Utica]
Zion's Herald [Boston]

Personal Papers

Papers of Elizur Wright. Manuscript Division, Library of Congress, Washington, DC.

Published Works

Abzug, Robert H. *Passionate Liberator: Theodore Dwight Weld and the Dilemma of Reform.* New York: Oxford University Press, 1980.

———. *Cosmos Crumbling: American Reform and the Religious Imagination.* New York: Oxford University Press, 1994.

Ahlstrom, Sidney E. *A Religious History of the American People.* New Haven and New London: Yale University Press, 1972.

Alexander, Jeffrey C. "The Binary Discourse of Civil Society." In *Cultivating Differences,* ed. Michele Lamont and Marcel Fournier, pp. 289–308. Chicago: University of Chicago Press, 1992.

Altschuler, Glenn C., and Stuart M. Blumin. "Limits of Political Engagement in Antebellum America: A New Look at the Golden Age of Participatory Democracy." *Journal of American History* 84 (1997): 855–85.

Altschuler, Glenn C., and Jan M. Saltzgaber. *Revivalism, Social Conscience, and Community in the Burned-over District: The Trial of Rhoda Bement.* Ithaca, NY: Cornell University Press, 1983.

Amenta, Edwin. *When Movements Matter: The Townsend Plan and U.S. Social Spending Challengers.* Princeton, NJ: Princeton University Press, forthcoming.

———. *Bold Relief: Institutional Politics and the Origins of American Social Policy.* Princeton: Princeton University Press, 1998.

Amenta, Edwin, Kathleen Dunleavy, and Mary Bernstein. "Stolen Thunder? Huey Long's Share Our Wealth, Political Mediation and the Second New Deal." *American Sociological Review* 59 (1994): 678–702.

Amenta, Edwin, and Yvonne Zylan. "It Happened Here: Political Opportunity, the New Institutionalism, and the Townsend Movement." *American Sociological Review* 56 (1991): 250–65.

American Anti-Slavery Society. *Declaration of Sentiments.* New York: W. S. Dorr, 1833.

———. *Annual Reports.* New York: William S. Dorr, 1836–38.

American Bible Society. *First through Thirteenth Report to the American Bible Society* 1816–1829.

American Board of Commissioners for Foreign Missions. *Reports Compiled from Documents Laid Before the Board at . . . Annual Meeting.* Boston: Crocker and Bewster, 1826–1830.

American Education Society. *The Quarterly Register and Journal of the American Education Sociey.* Boston: Perkins and Marvin, 1826–1831.

American Home Missionary Society. *Reports of the American Home Missionary Society*. New York: Claton and Van Norden, 1827–1830.

American Sunday School Union. *Reports of the American Sunday School Union*. Philadelphia, 1825–1830.

American Temperance Society. *American Quarterly Temperance Magazine*. 1833.

——. *Annual Reports*. Boston, 1828–1834.

American Temperance Union. *Permanent Temperance Documents*. Vol. 1. New York: American Temperance Union, 1852.

American Tract Society. *Annual Reports of the American Tract Society*. New York, 1824–1830.

——. *Tract No. 92. The Praying African: An Authentic Narrative*. New York, 1827–1831.

Anderson, Benedict. *Imagined Communities: Reflections on the Origin and Spread of Nationalism*. London: Verso, 1983.

Babb, Sarah. "'A True American System of Finance': Frame Resonance in the U.S. Labor Movement, 1866 to 1886." *American Sociological Review* 61 (1996): 1033–52.

Balmer, Randall Herbert, and John R. Fitzmier. *The Presbyterians*. Westport, CN: Green Wood Press, 1993.

Banner, Lois W. "Religion and Reform in the Early Republic: The Role of Youth." *American Quarterly* 23 (1971): 677–95.

——. "Religious Benevolence as Social Control: A Critique of an Interpretation." *Journal of American History* 60 (1973): 23–41.

Barnes, Gilbert H. *The Antislavery Impulse, 1830–1844*. New York and London: D. Appleton-Century Company, 1933.

Barnes, Gilbert H., and Dwight L. Dumond, eds. *Letters of Theodore Dwight Weld, Angelina Grimké Weld and Sarah Grimké*. 2 vols. Gloucester, MA: Peter Smith, 1934.

Beard, Charles A., and Mary Beard. *The Rise of American Civilization*. New York: Macmillan Co., 1927.

Beecher, Lyman. *The Government of God Desirable*. New London: Samuel Green, 1811.

——. *Autobiography*, ed. Barbara M. Cross. 1864. Cambridge, MA: Belknap Press of Harvard University Press, 1961.

——. *Six Sermons on the Nature, Occasions, Signs, Evils, and Remedy of Intemperance*. Boston: T. R. Marvin, 1828.

Beisel, Nicola. *Imperiled Innocents: Anthony Comstock and Family Reproduction in Victorian America*. Princeton: Princeton University Press, 1997.

Benford, Robert. "An Insider's Critique of the Social Movement Framing Perspective." *Sociological Inquiry* 67 (1997): 409–30.

Berg, Barbara J. *Remembered Gate: Origins of American Feminism: The Woman and the City, 1800–1860*. New York: Oxford University Press, 1978.

Blumer, Herbert. "Collective Behavior." In *An Outline of the Principles of Sociology,* ed. R. E. Park, pp. 221–28. New York: Barnes and Noble, 1939.

Blumhofer, Edith L., and Randall Balmer. Introduction. In *Modern Christian Revivals,* ed. Edith L. Blumhofer and Randall Balmer, pp. 1–16. Urbana and Chicago: University of Illinois Press, 1993.

Blumin, Stuart M. *The Emergence of the Middle Class: Social Experience in the American City, 1760–1900.* New York: Cambridge University Press, 1989.

Bodo, John R. *The Protestant Clergy and Public Issues, 1812–1848.* Princeton, NJ: Princeton University Press, 1954.

Boles, John B. *The Great Revival: Beginnings of the Bible Belt.* Lexington, KY: University Press of Kentucky, 1996.

Bourdieu, Pierre. *The Logic of Practice.* Stanford: Stanford University Press, 1980.

Boyer, Paul. *Urban Masses and Moral Order in America, 1820–1920.* Cambridge, MA: Harvard University Press, 1978.

Boylan, Anne M. "Women in Groups: An Analysis of Women's Benevolent Organizations in New York and Boston, 1797–1840." *Journal of American History* 71 (1984): 497–523.

Breinis, Wini. *Community and Organizing in the New Left, 1962–1968.* New Brunswick: Rutgers University Press, 1989.

Bristol, Sherlock. *The Pioneer Preacher: Incidents of Interest, and Experience in the Author's Life.* Urbana: University of Illinois Press, 1989.

Broekhoven, Deborah Van. "'Better than a Clay Club': The Organization of Anti-Slavery Fairs, 1835–1860." *Slavery and Abolition* 19 (1998): 24–45.

Brown, Richard D. "The Emergence of Urban Society in Rural Massachusetts, 1760–1820." *Journal of American History* 61 (1974): 29–51.

Burnham, Walter Dean. "The Turnout Problem." In *Election American Style,* ed. A. James Reichley, pp. 97–133. Washington, DC: Brookings Institution.

Butler, Jon. *Awash in a Sea of Faith: Christianizing the American People.* Cambridge, MA: Harvard University Press, 1990.

Buechler, Steven M. *Women's Movements in the United States: Woman Suffrage, Equal Rights, and Beyond.* New Brunswick: Rutgers University Press, 1990.

Calhoun, Craig. "Indirect Relationships and Imagined Communities: Large-Scale Social Integrations and the Transformation of Everyday Life." In *Social Theory for a Changing Society,* ed. Pierre Bourdieu and James S. Coleman, pp. 95–121. Boulder, CO: Westview Press, 1991.

———. "'New Social Movements' of the Early Nineteenth Century." *Social Science History* 17 (1993): 385–427.

Calvin, John. *Institutes of the Christian Religion.* Philadelphia: Westminster Press, 1960.

Carwardine, Richard. *Transatlantic Revivalism: Popular Evangelicalism in Britain and America, 1790–1865.* Westport, CN and London: Greenwood Press, 1978.

Ceplair, Larry, ed. *The Public Years of Sarah and Angelina Grimké: Selected Writings, 1835–1839.* New York: Columbia University Press, 1989.

Clemens, Elizabeth. *The People's Lobby: Organizational Innovation and the Rise of Interest Group Politics in the United States, 1890–1925*. Chicago: University of Chicago Press, 1997.

Clifford, Deborah Pickman. *Crusader for Freedom: A Life of Lydia Maria Child*. Boston: Beacon Press, 1992.

Cohen, Jean L. "Strategy or Identity: New Theoretical Paradigms and Contemporary Social Movements." *Social Research* 52 (1985): 663–716.

Cole, Arthur C. *The Irrepressible Conflict, 1850–1865*. New York: Macmillan Co., 1934.

Cole, Charles C. *The Social Ideas of the Northern Evangelists, 1826–1860*. New York: Columbia University Press, 1954.

Colton, Calvin. *Protestant Jesuitism*. New York: Harper and Brothers, 1836.

Conkin, Paul K. *The Uneasy Center: Reformed Christianity in Antebellum America*. Chapel Hill, NC: University of North Carolina Press, 1995.

Cott, Nancy F. *The Bonds of Womanhood: "Woman's Sphere" in New England, 1780–1835*. New Haven, CN: Yale University Press, 1977.

Cowing, Cedric B. *The Great Awakening and the American Revolution: Colonial Thought in the 18th Century*. Chicago: Rand McNally, 1971.

Craven, Avery. *The Coming of the Civil War*. New York: Scribner's Sons, 1942.

Cross, Whitney R. *The Burned-over District: The Social and Intellectual History of Enthusiastic Religion in Western New York*. Ithaca: Cornel University Press, 1950.

Cumberland Presbytery. "The Minutes of the Cumberland Presbytery, 1803–1806." In *The Presbyterians, 1783–1840: A Collection of Source Materials,* ed. William Warren Sweet, pp. 282–305. Vol. 2 of *Religion on the American Frontier*. New York and London: Harper & Brothers Publishers, 1936.

Dannenbaum, Jed. *Drink and Disorder: Temperance Reform in Cincinnati from the Washington Revival to the WCTU*. Chicago: University of Illinois Press, 1984.

Davis, David Brion. "The Emergence of Immediatism in British and American Antislavery Thought." *Mississippi Valley Historical Review* 49 (1962): 209–30.

———. *The Problem of Slavery in the Age of Revolution, 1770–1823*. Ithaca, NY: Cornell University Press, 1975.

———. "Perils of Doing History by Ahistorical Abstraction." In *The Antislavery Debate: Capitalism and Abolitionism as a Problem of Historical Interpretation,* ed. Thomas Bender, pp. 290–309. Berkeley: University of California Press, 1992.

Davis, Hugh. *Leonard Bacon: New England Reformer and Antislavery Moderate*. Baton Rouge: Louisiana State University Press, 1998.

———. *Joshua Leavitt: Evangelical Abolitionist*. Baton Rouge: Louisiana State University Press, 1990.

D'Emilio, John. *Sexual Politics, Sexual Communities: The Making of a Homosexual Minority in the United States, 1940–1970*. Chicago: University of Chicago Press, 1983.

Dewey, John. *A Common Faith*. New Haven: Yale University Press, 1934.

Dillon, Merton L. *Elijah P. Lovejoy, Abolitionist Editor*. Urbana, IL: University of Illinois Press, 1961.

——. "The Abolitionists: A Decade of Historiography, 1959–1969." *Journal of Southern History* 35 (1969): 500–22.

——. *The Abolitionists: Growth of Dissenting Minority*. New York: W.W. Norton and Co, 1979.

——. Book Review. *Journal of American History* 74 (1987): 484–86.

——. "Gilbert H. Barnes and Dwight L. Dumond: An Appraisal." *Reviews in American History* 21 (1993): 539–52.

Donald, David H. *Lincoln Reconsidered: Essays on the Civil War Era*. New York: Knopf, 1956.

Douglas, Ann. *The Feminization of American Culture*. New York: Alfred A. Knopf, 1979.

Duberman, Martin B. "The Abolitionists and Psychology." *Journal of Negro History* 47 (1962): 183–91.

Duberman, Martin B., ed. *The Antislavery Vanguard: New Essays on the Abolitionists*. Princeton, NJ: Princeton University Press, 1965.

Dumond, Dwight L., ed. *Letters of James Gillespie Birney, 1831–1857*. 2 vols. New York: D. Appleton-Century Co., 1938.

——. *Antislavery: The Crusade for Freedom in America*. Ann Arbor: University of Michigan Press, 1961.

Eisenger, Peter K. "The Conditions of Protest Behavior in American Cities." *American Political Science Review* 67 (1973): 11–28.

Elkins, Stanley M. *Slavery: A Problem in American Institutional and Intellectual Life*. Chicago: University of Chicago Press, 1959.

Ellingson, Stephen. "Understanding the Dialectic of Discourse and Collective Action: Public Debate and Rioting in Antebellum Cincinnati." *American Journal of Sociology* 101 (1995): 100–44.

Emerson, Ralph Waldo. "New England Reformers." In *The Selected Writings of Ralph Waldo Emerson,* ed. Brooks Atkinson, pp. 402–418. [1844]. New York: Modern Library, 1992.

Epstein, Barbara Leslie. *The Politics of Domesticity*. Middletown, CN: Wesleyan University Press, 1981.

Finke, Roger, and Rodney Stark. *The Churching of America: Winners and Losers in Our Religious Economy*. New Brunswick, NJ: Rutgers University Press, 1992.

Finney, Charles G. *Lectures on Revivals of Religion*. Cambridge, MA: Belknap Press of Harvard University, 1960.

——. *The Memoirs of Charles G. Finney: The Complete Restored Text*. Grand Rapids, Michigan: Zondervan Publishing House, 1989.

Fladeland, Betty. "Who Were the Abolitionists?" *Journal of Negro History* 49 (1964): 99–115.

——. *James Gillespie Birney: Slaveholder to Abolitionist.* New York: Greewood Press, 1969.

——. "Revisionists vs. Abolitionists: The Historiographical Cold War of the 1940s and 1950s." *Journal of the Early Republic* 6 (1986): 1–21.

Foner, Eric. *Free Soil, Free Labor, Free Men: The Ideology of the Republican Party Before the Civil War.* New York: Oxford University Press, 1995.

Formisano, Ronald P. *The Birth of Mass Political Parties: Michigan, 1827–1861.* Princeton: Princeton University Press, 1971.

——. 1983. *Transformation of Political Culture.* New York: Oxford University Press.

Foster, Charles I. *An Errand of Mercy: The Evangelical United Front, 1790–1837.* Chapel Hill: University of North Carolina Press, 1960.

Frankfurt, Harry. "Freedom of the Will and the Concept of a Person." *Journal of Philosophy* 68 (1971): 5–20.

Fraser, Nancy. "From Redistribution to Recognition? Dilemmas of Justice in a 'Post Socialist' Age." *New Left Review* 212 (1995): 68–93.

Freud, Sigmund. *Civilization and Its Discontents.* London: Hogarth Press, 1949.

Friedman, Lawrence J. *Gregarious Saints: Self and Community in American Abolitionism, 1830–1870.* New York: Cambridge University Press, 1982.

Fuchs, Thomas. 2003. "Shame, Guilt, and the Body: A Phenomenologic View." Unpublished Paper: Psychiatric Clinic, University of Heidelberg.

Gamson, William A. *Talking Politics.* New York: Cambridge University Press, 1992.

Garrison, Wendell Phillips, and Francis Jackson Garrison. *William Lloyd Garrison, 1805–1879: The Story of His Life Told By His Children.* [Vol. 1, 1885]. New York: Negro Universities Press, 1969.

Gaustad, Edwin. *Historical Atlas of American Religion.* New York: Harper & Row, 1962.

Geertz, Clifford. *The Interpretation of Cultures.* New York: Basic Books, 1973.

Gerteis, Louis S. *Morality and Utility in American Antislavery Reform.* Chapel Hill: University of North Carolina Press, 1987.

Giddens, Anthony. *Modernity and Self-Identity: Self and Society in the Late Modern Age.* Stanford: Stanford University Press, 1991.

Goffman, Erving. *Frame Analysis.* New York: Harper & Row, 1974.

Golightly, Cornelius L. "Race, Values, and Guilt." *Social Forces* 26 (1947): 125–39.

Goodheart, Lawrence. *Abolitionist, Actuary, Atheist: Elizur Wright and the Reform Impulse.* Kent, Ohio: Kent State University Press, 1990.

Goodman, Paul. *Of One Blood: Abolitionism and the Origins of Racial Equality.* Berkeley: University of California Press, 1998.

Goodwin, Jeff, James M. Jasper, and Francesca Polletta. "The Return of the Repressed: The Fall and Rise of Emotions in Social Movement Theory." *Mobilization* (2000): 565–84.

Gould, Roger V. "Patron-Client Ties, State Centralization, and the Whiskey Rebellion." *American Journal of Sociology* 102 (1996): 400–29.

———. "Collective Violence and Group Solidarity: Evidence from a Feuding Society." *American Sociological Review* 64 (1999): 356–380.

Griffin, Clifford. *Their Brothers' Keepers: Moral Stewardship in the United States, 1800–1865*. New Brunswick, NJ: Rutgers University Press, 1960.

Grimsted, David. *American Mobbing, 1828–1861*. New York: Oxford University Press, 1998.

Gusfield, Joseph R. *Symbolic Crusade: Status Politics and the American Temperance Movement*. Urbana: University of Illinois Press, 1963.

Habermas, Jurgen. *Between Facts and Norms: Contributions toward a Discourse Theory of Law and Democracy*. Cambridge, MA: MIT Press, 1996.

Hall, Peter Dobkin. *The Organization of American Culture, 1700–1900: Private Institutions, Elites, and the Origins of American Nationality*. New York: New York University Press, 1984.

Hammond, John L. "Revival Religion and Antislavery Politics." *American Sociological Review* 39 (1974): 175–86.

———. *Revivals in New York and Ohio, 1825–1835*. Computer file. Ann Arbor, MI: Inter-university Consortium for Political and Social Research (distributor), 1980.

Hampel, Robert L. *Temperance and Prohibition in Massachusetts, 1813–1852*. Ann Arbor: UMI Research Press, 1982.

Hardman, Keith J. *Charles Grandison Finney, 1792–1875: Revivalist and Reformer*. Syracuse: Syracuse University Press, 1987.

Haskell, Thomas L. "Capitalism and the Origins of Humanitarian Sensibility, Part 1 and 2." In *The Antislavery Debate,* ed. Thomas Bender, pp. 107–60. Berkeley: University of California Press, 1992.

Hatch, Nathan O. *The Democratization of American Christianity*. New Haven and London: Yale University Press, 1989.

Haydu, Jeffrey. "Business Citizenship at Work: Cultural Transposition and Class Formation in Cincinnati, 1870–1910." *American Journal of Sociolgy* 107 (2002): 1424–67.

Heidegger, Martin. *Being and Time*. New York: Harper & Row, 1962.

Heimert, Alan. *Religion and the American Mind: From Awakening to the Revolution*. Cambridge, MA: Harvard University Press, 1966.

Heimert, Alan, and Perry Miller. Introduction. *The Great Awakening: Documents Illustrating the Crisis and Its Consequences,* ed. Alan Heimert and Perry Miller. Indianapolis and New York: The Bobbs-Merrill Company, 1967.

Hepworth, Mike, and Bryan S. Turner. *Confession: Studies in Deviance and Religion*. London: Routledge and Kegan Paul, 1982.

Hewitt, Nancy A. *Women's Activism and Social Change: Rochester, New York, 1822–1872*. Ithaca, NY: Cornell University Press, 1984.

Hirrel, Leo P. *Children of Wrath: New School Calvinism and Antebellum Reform.* Lexington: University of Kentucky Press, 1998.

James, William. *The Varieties of Religious Experience: A Study in Human Nature.* 1902. New York: Penguin Books, 1982.

Joas, Hans. *The Creativity of Action.* Chicago: University of Chicago Press, 1996.

John, Richard R. *Spreading the News: The American Postal System from Franklin to Morse.* Cambridge, MA: Harvard University Press, 1995.

Johnson, Curtis D. *Redeeming America: Evangelicals and the Road to the Civil War.* Chicago: Ivan R. Dee, 1993.

Johnson, Paul. *A History of Christianity.* London: Weidenfeld and Nicolson, 1976.

Johnson, Paul E. *A Shopkeeper's Millennium: Society and Revivals in Rochester, New York, 1815–1837.* New York: Hill and Wang, 1978.

Johnson, Paul E., and Sean Wilentz. *The Kingdom of Matthias: A Story of Sex and Salvation in 19th Century America.* New York: Oxford University Press, 1994.

Kane, Anne E. "Theorizing Meaning Construction in Social Movements: Symbolic Structures and Interpretation during the Irish Land War, 1879–1882." *Sociological Theory* 15 (1997): 249–76.

Katz, Michael B. *The Irony of Early School Reform: Educational Innovation in Mid-Nineteenth Century Massachussetts.* Cambridge, MA: Harvard University Press, 1968.

Kent, John. *Holding the Fort: Studies in Victorian Revivalism.* London: Epworth Press, 1978.

Kraditor, Aileen S. *Means and Ends in American Abolitionism: Garrison and His Critics on Strategy and Tactics, 1834–1850.* New York: Pantheon Books, 1967.

Krout, John Allen. *The Origins of Prohibition.* New York: Alfred A. Knopf, 1925.

Kulikoff, Allan. *The Agrarian Origins of American Capitalism.* Charlottesville: University Press of Virginia, 1992.

Lerner, Gerda. *The Grimké Sisters from South Carolina: Pioneers for Women's Rights and Abolition.* New York: Schocken Books, 1971.

Lesick, Lawrence Thomas. *The Lane Rebels: Evangelicalism and Antislavery in Antebellum America.* Metuchen, NJ: The Scarecrow Press, Inc, 1980.

Loveland, Anne C. "Evangelicalism and 'Immediate Emancipation' in American Antislavery Thought." *Journal of Southern History* 32 (1966): 172–88.

Maier, Pauline. *From Resistance to Revolution: Colonial Radicals and the Development of American Opposition to Britain, 1765–1776.* New York: Knopf, 1972.

Magdol, Edward. *The Antislavery Rank and File: A Social Profile of the Abolitionists' Constituency.* New York: Greenwood Press, 1986.

Mann, Michael. *The Sources of Social Power.* Vol. 1, *A History of Power from the Beginning to A.D. 1760.* New York: Cambridge University Press, 1986.

———. *The Sources of Social Power.* Vol. 2, *The Rise of Classes and Nation State, 1760–1914.* New York: Cambridge University Press, 1993.

Matthews, Donald G. "Abolitionists on Slavery: The Critique behind the Social Movement." *Journal of Southern History* 33 (1967): 163–82.

———. "The Second Great Awakening as an Organizing Process, 1790–1830." *American Quarterly* 21 (1969): 23–43.

Mayer, Henry. *All on Fire: William Lloyd Garrison and the Abolition of Slavery.* New York: St. Martin's Press, 1998.

McAdam, Doug, Sidney Tarrow, and Charles Tilly. *Dynamics of Contention.* New York: Cambridge University Press, 2001.

McClelland, Peter D., and Richard J. Zeckhauser. *Demographic Dimensions of the New Republic: American Interregional Migration, Vital Statistics, and Manumissions, 1800–1860.* Cambridge: Cambridge University Press, 1982.

McCormick, Richard L. *The Party Period and Public Policy: American Politics from the Age of Jackson to the Progressive Era.* New York: Oxford University, 1986.

McDowall, John. *Memoir and Select Remains of the Late Rev. John R. McDowall.* New York, 1838.

McPherson, James M. *The Abolitionist Legacy: From Reconstruction to the NAACP.* Princeton: Princeton University Press, 1975.

Mead, George Herber. *Mind, Self, and Society from the Standpoint of a Social Behaviorist.* Chicago: University of Chicago Press, 1962.

Meinig, D. W. *The Shaping of America: A Geographical Perspective on 500 Years of History,* Vol. 2, *Continental America, 1800–1967.* New Haven: Yale University Press, 1993.

Merrill, Walter M., and Louis Ruchames, eds. *The Letters of William Lloyd Garrison, 1822–1840.* Cambridge, MA: Belknap Press, 1971.

Miller, Perry. *The New England Mind: From Colony to Province.* Cambridge, MA: Belknap Press, 1953.

———. "From the Covenant to the Revival." In *The Shaping of American Religion,* ed. James Ward Smith and A. Leland Jamison. Princeton: Princeton University Press, 1961.

———. *The Life of the Mind in America: From the Revolution to the Civil War.* New York: Harcourt, Brace and World, 1965.

———. *Errand into the Wilderness.* Cambridge, MA: Belknap Press, 1984.

Mills, C. Wright. "Situated Actions and Vocabularies of Motive." *American Sociological Review* 5 (1940): 904–13.

Mills, Samuel J., and Daniel Smith. *Report of a Missionary Tour Through That Part of the United States which Lies West of the Allegany Mountains; Performed Under the Direction of the Massachusetts Missionary Society.* Andover, MA: Flagg and Gould, 1815.

Moore, R. Laurence. *Selling God: American Religion in the Marketplace of Culture.* New York and Oxford: Oxford University Press, 1994.

Morgan, Edmund S. *Visible Saints: The History of a Puritan Idea.* Ithaca, NY: Cornell University Press, 1965.

Morris, Aldon D. *The Origins of the Civil Rights Movement: Black Communities Organizing for Change*. New York: Free Press, 1984.

Murrin, John. "The Great Inversion, or Court Verses Country: A Comparison of the Revolution Settlements in England (1688–1721) and America (1776–1816)." In *Three British Revolutions: 1641, 1688, 1776,* ed. J. G. A Pocock. Princeton: Princeton University Press, 1980.

Niebuhr, Reinhold. *An Interpretation of Christian Ethics*. San Francisco: Harper & Row, 1963.

Noll, Mark A. *America's God: From Jonathan Edwards to Abraham Lincoln*. New York: Oxford University Press, 2002.

Nord, David Paul. "The Evangelical Origins of Mass Media in America, 1815–1835." *Journalism Monographs* 88 (1984): 1–30.

Oliver, Pamela, Joge Cadena-Roa, and Kelley D. Strawin. "Emerging Trends in the Study of Protest and Social Movements." *Research in Political Sociology* 12 (2003): 213–44.

Perry, Lewis. *Radical Abolitionism: Anarchy and the Government of God in Antislavery Thought*. Ithaca: Cornell University Press, 1973.

Pierson, George Wilson. *Tocqueville in America*. [1938]. Baltimore: John Hopkins Press, 1996.

Polletta, Francesca. "Contending Stories: Narrative in Social Movements." *Qualitative Sociology* 21 (1998): 419–46.

Ramsdell, Charles W. "The Changing Interpretation of the Civil War." *Journal of Southern History* 3 (1937): 2–27.

Randall, J. G. "The Blundering Generation." *Mississippi Valley Historical Review* 27 (1940): 3–28.

Redding, Kent. "Failed Populism: Movement-Party Disjuncture in North Carolina, 1890 to 1900." *American Sociological Review* 57 (1992): 340–52.

Richards, Leonard L. *"Gentlemen of Property and Standing": Anti-Abolition Mobs in Jacksonian America*. New York: Oxford University Press, 1970.

Ricoeur, Paul. *Hermeneutics and Human Sciences: Essays on Language, Action, and Interpretation*. New York: Cambridge University Press, 1981.

Rorabaugh, W. J. *Alcoholic Republic: An American Tradition*. New York: Oxford University Press, 1979.

Roth, Randolph A. *Democratic Dilemma: Religion, Reform, and the Social Order of the Connecticut River Valley of Vermont, 1791–1850*. New York: Cambridge University Press, 1987.

Rothman, David J. *The Discovery of the Asylum: Social Order and Disorder in the New Republic*. Boston: Little, Brown and Co., 1971.

Rumbarger, John J. "The Social Origins and Function of the Political Temperance Movement in the Reconstruction of American Society, 1825–1927." Ph.D. diss., University of Pennsylvania, 1969.

——. *Profits, Power, and Prohibition: Alcohol Reform and the Industrializing of America, 1800–1930*. Albany: State University of New York Press, 1989.

Ryan, Mary P. *Cradle of the Middle Class: The Family in Oneida County, New York, 1790–1865*. New York: Cambridge University, 1981.

———. *Women in Public: Between Banners and Ballots, 1825–1880*. Baltimore: Johns Hopkins University Press, 1990.

Schermerhorn, John F., and Samuel J. Mills. *A Correct View of that Part of the United States which Lies West of the Allegany Mountains, with Regard to Religion and Morals*. Hartford: Peter B. Gleason, 1814.

Scott, Donald M. *From Office to Profession: The New England Ministry*. Philadelphia: Unversity of Pennsylvania, 1978.

———. "Abolition as a Sacred Vocation." In *Antislavery Reconsidered: New Perspectives on the Abolitionists*, ed. Lewis Perry and Michael Fellman, pp. 51–74. Baton Rouge: Louisiana State University Press, 1979.

Sellers, Charles. *The Market Revolution*. New York and Oxford: Oxford University Press, 1991.

Sewell, Richard H. *Ballots for Freedom: Antislavery Politics in the United States, 1837–1860*. New York: Oxford University Press, 1976.

Sewell, William H., Jr. "A Theory of Structure: Duality, Agency, and Transformation." *American Journal of Sociology* 98 (1992): 1–29.

———. "Political Events as Structural Transformations: Inventing Revolution at the Bastille." *Theory and Society* 25 (1996): 841–81.

Sherkat, Darren E., and Christopher G. Ellison. "The Cognitive Structure of a Moral Crusade: Conservative Protestant Opposition to Pornography." *Social Forces* 75 (1997): 957–80.

Skocpol, Theda. *Protecting Soldiers and Mothers*. Cambridge MA: Belknap Press, 1992.

———. "The Tocqueville Problem: Civic Engagement in American Democracy." *Social Science History* 21 (1997): 455–79.

Skotheim, Robert Allen. "A Note on Historical Method: David Donald's 'Toward a Reconsideration of Abolitionists." *Journal of Southern History* 25 (1959): 356–65.

Skowronek, Stephen. *Building a New American State: The Expansion of National Administrative Capacities*. New York: Cambridge University Press, 1982.

Smelser, Neil J. *Theory of Collective Behavior*. New York: Free Press, 1962.

Smith, Christian. *Moral, Believing Animals: Human Personhood and Culture*. New York: Oxford University Press, 2003.

Smith-Rosenberg, Carroll. *Religion and the Rise of the American City: The New York City Mission Movement, 1812–1870*. Ithaca, NY: Cornell University Press, 1971.

Snow, David A., et al. "Frame Alignment Processes, Micromobilization, and Movement Participation." *American Sociological Review* 51 (1986): 464–81.

Snow, David A., and Robert D. Benford. "Master Frames and Cycles of Protest." In *Frontiers in Social Movement Theory*, ed. Aldon D. Morris and Carol McClurg Meuller, pp. 133–155. New Haven: Yale University Press, 1992.

Sprague, William B. *Lectures on Revivals of Religion*. Albany: Webster and Skinners, 1832.

Stewart, James B. *Holy Warriors: The Abolitionists and American Slavery*. New York: Hill and Wang, 1996.

Stout, Harry S. "Religion, Communication, and the Ideological Origins of the American Revolution." *William and Mary Quarterly* 34 (1977): 519–41.

Sweet, William Warren. *The Presbyterians, 1783–1849: A Collection of Source Materials*. New York and London: Harper and Brothers, 1936.

———. *Revivalism in America: Its Origin, Growth and Decline*. New York: Charles Scribner's Sons, 1945.

Synod of Kentucky. "Minutes of the Synod of Kentucky." In *Religion on the American Frontier: The Presbyterians, 1783–1840*, ed. William Warren Sweet, 2: 306–92. New York and London: Harper & Brothers Publishers, 1936.

Szatmary, David P. *Shay's Rebellion: The Making of an Agrarian Insurrection*. Amherst: University of Massachusetts Press, 1980.

Tarrow, Sidney. "Modular Collective Action and the Rise of the Social Movement: Why the French Revolution Was Not Enough." *Politics and Society* 21 (1993): 69–90.

———. *Power in Movement: Social Movements, Collective Action and Politics*. New York: Cambridge University Press, 1994.

Tarrow, Sidney. "'The Very Excess of Democracy': State Building and Contentious Politics in America." In *Social Movements and American Political Institutions*, ed. Anne N. Costain and Andrew S. McFarland. Lanham, MD: Rowman and Littlefield, 1998.

Taylor, Charles. *Sources of the Self: The Making of the Modern Identity*. Cambridge, MA: Harvard University Press, 1989

Taylor, George R. *Transportation Revolution, 1815–1860*. White Plains, NY: M. E. Sharpe, 1951.

Taylor, Verta. *Rock-A-By Baby: Feminism, Self-Help, and Postpartum Depression*. New York and London: Routledge. 1996.

Thomas, George M. *Revivalism and Cultural Change: Christianity, Nation Building, and the Market in the Nineteenth-Century*. Chicago: University of Chicago Press, 1989.

Thompson, E. P. *Customs in Common: Studies in Traditional Popular Culture*. New York: New Press, 1993.

Tilly, Charles. "Collective Action in England and America, 1765–1775." In *Tradition, Conflict, and Modernization: Perspectives on the American Revolution*, ed. Richard Maxwell Brown and Don Fehrenbacher. New York: Academic Press, 1977.

———. *From Mobilization to Revolution*. Reading, MA: Addison-Wesley, 1978.

———. "Repertoires of Contention in America and Britain." In *Dynamics of Social Movements*, ed. Mayer N. Zald and John D. McCarthy. New York: Academic Press, 1979.

———. *The Contentious French*. Cambridge, MA: Belknap Press of Harvard University Press, 1986.

———. *Popular Contention in Great Britain, 1758–1834*. Cambridge, MA: Harvard University Press, 1995.

———. "The Parliamentarization of Popular Contention in Great Britain, 1758–1834." In *Roads from Past to Future, Legacies of Social Thought*, ed. C. Lemert, pp. 217–44. Lanham: Rowman & Littlefield Publishers, Inc., 1997.

———. "From Interactions to Outcomes in Social Movements." In *How Social Movements Matter*, ed. Marco Giugni, Doug McAdam, and Charles Tilly. Minneapolis: University of Minnesota Press, 1999.

———. "Buried Gold." *American Sociological Review* 67 (2002): 689–92.

Tocqueville, Alexis de. *Democracy in America*. Chicago: University of Chicago Press, 2000.

Tyler, Alice Felt. *Freedom's Ferment*. Minneapolis: University of Minnesota Press, 1944.

Tyrrell, Ian R. *Sobering Up: From Temperance to Prohibition in Antebellum America, 1800–1860*. Westport, CN: Greenwood Press, 1979.

United Domestic Missionary Society. *Fourth Annual Report*. New York, 1826.

U.S. Bureau of Census. *Historical Statistics of the United States from Colonial Times to 1970*. Washington, DC: U.S. GPO, 1975.

———. *The Statistical History of the United States From Colonial Times to the Present*. Part 2. Washington, DC: U.S. GPO, 1976.

Voss, Kim. *The Making of American Exceptionalism: The Knights of Labor and Class Formation in the Nineteenth Century*. Ithaca, NY: Cornell University Press, 1993.

Walters, Ronald G. *American Reformers, 1815–1860*, ed. Eric Foner. New York: Hill and Wang, 1997.

Warner, Stephen R. "Work in Progress toward a New Paradigm for the Sociology of Religion in the United State." *American Journal of Sociology* 98 (1993): 1044–93.

Weber, Max. "Science as a Vocation." In *From Max Weber: Essays in Sociology*, ed. H. H. Gerth and C. Wright Mills, pp. 129–56. New York: Oxford University Press, 1946.

———. "Soteriology of the Underprivileged." In *Max Weber: Selections in Translation*, ed. W. G. Runciman. New York: Cambridge University Press, 1978.

Weisberger, Bernard A. *They Gathered at the River: The Story of the Great Revivalists and Their Impact upon Religion in America*. Boston: Little, Brown and Company, 1958.

Westerkamp, Marilyn J. *Triumph of the Laity: Scots-Irish Piety and the Great Awakening, 1625–1760*. New York and Oxford: Oxford University Press, 1988.

Wilentz, Sean. *Chants Democratic: New York City and the Rise of the American Working Class, 1788–1850*. New York: Oxford University Press, 1984.

Wosh, Peter J. "Bibles, Benevolence and Emerging Bureaucracy: The Persistence of the American Bible Society, 1816–1890." Ph.D. diss., New York University, 1988.

Wyatt-Brown, Bertram. *Lewis Tappan and the Evangelical War against Slavery.* Baton Rouge: Cleveland: Press of Case Western Reserve University, 1969.

——. *Yankee Saints and Southern Sinners.* Baton Rouge: Louisiana State University Press, 1985.

Young, Michael P. "Tocqueville's America: A Critical Reappraisal of Voluntary Associations before the Civil War." Paper presented at the 2001 ASA meeting in Anaheim, 2001.

Zimmerman, Bonnie. "The Politics of Transliteration." In *The Lesbian Issue,* ed. Estelle Freedman et al., pp. 251–270. Chicago: University of Chicago Press, 1985.

Index